A History of 1970s Experimental Film

A History of 1970s Experimental Film

Britain's Decade of Diversity

Patti Gaal-Holmes
Independent Artist/filmmaker and Historian, UK

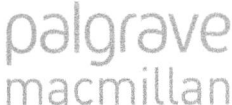

First published 2015 by
PALGRAVE MACMILLAN

Palgrave Macmillan in the UK is an imprint of Macmillan Publishers Limited,
registered in England, company number 785998, of Houndmills, Basingstoke,
Hampshire, RG21 6XS.

Palgrave Macmillan in the US is a division of St Martin's Press LLC,
175 Fifth Avenue, New York, NY 10010.

Palgrave is the global academic imprint of the above companies
and has companies and representatives throughout the world.

Palgrave® and Macmillan® are registered trademarks in the United States,
the United Kingdom, Europe and other countries.

ISBN 978–1–137–36937–6

This book is printed on paper suitable for recycling and made from fully
managed and sustained forest sources. Logging, pulping and manufacturing
processes are expected to conform to the environmental regulations of the
country of origin.

A catalogue record for this book is available from the British Library.

A catalog record for this book is available from the Library of Congress.

Typeset by MPS Limited, Chennai, India.

For Marcus, Tarquin, Benjamin and Zsuzsa: for the wonderful adventures ... long may they continue ...

Contents

Table

Foreword

To experience experimental film in Britain in the 1970s meant – for that rare creature the serious devotee – regular visits to the London Filmmakers Co-operative (LFMC), in whatever obscure venue it might be housed: The New Arts Lab, Robert Street (1969–71); the Dairy (1971–5), a semi-abandoned factory building in Prince of Wales Crescent, where SPACE studios had secured temporary use of a short-life building from Camden Council; then The Piano Factory (1975–7) in Fitzroy Road (in fact what might have been the works canteen in the yard behind the factory), again a mix of artists' studios and workspaces; and, finally, 42 Gloucester Avenue (1977–), another ex-industrial building formerly belonging to British Rail, reached by climbing a metal fire-escape-like staircase to a leaking space above an abandoned laundry (where presumably British Rail staff uniforms were washed). There were other venues in London where experimental film was occasionally shown – the Institute of Contemporary Art (ICA), the National Film Theatre (NFT), the New Cinema Club – and towards the end of the decade new artist-led venues appeared, dedicated to video, installation and performance, such as 2B Butlers Wharf (1975–78), the ACME Gallery (1976–81) and the adopted spaces of London Video Arts (LVA), such as the Air Gallery (1977–). There were even a few galleries that showed the moving image from time to time – commercial galleries (perhaps more altruistic than truly commercial) such as The Lisson, Nigel Greenwood, Jack Wendler and Situation – and publicly funded ones such as Camden Arts Centre, the Whitechapel Gallery, and outside London the Arnolfini (Bristol), the Museum of Modern Art (MOMA; Oxford), the Bluecoat and Walker Galleries (Liverpool). All these – and many others – contributed to the rise in public awareness of the moving image as an artists' medium during this decade, and their individual contributions have yet to be properly acknowledged. Yet, a listing of the regular once/twice-a-week screenings of the LFMC throughout this period surely provides the fullest account anywhere of the sheer diversity of the British contribution to the art form, which is the subject of Patti Gaal-Holmes' invaluable study.

Spawned in the freewheeling 1960s international underground culture, by the early 1970s experimental film had taken root in the UK's art schools, sharing their ethos of direct hands-on production. Whereas the classic film or television studio was based on the specialist division of labour, the art school studio fostered individual authorship and the experimental exchange of views, processes and ideas. Some offered courses in new media, both in graphic design and fine art; others simply had 'the Bolex in the cupboard', which enterprising souls would discover and use. By the 1970s, art schools were less training grounds than places where new art was made directly. Much of the work of this period went far beyond the student film category; for example, John Smith's *The Girl Chewing Gum* (1975), made at the Royal College of Art and still generating variations and riffs by new makers.

In another view, this whole period is often unfairly characterised as narrow, didactic and partisan – Smith providing a clear exception – reflecting a hardening of cultural and political attitudes more widely across the arts and society. Despite this, the LFMC screening programme was remarkably consistent in its diversity, responding to two vital yet unwritten objectives: (1) showcasing new work as it was made (a priority that benefited those running the place most immediately), and (2) honouring the repertory of avant-garde classics, the latter as much for the pragmatic reason that 'that's what will bring in the paying punters', as for the more noble and far-sighted 'because that's how we build an audience for our work'. Patti's study covers the period that begins when the LFMC was associated most closely with Structural Materialism (Peter Gidal's formulation) and ends with the linked events on the South Bank – the exhibition 'Film as Film' (Hayward Gallery 1979) and the 'Film London: 3rd International Avant-garde Festival', (NFT 1979); one (Film as Film) attempting to construct a history of 'where we have come from' (which proved highly controversial, as Patti shows), and the other (Film London) celebrating the diversity of the moving image 'now'. Between these poles, the LFMC exhibited an extraordinary variety of works, reflecting the curatorial interests and insights of many artists and programmers: Peter Gidal, Annabel Nicolson, Lis Rhodes, David Curtis, James Mackay, Deke Dusinberre, Anna Thew and others. Patti quotes Malcolm Le Grice's call – made in *Studio International* in 1973 – for the Tate to commit to showing 'an historical repertory of avant-garde film, regularly presented as an aspect of the Tate's permanent art exhibition'. In its absence, the LFMC dutifully filled that gap.

In an age before home-video recording, before DVD publishing, before YouTube and Ubuweb, before Facebook and Twitter, you saw an artist's work when it had its first screening – or you didn't see it, and indeed might never see it again. The only forms of advance notice of a screening were the roughly printed flyers you picked up at some sympathetic sister venue, or – if you were lucky – a *Time Out* or *City Limits* listing (usually written by the filmmaker, sometimes illuminating, often not). Even the early film works of B. S. Johnson, already a much discussed novelist in the 1960s – had just one showing at NFT (July 1967), before returning to long-term obscurity. The experimental film works of another novelist, W. S. Burroughs were first shown in his filmmaking partner Anthony Balch's Oxford Street cinema, entirely off the LFMC radar, though they soon entered distribution and became part of the repertory. Derek Jarman's first screenings of his Super-8 films took place in his studio and were attended only by close friends, until he showed them more publicly at the LFMC and ICA towards the end of the decade. No wonder the sense prevailing among groups such as the LFMC, LVA and Circles (1979–) was that you should organise your own screenings and support your peers by religious attendance. Film-viewing was an act of pilgrimage. Jarman would have admitted the same of his own studio screenings, even though he mocked the LFMC's air of seriousness.

That seriousness was in part illusory – there was plenty of fun at the LFMC (what was expanded cinema if not at least, in part, joyous and celebratory?) Where it existed, seriousness was associated with the critical writing of the period and its response to high (film) theory. Before the liberating impact of feminism and gender studies took hold at the end of the decade, before *Undercut* and *Independent Media* arrived to give more power to artists' own voices, before the 'image' returned (not that it ever went away, as Patti demonstrates), 'serious' debate in England was led by the British Film Institute's (BFI) journal, *Screen*. This remarkable development is so familiar now that it deserves a brief step back to focus on what was going on, especially as film and/or media studies were not then academic disciplines. At best they were add-ons to another new topic – 'popular culture', a subset of English and General Studies for 16–19-year-old further education students.

That all changed on a massive scale in the early 1970s when *Screen* – up until then a rather staid journal promoting film and media education, such as it was – was taken over by an ambitious group of Oxbridge graduates, '68-ers for whom culture was a zone of contestation and struggle. As the most popular medium of the twentieth century, com-mercialised and led by the USA, cinema had shaped the imagination of global mass audiences. Its mechanisms – industrial, psychological, ideo-logical – demanded attention, with the 'new science' of structural analysis as a guiding model. Next, unknown or obscure critical alternatives were translated into English (notably the 1920s Russian Formalists and Futurists with their deep commitment to montage cinema, and the radical Brechtian legacy of the 1930s freed from its official fetters). In addition, 'the news from Paris' – cultural critiques by Barthes, political critiques by Althusser – updated and expanded Marxism and modernism for English readers.

Screen's interest in the avant-garde was limited, but significant. Art schools had regularly shown avant-garde classics by Leger, Man Ray and other pioneers; and some, such as the Slade, had substantial screening programmes long before the universities targeted by *Screen*. The films actually made in this milieu were clearly radical and demanding, undermining every convention of film form and – in expanded cinema – breaking open its borders. Even the (accidental?) chime between 'structural film' and 'structuralist theory' added to the mix. Connections beckoned, so that by the mid- to late-1970s, *Screen* had published texts on the avant-garde by Peter Wollen, Peter Gidal, Stephen Heath, Deke Dusinberre, Annette Kuhn, A.L. Rees, Malcolm Le Grice, Ben Brewster, Paul Willemen and Paul Marris. Parallel to this, avant-garde film was featured in *Screen*/BFI events at the Edinburgh Film Festivals and many other conferences and gatherings.

The gains and losses of this brief and rare conjunction between advanced film theory and radical film practice are weighed and assessed in Patti's book. It is hard to think of a precedent to the brief, if intense, debates of the 1970s. Earlier writers such as Kracauer and Arnheim – sadly neglected in this era – took the avant-gardes of their time seriously, but found them wanting; too painterly, too many 'tricks'. The best US critics, from Parker Tyler to P. Adams Sitney and Annette Michelson, forged a new film aesthetic from the models of literature and poetics. *Screen* itself paid a price for its revaluation – sometimes overvaluation – of Hollywood films by finding in them ever more ingenious psychoanalytic depths. The rise of defiantly celebratory accounts of popular culture in the 1980s blunted the edge of this kind of critical theory, and mocked avant-garde aspirations (post-structural enthusiasms migrated elsewhere, to the fringes of an expansionist media culture). A decade later, ironically enough, 'artists' film' dominated the gallery world from the late '90s, led by new generations mostly wholly unaware of any predecessors.

As we look to perspectives on our recent cultural context and its histories, the 1970s avant-gardes prove to be illuminating, provocative and suitably contradictory. Critical discussion of the artists' work of this period is often over-assigned to Le Grice and Gidal; their voices were indeed important, but the film viewing culture was more catholic, as was the writing in other journals: Simon Field on David Larcher and Dwoskin and Nicolson on films by conceptual artists in *Art & Artists*; John Du Cane on Larcher, Le Grice, EXPORT and others in *Time Out* (a listing magazine then capable of serious reviews), Tony Rayns on Jeff Keen, Kenneth Anger and others in his magazine *Cinema Rising*, and not least Nicolson's own magazine *Readings* (1977) which boldly proclaimed its interest in new music and performance art – subjects far beyond any supposed LFMC orthodoxy. The range of essays in the exhibition catalogues of the confusingly similarly titled 'Perspectives on British Avant Garde Film' (1977) and 'A Perspective on English Avant Film' (1978), was equally catholic. Video was a real force for change during this decade, following the inaugural fanfare of 'The Video Show' (Serpentine Gallery 1975), a show that was itself a proclamation of diversity that encompassed agitprop, community video and artists' works from the UK, USA and across Europe. Video brought its own critical agendas, and certainly helped to re-contextualise 'the image'. Subsequent accounts of developments in this diverse decade by Mike O'Pray, Nicky Hamlyn, Le Grice, Cate Elwes, Jackie Hatfield and our own published histories – have inevitably attached labels and constructed narratives that oversimplified the chaos and contradictions of the reality, in their attempt to impose some kind of narrative flow. Patti Gaal-Holmes' welcome addition to this field benefits enormously from being seen through the eyes of an artist from another generation, free of the blinkers of direct personal involvement at the time, so bringing fresh insights to the works. It challenges us to think again, and more importantly, to look again – to reconsider and re-value the works of these still underappreciated artists.

A.L. Rees
Royal College of Art (1996–2014)

David Curtis
British Artists' Film & Video Study Centre (BAFVSC)
at Central St Martins School of Art and Design

Acknowledgements

This book could not have been written without the assistance and kindness of numerous individuals. Many kind thanks to David Curtis for his generous support, for reading through chapters and offering invaluable advice. To A. L. Rees for his encouragement to pursue the final stages of the doctoral research and to publish these findings; and generally for his good humour and generosity of spirit. It is with great sadness that his passing was noted on 28 November 2014: the loss of a great voice in the field. Thanks to Professors Sue Harper and Paul MacDonald for guiding and steering me through the doctoral research informing this book, to Dr Dave Allen for support in the initial research phase and to Dr Duncan White for his expertise in supporting the final stages of the doctoral writing process. Grateful thanks also to my examiners A.L. Rees and Dr Esther Sonnett for advising publication. Kind thanks to Steven Ball, Duncan White and David Curtis for assisting with research at the British Artists Film and Video Study Collection at Central St Martins: an exemplary resource! With thanks to the BFI library for assistance; and to Benjamin Cook at LUX and all the filmmakers who kindly gave their time in interviews, informal discussions and email correspondence.

Acknowledgement is made to the Arts and Humanities Research Council for funding the doctoral research informing this book and the Hosking Houses Trust for financial support and residency in 2014.

Thank you to fellow doctoral researchers, Sian Barber and Sally Shaw, who have provided inspirational support and friendship on the long trajectory from initial research to publication. Immensely grateful thanks to the numerous friends who have been supportive throughout and endured listening to the joys and quandaries of this long journey. Special thanks to Birgit and Tina Gaal and the extensive family Holmes, for continued long-distance love from Africa...

Image credits for book cover

Patti Gaal-Holmes:
just looking, 2004, 8mm
Courtesy of the artist

Guy Sherwin:
Flight, 1998, 16mm
Courtesy of the artist

Ben Rivers:
Sørdal, 2008, 16mm
Courtesy of the artist and Kate MacGarry Gallery

David Larcher:
Monkey's Birthday, 1975, 16mm
Courtesy of the artist

Derek Jarman:
Journey to Avebury, 1973, S8mm
Courtesy of James Mackay © LUMA Foundation

Tacita Dean:
FILM, 2011, 35mm film still (detail)
Courtesy of the artist, Frith Street Gallery, London and Marian Goodman Gallery, New York/Paris

Jeff Keen:
Rayday Film, 1968–70 and 1976, 16mm
Courtesy of the artist's estate

Annabel Nicolson:
Sweeping the Sea, 1975, black-and-white photograph
still from performance
Courtesy of the artist

John Akomfrah:
The Unfinished Conversation, 2012, video
Courtesy of the artist © Smoking Dogs Films 2012

List of Abbreviations

ACGB   Arts Council Great Britain
BAFVSC   British Artists' Film and Video Study Collection
BFI   British Film Institute
BFIPB   British Film Institute Production Board
CND   Campaign for Nuclear Disarmament
FMOT   Film-makers on Tour
GLC   Greater London Council
ICA   Institute of Contemporary Art
IFA   Independent Filmmakers Association
LEA   London Electronic Arts
LFMC   London Filmmakers Co-operative
LVA   London Video Arts
NFT   National Film Theatre
RCA   Royal College of Art

Introduction

This book acts as a form of historical reclamation, demonstrating the complex and rich diversity in 1970s British experimental filmmaking. The intention is to integrate films that have not received adequate recognition into the field alongside those that stand as accepted texts. While filmmakers such as Derek Jarman, Ian Breakwell, Jeff Keen, David Larcher, Margaret Tait and Peter Whitehead have been recognised in 1970s histories, this collectively extensive (image-rich and representational) body of work has been overshadowed by structural and material film experimentation taking place predominantly at the London Filmmakers Co-operative (LFMC). I also advocate for the recognition of films by Jane Arden and B. S. Johnson – albeit perhaps awkwardly situated within this history – as these are sufficiently innovative and experimental to warrant inclusion. This re-evaluation of the history, situating more personal, poetic or expressive forms of filmmaking *alongside* the already well-established history of formal, structural/material film, brings unique insights to the fore and importantly recognises the richness and diversity in 1970s experimentation. While LFMC histories are already fairly well-documented, they also, in my mind, problematically focus too much on 1970s filmmakers/ theoreticians Peter Gidal and Malcolm Le Grice's structural/material(ist) theoretical positions, thereby also belying the rich seam of material produced at, and affiliated to, the LFMC during the decade. The particular 'culprit' which I argue is responsible for numerous biased historical accounts is the term embodying the myth that a *'return* to image' (that is personal, visionary and expressive forms of filmmaking) occurred at the *end* of the 1970s, whereas in fact these types of filmmaking existed *throughout* the decade. 'Image' never disappeared in the 1970s, and thus made no return.

1

Most of the filmmakers discussed in this book took an anti-Hollywood stance to filmmaking, identified by the very nature of working with small (or no) budgets and the use of 16mm or 8mm formats. Contextualisation took place within visual art practices such as painting, photography, sculpture, etc., and in earlier artists' film experimentation, rather than in the field of commercial cinema (although this also informed filmmaking). These films are differentiated from the dominant, narrative cinema and independent film production by their small budgets and their personal engagement with discourses in the arts, poetry or personal, diaristic investigations with film. The films discussed here were also mostly single-authored, with filmmakers often working on all aspects of production, including initiating ideas, filming, acting, processing, printing, editing, distributing and screening films.

While Marxist-informed attempts were made in the 1970s to argue against personal subjectivity in films made in opposition to industrial, commercially produced dominant cinema, the fact that these were mostly single-authored films indicates that there was no escaping their existence as individual, subjectively informed films. Sam Rohdie identified that '[t]he film in "the *final* analysis", was the expression of the author and the author's world ... Behind the film, waiting to be recognized, waiting to tear the mask of the film and to appear, was the filmmaker.'[1] It is, therefore, important to be aware of the finer details determining personal filmmaking practices in order to also understand how these films have been critically engaged with and historicised, as Vanda Carter points out:

> The reasons why people adopt particular filmmaking techniques are often overlooked in critical appraisal/s of work. The relationship between filmmaker and equipment, and with film itself, is one of the foundations on which individual style is developed. It is frequently assumed that purely aesthetic decisions govern filming and editing choices at every stage, whereas all filmmaking practice is pre-formed by the amount of money available, what equipment one has access to and by the practical situation and social context in which one works. 'Aesthetic' decisions are made within these boundaries, struggling constantly to push resources to the very limits, but never escaping these basic constraints.[2]

These factors are important to recognise as they essentially inform how a film might be interpreted beyond considerations of content and aesthetics. Alongside these, an awareness of critical or theoretical discourses framing a film also instrumentally informs its reading, as critic Rod Stoneman noted:

> The critical context involves a series of discourses which serve to interpret, mediate and locate the film. They offer the terms in which the text can be read. A work of art, like any other cultural and social discourse, has no meaning outside of its context and a number of complex and reciprocal determinations operate at the point of meaning production.[3]

Certainly, critical, aesthetic and theoretical contexts are central for situating a film within wider art/film/cultural frameworks, but an air of caution is needed in order not to over-determine these contextual issues. With regard to certain 1970s films (LFMC), framing within specific discourses, according to LUX director, Benjamin Cook, also had some more unwelcome effects:

> It was all about the frame. It was about the whole social, cultural framing of works. I've always strongly believed that it is a lot more accessible and has a lot to offer people, but the problem is once it gets framed in a particular way – with semantics really – it has the potential to kind of shut it down for people.[4]

The significance of discourses framing many of the films discussed here – such as the structural/material(ist) theoretical position – was therefore instrumental in shaping how these were read and how they continue to be historicised.

Many of the issues raised by experimental filmmakers in the 1970s are as pertinent today with the rise of accessible digital moving image technologies. The longer histories informing diverse forms of experimentation within the moving image are therefore important for contextualising contemporary practices. However, as David Curtis outlined, this recognition has not always been forthcoming:

> The common perception that the video installation is an invention of the 1990s – born miraculously free of any evolutionary history – is understandable, if wholly wrong ... the modern form of the installation in all its diversity was the product of a long period of experiment shared by the post-Caro generation conceptualists with their commercial gallery shows, and by members of the Co-op and future LVA groups, exhibiting mostly in artist-run and public-sector spaces.[5]

The lack of historical recognition not only empties the field of its richness but also fails to give filmmakers the credit they deserve. Le Grice, for example, observed that perceiving contemporary moving image work as 'groundbreaking', when it failed to recognise important historical precedents, was especially problematic:

> I saw a triple projection piece by [Steve] McQueen at the ICA, but a triple projection that could easily have been done in the 1970s. One has to ask oneself the question: why is this contemporary film practice taken up and given some celebrity when the work of people who had created a sort of long term language or practice is still marginalised.[6]

While Le Grice could be viewed as a disgruntled filmmaker, lamenting a sense of historical recognition, his comment does indeed raise some very important questions about the need for the historical contextualisation of contemporary moving image practices. Le Grice acknowledged that his work had been historically situated within Greenbergian modernist developments which, in his mind, were unsustainable 'in the framework of either digital technology or the present hybridisation of technology and culture'.[7] He also expressed difficulty 'with the gestural eclecticism that seems to be fundamental in postmodern work'.[8] It is perhaps this eclecticism that poses particular problems with regard to singling out specific historical lineages. Certainly, one could not propose to 'rule out' eclecticism, as this would serve no purpose and clearly be impossible. And it is in the nature of art that it imbibes, builds on and transmutes what has come before. But perhaps there is, in fact, a need to once again understand these histories within their specificity and not just within the broader scope of moving image practice.

This realignment of 1970s history therefore recognises the importance of identifying experimental film within its medium-specific capacity; this is not to elevate its hierarchy above video or other important 1970s art forms, but because this is a sufficiently rich history in need of clarification. With a resurgence of interest in these histories, filmmakers, critics and theorists can re-engage with some of the foundational issues that shaped these histories and which continue, as Vicente Todolí identified, to intrigue beholders: '[t]he art of the 1960s and 1970s continues, even some forty years later, to fascinate and provoke ... One thing is certain – the innovations of then are regarded as the foundations of art now'.[9] A clearer understanding of the rich diversity in 1970s film experimentation, which this book promises, thus also sets the precedent for examining subsequent decades: the 1980s, 1990s, 2000s, etc., therefore opening up pathways for understanding the extensive histories of contemporary moving image practices.

Note on terminology

Terminology in this field is in itself complex, and the reasons for using 'experimental film' over other terms of usage here requires a brief explanation. Film's uneasy placement between the fields of art and cinema became an important concern for 1970s funding bodies, with a need to distinguish different types of filmmaking arising early on in the decade. According to Curtis, the term 'artists' film' first emerged in 1972 when it was used to identify a particular Arts Council sub-committee funding artists' films.[10] The term 'experimental film' was similarly popularised in the 1950s, with films supported by the British Film Institute's (BFI) Experimental Film Fund.[11] In his recent history of underground cinema, filmmaker/activist Duncan Reekie noted the open-ended possibilities for 'experimental film':

> It refers to both process and product, adapts easily as a noun and an adjective, and it has been accepted by a significant number of divergent film movements and theorists as a transcendent historical term. Experimental in this context would not be limited to formal experimentation but would include experiments in narrative, acting technique, sound, *mise-en-scène*, technology, working practices, distribution, exhibition.[12]

Both 'artists'' and 'experimental' film fall under the broader term 'independent' film and refer to films identified from larger commercial studio systems due to their smaller budgets and cultural or socio-political (rather than commercial) motivations and values. The British Film Institute and the Arts Council of Great Britain (ACGB) were the main funders of independent and experimental films in the 1970s, and these included 'experimental film', 'art house' or 'counter cinema', with the latter two often defined by the distinctive individual visual styles of the directors. 'Counter cinema' was described by filmmaker/theorist Peter Wollen as having a 'militant hostility to commercial, narrative cinema as well as a commitment to radical politics and formal experimentation'.[13] The terms 'avant-garde' and 'independent' were sometimes used interchangeably in the 1970s. However, some forms of independent filmmaking took more conventional approaches to documentary or narrative filmmaking, while others, such as 'experimental' or 'counter cinema', took oppositional approaches to attack the illusionism and seamless narrative structures of commercial, dominant cinema. The term 'underground film', closely affiliated to 1960s American and British countercultural movements, had the filmmaker Steve Dwoskin defining these films as having 'no fixed scope, no fixed budget, no fixed audience, no fixed style and often no fixed script' with the '[t]he painters and poets hav[ing] become film-makers'.[14] 'Avant-garde', a term historically affiliated with military and political activity, identified the principal force in combat or political revolution. Its use in the arts and filmmaking dates from the 1920s, but the early 1970s substitution of the term 'underground' for 'avant-garde' resituated filmmaking within more academic (rather than oppositional, countercultural) spheres. The term 'experimental' is used here as I feel it accommodates the broadest forms of experimentation and is a good enough compromise, but its use should be understood to encompass all other cited terms of usage. 'Moving image' is used as an all-encompassing term referring to contemporary film, video and digital technologies.

Socio-political and theoretical contexts

The rich diversity in 1970s British experimental filmmaking did not, of course, occur in a self-informed vacuum, and it is important to recognise longer histories with broader international contexts. These include countercultural developments emerging first in 1950s America; the turn to theory in international film/art and intellectual circles in the 1970s; and the formation of co-operatives and workshops in Britain providing centres for art and filmmaking. In the first of these, countercultural influences, which emerged in America in response to increased 1950s capitalist growth, Cold War anti-communist McCarthyism, the Korean and Vietnam Wars and campaigns for racial and gender equality, would take different – and somewhat more militant – forms in 1970s Britain. These included challenging the increasing influence of American impe-rialism (cultural and capitalist) by taking a firm Marxist and socialist stance. The loss of Empire, with the impact of decolonisation rendering Britain as the small island it was (rather than the imperial power it had been when ruling over a quarter of the world), also resulted in a crisis of identity for the nation. This was further increased by the Campaign for Nuclear Disarmament (CND), with Jeff Nuttall identifying that the atom bomb – and specifically the attacks on Hiroshima and Nagasaki – acted as defining moments in the turn against seemingly 'progressive' Western developments relating to modernity.[15]

Although the media concept of the 'Swinging Sixties' was presented as a harmonised idea of hip and cool bohemia, filmmaker and activist Peter

Whitehead maintained that it was invented by *Time* magazine, obscuring the burgeoning counter-revolutionary activity and true sentiments of the decade. In his film, *Tonite Let's All Make Love in London* (1967), Whitehead presented 'a dark version of a city at war with itself' and a more politicised account of events:[16]

> With *Tonite* I was trying to examine the mythology that everybody in London was having fun. Ginsberg's poem, which is very much about the theft of British culture by American cultural and capitalistic imperialism, is actually, very dark. For me the 1960s was the Aldermaston march, the war in Vietnam and the Dialectics of Liberation. The only miracle about those years is that it was a moment of extreme change that managed to get through without savage violence.[17]

Whitehead's hostile interpretation of 1960s London was not unique, as attempts were made to avert American imperialism through more hardline socio-political Marxist ideologies. A radical rethinking of socialism by the New Left, challenging American imperialism, resulted in socialist and Marxist theories informing many aspects of social and cultural investigation and wielding a significant influence on independent filmmaking circles.

While the 1960s countercultural ethos formed the bedrock for initial film experimentation, certain 1970s developments shifted in subsequent years by taking more theoretical and academic approaches and leading to institutionalisation in some sectors, as outlined by Duncan Reekie:

> The New Left gathered around the development of the journal *New Left Review* (1959), the Campaign for Nuclear Disarmament (CND) and the London New Left Club in Soho. An essential component of the movement was the reciprocal allegiance and involvement of the Free Cinema group. The central thematic of the New Left was that socialism had to be radically reconceived if it was to challenge the new forms of post-war corporate and consumer capitalism and that this reconception had to be based on the development of a rigorous intellectual investigation into contemporary society.[18]

The theorisation and intellectualisation of oppositional approaches (to the condition of Western society and increasing American imperialism) therefore undoubtedly informed many aspects of 1970s society and culture, including the fields of independent and experimental film

experimentation. Film critic D. N. Rodowick, writing in 1982 and referring to the previous ten years, noted that '[n]ot since the 1920s, in
Weimar Germany and Soviet Russia, has there been a time in which
the inter-relationship between theoretical work, political activity, and
avant-garde artistic practices been so thoroughly argued'.[19]

Broader theoretical contexts informing 1970s independent filmmaking
included Marxism, feminism, psychoanalysis, structuralism and semiotics. For some filmmakers, particularly those affiliated with the film journal
Screen, these were informed by continental theories relating to structuralism, psychoanalysis and the French literary journal *Tel Quel* (1958–1982).
For artists/filmmakers emerging from the art school context – notably
conceptual artists or those affiliated with the LFMC – theories relating to
modernism in the arts and the privileging of 'form over content' would
also prove to be important. In this respect, Clement Greenberg's seminal
essays, written between the 1940s and 1960s connected artists and critics
'to the never-ending debates about whether and how far an art form
is determined by the media it employs'. This would be important for
informing certain experimental film practices, particularly those established by filmmakers/theorists Gidal and Le Grice at the LFMC, discussed
in some depth in Chapter 3.

It is important to note that certain filmmakers had little or no
involvement within Marxist- and theoretically informed experimental
filmmaking circles. These critically – informed positions did, however,
influence 1970s *readings* of films, resulting in filmmakers taking more
personal, expressive approaches (and falling outside the main theoretical
Marxist-informed frameworks) sometimes lacking the adequate recognition they deserved. This was, however, not only due to the problematic
'return to image' myth identified in this book but was also due to the
lack of a collective voice held by these filmmakers. Unlike structural/
material filmmakers who were part of workshops such as the LFMC
(providing opportunities to be part of a collective movement or 'voice'),
these personal, expressive or visionary filmmakers, demonstrated a true
independent spirit with no overarching theories or positions offering
cohesion. Instead, they worked on their own terms with the camera as
their tool to 'stalk' images, recording their world for perpetuity or bringing their imaginary visions to filter through their films.

Methodologies and structure

The diverse and extensive resources informing this research meant that
no simple methodological process could adequately reveal the complexity of experimental filmmaking in the decade. There was, for example,

no set number of film and production companies, governed by commercial directives, shaping the decade's production. Instead, these personal films – situated uncomfortably between the fields of art and cinema – were often made in improvised spaces, with limited resources, using friends for actors where necessary, and with often nothing more than an inspired moment to capture the world around them. As the (often short) films were usually screened alongside other films, an understanding of the curatorial role and discourses surrounding the films also played an important part in contextualisation. In approaching this history, I wanted to take the films themselves as my starting point to determine the diversity in filmmaking; and initially it was important to consider these as the key primary sources. Textual analysis, however, also required considerations of production contexts and screening conditions. For the latter, a reading of a film could differ significantly if it was screened within a specific programme of films, as an installation piece or as a live 'expanded cinema' event. Assessing film content included analyses of what was represented in-frame, relating to technicalities such as camera work, lighting, framing and composition, with recognition of the processes of production being essential for understanding the film texts.

Numerous written sources, taking the form of books, articles, doctoral theses and more ephemeral archival materials (short-run magazines, programme notes, interviews, filmmakers' notes and notebooks, funding applications, film stills and photographs) provided the breadth of research required to get an in-depth understanding of the decade's filmmaking. Recordings of audio and filmed interviews (1970s and retrospective), actual interviews and informal conversations with filmmakers and historians who generously gave up their time were instrumental in helping to steer my research. The 'return to image' thesis made itself apparent early on in my investigations and I held this in mind as I navigated through this history, questioning how films had been framed and asking why some films were more 'officially' included, while others were excluded or only partially recognised, obscuring the true richness of the decade's experimentation.

My initial training as a Fine Artist and my insights as an artist/filmmaker have to a large extent informed this research. Working with film in an artisanal manner – shooting, hand-processing, editing, printing and projecting – has, I hope, brought a depth of understanding which is evident in the analyses and appreciation of the challenges, frustrations and exhilarations experienced by the filmmaker in taking an idea from conception to projection. The decision to focus principally on film in this historical assessment is in no way due to a lack of appreciation for the video medium and its history. As it is, video histories have been extensively covered in diverse film and video histories (Rees, Curtis, Hatfield, etc.) and in histories focused on video only (Elwes, Meigh-Andrews, REWIND project, etc.). These video histories should be read alongside the film histories for a more extensive understanding of the decade's moving image production.

This book could have been presented in a chronological, linear format, as if the history unfolded seamlessly from the beginning of the decade until the end. 1970s filmmaking, however, did not evolve synchronously in a measured and sustained manner across the decade. Instead, there were diverse types of activity – occurring simultaneously or separately – fuelled by individual or collective interests, accessibility to production facilities, funding and socio-political or theoretical concerns. For this reason, a thematic approach provides a more useful way of examining this history, enabling closer investigation into specific contexts or discourses informing filmmaking. The structure of this book approximates a two-part structure. Firstly, Chapters 1 and 2 consider the wider frameworks historicising and enabling the growth of 1970s filmmaking; and secondly, Chapters 3–6 pay close attention to a range of film texts by contextualising these within specific discourses.

It seemed important at the outset to leap straight into the problem identified with this history – namely the 'return to image' thesis, which I believe has misrepresented the decade in previous accounts. Chapter 1 therefore considers the complexities of historiography related specifically to 1970s filmmaking and gives a detailed account of the 'return to image' thesis, identifying it and demonstrating how this biased position has been perpetuated. It then seemed vital in Chapter 2 to provide information about the organisational strategies and institutional frameworks in order to better understand the broader contexts enabling filmmaking, particularly as this resulted in a veritable 'explosion' in 1970s filmmaking which has ricocheted through the decades and is still evident in contemporary moving image practices. In the subsequent four chapters I go into more detail about specific aesthetic, theoretical or socio-political contexts informing filmmaking and provide close textual analyses of a range of films. Chapter 3 considers relationships between experimental filmmaking and other visual art practices, with a number of examples revealing relationships to painting, photography, sculpture and genres such as landscape and still life. In Chapter 4 more personal, expressive British films informed by aspects of the counterculture, psychoanalysis, mythology or 'diary' filmmaking are explored, using the American critic, P. Adams Sitney's taxonomical distinctions ('psychodramatictrance', 'lyrical', 'mythopoeia', and 'diary') as outlined in his seminal *Visionary Film: The American Avant-garde* (1974). My approach to this aspect of 1970s history provides a distinctly original contribution, particularly as these types of filmmaking were marginalised or seemingly militated against by the overriding Marxist ethos informing more theoretically informed filmmaking. Chapter 5 focuses on the already well-established history of experimentation with film structure and material, revealing the diversity in experimentation. Reasons for the dominance of structural and material filmmaking are also considered, in order to reveal why this has overshadowed the diverse forms of personal, more individual forms of filmmaking. In the final chapter the impact of feminism and discourses surrounding women's filmmaking are discussed with a focus on the 'feminine aesthetic' – an issue preoccupying filmmakers, artists and theorists in the decade – which provides engaging frameworks for discussion. The choice of films discussed in each chapter neither identifies the most important 1970s films, nor attempts to form some kind of canon. Instead, films were chosen because they best illustrated the points made, revealed the creative approaches used by filmmakers, or just simply because they piqued my interest enough to want to share them in illuminating this history.

The dominant view that personal or visionary forms of experimental filmmaking fell away during the decade, only to make a return at the end of the 1970s and the beginning of the 1980s, has been reinforced by the numerous written accounts of 1970s history. My central argument – that there was no *return* and this work existed *throughout* the decade – is supported by further evidence in the diverse range of films under discussion in this book. This review of the decade's filmmaking takes an alternative position, developing new forms of categorisation in order to show that dominant accounts of 1970s experimental film history have papered over a diversity of filmmaking approaches, particularly where the image was centrally placed within the texts. I believe this unprecedented re-examination forms an essential part in understanding the rich diversity in 1970s experimental filmmaking, and in giving *all* filmmakers the recognition they deserve: centrally placed, on an equal footing and within the lamplight beam illumination of history.

1
Questions of History

What are the decisions made when a historical moment is selected, contextualised within particular frameworks and used to narrate the past? What exactly is the evidence determining the 'facts' of history? Should history, as cultural historian Marius Kwint suggests, 'fully admit to its illusory and constructed nature, and stop pretending that it refers to a real process which is amenable to systematic analysis and even prediction'?[1] Should it admit to the sometimes arbitrary choices made by the historian who follows a hunch or a path with a head already full of ideas, but who through necessity gets momentarily side-tracked as new discoveries make themselves visible? What are the positioned approaches taken by historians, bringing their world-views to shadow the table where chosen sources are spread out for examination? How are these sources revealed in the light of the future moment of the new history's arrival? These questions raise possibilities which the practice of history brings to the fore, and to my mind these positioned approaches cannot pretend to exist within the certainties of a definitive methodology. Instead, I believe they should embrace an openness required for a methodology of discovery more akin to Paul Feyerabend's 'conviction that *anarchism*, while perhaps not the most attractive *political* philosophy, is certainly excellent medicine for *epistemology*' (Feyerabend's italics).[2] I believe that an openness to chance findings within and outside of the established historical paradigm is required by the researcher, whose approaches necessitate a passion for the subject of exploration equalled by a rigour to bring a new history to cohesion. These approaches to history are more akin to Robert Musil's 'Digression Three or Answer Number Four':

> The course of history was therefore not that of a billiard ball – which, once it is hit, takes a definite line – but resembles the movement of

clouds, or the path of a man sauntering through the streets, turned aside by a shadow here, a crowd there, an unusual architectural out-crop, until at last he arrives at a place he never knew or meant to go to. Inherent in the course of history is going off course.[3]

The 'going off course' but remaining within the radar signal of inten-tion has been my chosen historical method. I wanted, at the outset, to bring the films to the fore as readings of this 1970s history but without a doubt to also recognise the necessary contexts of the films and his-tories preceding this one. It has, therefore, been important to consider historiography and the way in which canons or dominant readings can problematically be shaped and remain unchallenged. These considera-tions underpin the discussions here together with some pertinent ques-tions asked about the roles of curation, the responsibility of national collections in accumulating representative histories of experimental film, and how we might look to untangle the complex histories making up contemporary moving image.

An initial discussion in the first half of this chapter is framed by a number of essays whose titles reveal ongoing questions which are still urgent for this history today. These are Malcolm Le Grice's 'The History We Need', Lis Rhodes' 'Whose History?' (both 1979) and David Curtis's more recent Tate symposium paper 'Which History?' (2001).[4] The sec-ond half of this chapter is central to the argument put forward in this book, namely that 1970s experimental filmmaking was far more diverse than accounts have determined. It importantly challenges the 'return to image' thesis, a myth continuing to dominate accounts of this history. This flawed myth, problematically privileging formal investigation over others types of experimentation, has offered a biased account of events. Evidence to dispel this claim and inconsistencies within some written accounts are provided in order to highlight problems with the 'return to image' thesis and how this argument has been perpetuated since the early 1980s.

Historiography and history through curation

While the study of history is a long-established discipline, more recent approaches raised in the late 1960s by historical theorists such as E. H. Carr and Hayden White, and in the 1990s by Keith Jenkins, provide useful considerations about the positioned nature of the historian. These approaches have informed an understanding of the vagaries of historical analysis in determining the impossibility of truly objective accounts of history. Jenkins' assertion that a single, 'true' history is unfeasible – 'the same object of enquiry can be read differently by different discursive practices [...] whilst, internal to each, there are different interpretive readings over time and space' – identified analyses of the same period as being dependent on choices of critical framework, subjective interpretation and methodological process.[5] Despite arguments for the reliability of sources as evidence, Jenkins also noted that the writing of history was never an impartial task – an unpositioned history – no matter how objectively a historian attended to the sources or intended the analysis to be:

> The empiricist claim – that one can detect bias and expunge it by attending scrupulously to 'what the sources' say – is undercut by the fact that sources are mute. It is historians who articulate whatever the 'sources say', for do not many historians all going (honestly and scrupulously in their own ways) to the same sources, still come away with different accounts; do not historians all have their own many narratives to tell?[6]

The different narratives that historians have to tell are also invariably informed by institutional or ideological reasoning.

In his curatorial essay for 'The Elusive Sign' (1987) exhibition, the critic Michael O'Pray similarly asserted Jenkins' claims about the positioned nature of the historian, acknowledging how choices are often made to accommodate certain historical accounts by potentially omitting works sitting less comfortably within the arguments presented:

> To this extent, the history of the avant-garde is always elusive. Art is continually re-writing its own history in order to provide an alibi for its contemporary ideas, strategies and tastes. Inevitably and necessarily, in such critical re-writings, aspects of the past are elided, and the present floods the future with its projects, ambitions and prejudices.[7]

Similar sentiments were also identified in an essay focusing on the theoretical, institutional and ideological approaches informing any historical analysis. The curator, Walter Grasskamp, for example, discussed the contexts shaping the acceptance of artworks into the historical paradigm and the selectivity inherent within any historical assessment:

> Of course, historiography, including art historiography, is only possible if a few events are selected from the chaos and peddled. Historiography

pretends to go by the worth of events, as contemporaries supposedly saw it, but uses its own evaluation.[8]

Grasskamp revealed how historical analyses were shaped by an array of complex discourses, decisions and intentions, providing as an example curator Wulf Herzogenrath's 1978 restaging of a 1949 exhibition, whereby he hoped to offer new perspectives on art history. It was anticipated that the 30-year distance would provide a more representative history than the limited exhibits presented in the earlier exhibition. However, acquiring some of the work by 'artists who had fallen through the sieves of art history' became problematic for the reconstruction:[9]

> How many forgotten paintings and sculptures are there for each painting that makes a career for itself in the colour reproductions of the standard works of art history? When do these decisions (which art historians take in order, they think, to separate the chaff from the wheat) start to be taken for granted? How often do these works remain unchallenged merely because the other works have simply been overlooked, forgotten or even frittered away by the heirs?[10]

Thus, unrepresentative histories are not only determined by a historian or curator's intentions but are also dependent on the availability of artefacts/artworks or sources available for inclusion. This is a particularly important issue for this 1970s history as many of the films I argue for here were not in distribution during the decade, or the filmmakers were not within the boundaries of dominant screening/exhibition circles, as was the case with B. S. Johnson, for example. Many of Derek Jarman's Super-8 films were only screened to a small coterie of friends or fellow-artists before receiving wider viewing, or only emerged when funding opportunities materialised, as he clarifies here:

> During the summer of 1973 I filmed the main sequences of a full-length Super 8 film – *In the Shadow of the Sun*, which was to wait eight years before it saw the light in 1980 at the Berlin Film Festival.[11]

Jarman's films were not the only ones out of circulation in the 1970s. David Larcher's two films were also rarely shown and not in distribution; as was the case with the films of Jane Arden and B. S. Johnson (possibly also related to their suicides). Margaret Tait's films were also only screened in England in the late 1970s, once she had been 'discovered' at a 1975 film festival.

The screening of experimental films was often a rare occasion – 'few films are likely to have more than one showing in a year even in London. So arrive 5 minutes late and you may have missed that masterpiece for ever' – and written accounts were often wrought through single screenings.[12] Critical essays and reviews have therefore held a great deal of significance, becoming central to readings of experimental film histories.[13] It is perhaps stating the obvious, but if films were not available – or so fleetingly available – there was less likelihood that they could be written about, critiqued or included in contemporary or retrospective screenings.

Accessibility to films

While digitisation and access to on-line materials has significantly changed things for the researcher, not all resources available on-line are representative of a given period as they have (prior to being uploaded) already been selected for dissemination. Before digitisation experimental films were also difficult to see as the following two examples indicate: D. N. Rodowick mentioned discovering (in 1989) that Pasolini's whole oeuvre was available at his local video store whereas 'five years earlier, I might have prioritised my life around a trip to New York to fill in the one or two Pasolini films I hadn't seen, or to review *en bloc* a group of his films'.[14] Curtis, similarly, noted: 'I knew about Warhol, and was even prepared to go to New York to try and see what he was on about'.[15] These details are significant for the way in which written texts about experimental film have dominated – and continue to in some respects – accounts of filmmaking. While the digital availability of films is certainly wonderful, providing access to a rich diversity of films, it does not account for the majority of 1970s films discussed here and it *cannot* stand in for the actual viewing of a film in a darkened room (and not on a computer screen) with projection mechanisms made visible where necessary.

Film also differs significantly to still artworks in its durational aspect, and it is therefore essential that the *whole* film be seen in order to grasp the work, differing significantly to the viewing of a drawing, painting or photograph. And this is where access has also been an issue, as LUX director Benjamin Cook identified:

> It is easier to see a painting than it is to see a film for the basic reason a film has no secondary representation like a painting does. You could theoretically study painting from pictures and books and obviously that is not ideal but you could, to a degree, know these works. Now

without seeing a film from beginning to end, you couldn't know it. And there is a whole complex system of how works are circulated. How value is imbued in works that also affects them.[16]

One of the issues specifically overshadowing historical accounts of 1970s experimental film is that many of these to a large extent became prejudiced by a lack of – and inaccessibility to – the primary sources: the films. Reliance on accepted written texts therefore became problematically intensified as these inadvertently became representative of the period, as Cook continues:

> There is a problem in discourse that lacks quite far behind in the practice in this particular area because of this particular phenomenological issue with these kinds of work and their inaccessibility. So the problem is because there is such a lack of writing and scholarship in this area. I mean in relation to other kinds of art history generally. What happens is that the books and the work that was made – maybe not meaning to – establishes a kind of canon or key texts become by default key texts.[17]

These issues have, since my discussion with Cook, begun to be addressed – and I do this here with the 'return to image' thesis below – but there are still gaps and challenges to the established histories.

Another concern raised by filmmaker/curator Lucy Reynolds is that most of the 1970s histories have to date been written from within. While this may give a certain depth of detail, they could also lack the necessary objectivity an 'outsider' might bring. In her review of two experimental film histories she identified issues where both writers (David James and David Curtis) were, in effect, writing from the inside:

> Of course, it could be argued that academic texts are always palimpsests, as the unfolding story of the writing and the writer become overwritten, yet remain discernible, beneath the subject material. In the canons of experimental cinema, it may be that these two texts are more closely written and harder to untangle because the chronicle often occupies the same temporal space as the chronicler; as friends become subject matter and events experienced become historical evidence.[18]

Thus, all these issues can seriously impede understandings of a period as reliance on key texts or accepted sources, inaccessibility to films and insider histories may distort historical readings, perpetuating certain accounts or failing to recognise other positions. These should be kept in mind as we turn to more specific examples to further consider these questions of history.

Whose history do we need?

Before turning to more in-depth discussions on the 'return to image' thesis, the three polemical texts – 'The History We Need', 'Whose History?' and 'Which History?' – will be considered, as they shed light on the complexities of curatorial decision-making and historical analysis. The first two essays relate to the controversial 'Film as Film: Formal Experiment in Film 1910–1975' (1979) retrospective exhibition, and Curtis's paper (presented more recently) focuses on the problematic absence of 1970s experimental film and video held in public collections.

'Film as Film', as the title suggests, focused on formal experimentation, identifying particular historical developments. The initiative was born out of the German *'Film als Film: 1910 Bis Heute Vom Animationsfilm Zum Filmenvironment Der Siebziger Jahre'* (1977) exhibition, co-curated by Birgit Hein and Wulf Herzogenrath, setting up an international art historical polemic focused on relationships between experimental film and related artefacts (drawings, paintings and archival documentation). This provided a critical context for experimental filmmaking within the broader contexts of cinema and German art.

The Hayward Gallery exhibition differed in not 'simply reproducing the excellence of the German model' but expanded on related concepts in film aesthetics, thereby presenting new historical perspectives and emphasising formal investigation focused on cinematography, editing and the projection event.[19] The British curatorial team sought to re-examine the history, taking into account recent British experimentation and including previously omitted international material:

> In following the German model, but re-interpreting it within a slightly later, British context, we have therefore understood our task as that of extending the range of issues – not only aesthetic or historical, but theoretical and political – which is implied in the very notion of the avant-garde, or of avant-gardes, at large.[20]

The intention was to include early European and Soviet films and the previously hidden history of women's experimental filmmaking.

In his catalogue essay Le Grice outlined 'The History We Need' as recognising the impossibility of 'a neutral and inclusive history', but suggested that 'the historical enterprise should be aimed at aiding the development of contemporary practice' rather than the 'nebulous general public'.[21] At stake was the presentation of a history most clearly aligned to formal, material and structural experimentation, with Le Grice positing a decisive rejection of films with a symbolist or narrative basis:

> What is designated form or structure in film is primarily related to the pattern of its temporal construction [...] Rejection of symbolist/surrealist practice does not eliminate the issues of signification from 'formal' cinema but may encourage a false assumption in the practice that it does.[22]

While Le Grice justified reasons for inclusion or exclusion, problems emerged for women on the curatorial team who found the history unrepresentative of women's filmmaking prior to 1975.[23] Despite recognising that 'Film as Film' dealt with specific formal practices, it was felt that the inclusion of this historically marginalised group would contribute important breadth and context to the exhibition, thereby offering a more representative history.

Problematically, no resolution could be found to the dispute, leading to the well-documented controversial withdrawal from the project and an exhibition devoid of the women's contribution (although essays and statements were importantly included within the exhibition catalogue). Rhodes raised particularly incisive questions in her polemical essay:

> Women appear, but on whose terms? Within whose definitions? Apparently historical accuracy is based upon acceptable 'facts', that is those facts that are the concern of men. Unacceptable 'facts' are forgotten and rearranged.[24]

Rhodes ended by pertinently asking '*who* makes history for *whom*?' (Rhodes' emphasis).[25] While the research gathered for 'Film as Film' was later used to ameliorate some of the omissions in women's film history with 'Her Image Fades and her Voice Rises' (1983), Rhodes important question, speaking a universality, is useful to hold in mind as this history is outlined and deliberated.

'Which History?'

Curtis's 'Which History?' paper (presented as part of a Tate International Council Conference, 2001) challenged public institutions such as the Tate, Arts Council England (ACE) and the British Council on the unrepresentative moving image histories held in their collections. With reference to

Le Grice's earlier essay, Curtis asked 'Where does this art come from? What is its past?', and identified that almost 30 years later this was still a pertinent and largely unanswered question.[26] Curtis discussed works made for the gallery, single-screen works for cinema or monitor screening, works commissioned for television and site-specific or performative works. He revealed that the rich diversity of works, dating back to the early days of cinema, were presented by sparse historical collections and that these suddenly burgeoning at a late point as if these art forms had been 'immaculately conceived at some point in the mid-1990s'.[27]

The Tate collection, for example, included three 1970s films by Gilbert and George, mid-1980s works by Susan Hiller and Mona Hatoum, and a sudden mid-1990s expansion including the acquisition of a relatively substantial collection including Steve McQueen's *Deadpan* (1990) and Douglas Gordon's (*24-Hour Psycho* 1993). In Curtis's estimation the ACE collection was equally unrepresentative with a few 1970s conceptual films by Darcy Lange, Liliane Lijn, David Dye, David Lamelas and Gilbert and George, a single 1980s film represented in Rose Finn-Kelcey's *Glory* (1983), and a similar noticeable mid-1990s expansion as this type of work became more collectible:

> It reflects the fact that there was (briefly) a market for the moving-image in the early 1970s (or at least a belief that there *might* be one), and that there certainly *wasn't* a market in the 1980s and early 1990s, but that one finally took off in the mid 1990s.[28] (Curtis's emphasis)

The rich productivity in 1970s and 1980s filmmaking was shown in both publicly funded galleries, such as the Ikon (Birmingham), Museum of Modern Art (Oxford), Serpentine and Institute of Contemporary Art (ICA) (London) and the Arnolfini (Bristol), and in artist-run spaces like 2B Butlers Wharf and ACME Gallery (London). Problematically, as with the single-screen films, this abundant history was almost non-existent in state collections:

> These were the key players in the late 1970s [and] early '80s. It was in these galleries that the film and video installation as we now know it – single-screen, multi-image or mixed media – was born. And yet despite the fact that the work produced in these venues during these decades was designed for the gallery space, it is almost wholly absent from our national collections.[29]

Curtis went on to discuss the wide range of site-specific or live-cinema film works shown in public-sector galleries, lamenting their exclusion from collections. While Curtis admitted that there were inherent difficulties in the presentation of such works – due to their site-specific, multi-screen or performative nature – he firmly believed that at least some form of documentation should be represented in the collections. But the question of obsolete technologies also raised some pertinent issues:

> The technology used by David Hall's *Progressive Recession* [1974] is now completely obsolete. Do you fake it with modern equivalents? Malcolm Le Grice may not be with us forever to perform in *Horror Film* [1971], and a site-specific work such as Judith Goddard's *Television Circle* [/*Electron*, 1987], misses its point when removed from the forest location for which it was conceived.[30]

Curtis was concerned that these works should not be lost to history, suggesting that even if technology needed to be faked or documentation exhibited in glass cases this would be better than having no record of the work at all. Similar concerns were also reiterated by Rees when he noted that '[o]nly a few works are likely to survive in their original state, permanently installed in museums'.[31] These, he said, would in all likelihood be determined by the different media rather than on creative merit. He gave the example of the artist, Dan Flavin's mass-produced neon tubes which 40 years later have to be hand-produced to preserve the work. Rees wondered how 'many artists will get that kind of treatment when the factories run out of 8mm film, VHS recorders and CD-Roms?'[32] Both Curtis and Rees acknowledged the challenges involved in acquiring or documenting such works for posterity but urged that this was not a call for complacency. They argued that compromises should be sought where actual works could not be displayed, as the misleading histories held in public collections did little to accommodate the diversity of works produced prior to the mid-1990s, thereby offering a problematically unrepresentative view of moving image history.

Interestingly, Le Grice had already urged the Tate to collect experimental film in the 1970s:

> There are three important areas for which the Tate could be the ideal screening context: (1) an historical repertory of avant-garde film, regularly presented as an aspect of the Tate's permanent art exhibition; (2) a regular series of showings by individual film-makers, introduced by them, beginning with a complete review of home-grown production; (3) occasional special presentations of installation and cinema in the round, work prepared for the gallery situation.[33]

Le Grice justified his reasoning as the BFI collected more commercial cinema and no equivalent to New York's Anthology Archives existed in Britain. Le Grice's recommendations were, however, largely disregarded at the time and have yet to be fully addressed over 40 years later. In his interview with Mazière, Le Grice said he was critical of the Tate as it 'had a responsibility to build up a collection of artists' film and video'.[34] Mazière pointed out that he too had approached the Tate, asking them why they weren't collecting the work, with their responses from the late 80s being: '[w]e are not a museum of modern art. We are a museum of British art so it's not in our remit. And also our trustees don't want to collect reproducible media'.[35]

Curtis hoped that the publication of his recent A History of Artists' Film and Video in Britain (2007), informed by his extensive 100-year historical Tate survey, would (alongside other histories) help to invigorate interest in this work, but at the time of presenting his paper he noted that:

> Tate purchases have played their part in confirming the importance of the YBA generation of filmmaking artists, though the museum has yet to show that it recognises the significance of the older generations (these artists' spiritual parents), such as (to name but a few) Dye, Gidal, Larcher, Le Grice, Rhodes and Parker, or even Lye and Jennings.[36]

But to date, many of the 1970s films representative of this influential and formative decade – where a veritable 'explosion' in experimental filmmaking took place – have yet to be included in the Tate's collections.

Certainly, issues around reproducibility and limited editions have been of concern to public collections with the collecting of historical work. Curtis sheds some important light (and I will quote in full) on how these issues were also of concern to many 1970s and 80s artists and experimental filmmakers:

> [F]ilm remained the responsibility of the education department, with only rare excursions into the territory by the exhibitions and collections staff over the next two decades. One apparent obstacle was the Tate Trustees' decision only to collect works published in limited editions. To many artists, the idea of a limited edition of films was anathema; film's infinite reproducibility was one of its attractions, offering an escape from the trap of the unique, therefore materially valuable art-object, also making film a conceptually purer and (arguably) more democratic medium [...] The Arts Council, which saw purchasing works for its Collection as a primary means of

supporting living artists, similarly failed to include film and video till the mid-1990s. It had the excuse that from the 1970s it was already supporting film-making artists with grants of production and exhibition funds. None the less, the absence of film and video works from the 1970s and 1980s in the Arts Council Collection of contemporary British art – which in size exceeds that of the Tate – was, and is, anomalous.[37]

While the need to collect moving image work was already mooted by Le Grice in the 1970s as a matter of urgency, it is interesting to see how little this has been addressed by national collections. The hope, of course, is that this will change in due course. There is no doubt that this seminal decade has informed subsequent developments. Conrad Atkinson, for example, identified that '[t]he British art of the 70s made the British art of the 90s possible. The 80s were a reaction to the 70s, but the 90s built on the lessons of the 70s'.[38] With Tacita Dean's recent call (to UNESCO) for the recognition of film as a cultural product in its own right, and more recent interest and activity in the decade, it may also be a timely moment to reconsider the important developments in 1970s experimental filmmaking and the longer histories lying either side of the decade.

The 'return to image' thesis

The 'return to image' thesis, arguing that more representational and image-rich forms of filmmaking occurred at the *end* of the 1970s included the use of various terms such as 'autobiographical', 'personal' filmmaking, 'narrative', 'celebratory cinema', 'visionary cinema', 'cinema of excess', and 'poetic' filmmaking.[39] 'Autobiographical' and 'personal filmmaking' – more self-explanatory – referred to filmmakers drawing on personal biographical references; 'narrative' referred to films taking a more linear, narrative format. The 'film poem' was described by P. Adams Sitney as being made by filmmakers who 'like poets, produce their work without financial reward, often making great sacrifices to do so' but also refers to more poetic filmic forms (rather than more abstract, minimalist texts).[40] Sitney likened the relationship of the 'film poem' to commercial narrative cinema as being similar to that of poetry to fiction.

The word 'image' also requires a brief moment of consideration here as film is, arguably, always about image whether the image revealed is the grain of the film, a Colour Field or recognisable figurative imagery.

Exceptions to this could be conceptual works, discussed in Chapter 3 as 'no film' films, where no actual film exists but the works explicitly refer to the filmed image in their conceptualisation and exhibition. 'Image' is, therefore, a problematically complex term, but in the context of its 'return' here it relates to more expressive, personal and potentially symbolic or metaphoric use of image, possibly also serving a narrative purpose. This 'return' to more representational forms of visual excess was identified as being a surplus of imagery sometimes arrived at through formal or technological procedures and content which might include multiple exposures, the use of images from popular culture sources, the prevalence of the human figure or an excessive use of colour. Or these films were simply personal films expressing individual responses to the world with images being recognisably figurative rather than abstract.

I will begin with film historian, A.L. Rees's Tate symposium paper, 'No Psychodrama Please, We're British' (2002), in which he identified film experimentation emerging from 1960s and 1970s British underground counterculture and film schools, with a particular focus:

> Aesthetics is a kind of ethics. All explored the medium as material. Artisanal work came, not through drama, but only film as process, something not fixed and always in a state of deferral.[41]

US influence, Rees said, came through Warhol – a few illegal dubs had made their way to the LFMC – whose portraits were 'cool, objective, rejecting the interiority of the psychodrama, which was seen as phoney and pretentious'.[42] While Rees acknowledged the influence of US structural filmmakers on their British counterparts, he professed that 'psychodrama' or 'mythopoeia' (two types of US image-rich experimental filmmaking identified by Sitney) were not widespread in Britain as filmmakers were against the spectacle of cinema. While this may have been the case with filmmakers affiliated to the LFMC, this cannot be said to be true of other filmmakers such as Jeff Keen, David Larcher, Steve Dwoskin or Derek Jarman whose films were instead sometimes ablaze with imagery, often subjectively informed or filled with psychological drama. Whether they were 'phoney and pretentious' was down to the critical reading.[43]

In Rees's earlier 'Re-viewing the Avant-Garde' (1983) he described some changes in experimental filmmaking which he said were evident by the end of the 1970s, suggesting that '[s]ome of the *bêtes noires* of avant-garde theory in previous years – including narrative and autobiography – have been reworked in a number of excellent films made in a less "formalist" mode than those of the earlier 70s' (Rees's emphasis).[44] Rees also noted that:

> There has also been a crop of Neo-Romantic work, promoted by the energetic B2 group (Wapping and the Regent's Park Diorama). Its exponents include John Maybury, Cerith Wyn Evans and Julia Hotspur Percy, working on cheap and occasionally nasty low-gauge tape and film. The whole enterprise suggests a folk memory of Jack Smith and might prove the success of excess – or just as quickly disappear into an ever-growing market for style, glitter and pose.[45]

Although Rees's criticism of films emerging in the 1980s did not preclude their existence during the 1970s, he also indicated that a renewed change of direction occurred at the end of the 1970s. In his related review of Will Milne's *Same* (1981) he suggested the film was 'evidence of a revival of interest in the codes of editing and composition, of a need to extend and re-think film language' which followed 'a period of minimalist paring down of the image by experimental filmmakers'.[46] It should be pointed out, however, that not all experimental filmmakers went through this period of 'minimalist paring down of the image' and that the '*bête noires* of avant-garde theory [...] narrative and autobiography' were in evidence throughout 1970s films.[47] Anne Rees-Mogg's *Real-Time* (1971–74), Margaret Tait's *Place of Work* (1976) (reviewed in the same journal issue) and B. S. Johnson's *Fat Man on the Beach* (1973) are a few examples which could hardly be described as minimalist. David Larcher's *Monkey's Birthday* (1975) was anything but pared down with its multi-layered imagery, montage-style and hand-worked frames.

In a further example, Michael O'Pray's unambiguously titled 'The Elusive Sign: From Asceticism to Aestheticism' (1987), mentioned David Larcher's 'classic "underground" films', as 'unequalled in their rich visionary quality', yet O'Pray only mentioned *Mare's Tail* (1969) and not *Monkey's Birthday* (1975).[48] In this essay O'Pray possibly did more than most to begin consolidation of the 'return to image' thesis, which has since been propagated to fulfil the problematic myth. O'Pray identified the 'return to image as an avant-garde component' by taking a retrospective view of ten years of film and video production:

> That the past decade has seen a return to such kinds of cinema – surrealist, documentarist, poetic, and experimental narrative – should not be surprising, it is precisely the recovery of traits in avant-garde

film history that have been allowed to slip out of sight for some time, and that have not been the root of influence.[49]

There are some interesting discrepancies in O'Pray's review as he discusses filmmakers working within experimental traditions he suggests have slipped out of sight for some time, yet he mentions, for example, Jarman's 'Super 8 "home movies" which he had been working on *since* 1970'.[50] He also described the 'avant-garde's two oldest practitioners', Jeff Keen and Margaret Tait, as 'a surrealist' and 'a poetic documentarist', respectively.[51] In a more recent account O'Pray said that '[i]n many ways, Jarman had always, notwithstanding the "constructed" cinema of *In the Shadow of the Sun* 1972–1981, been a documentarist, filming his friends, social events and his milieu'.[52] Surely, calling Jarman a 'documentarist' stretches the term somewhat. One could then even go so far as to call Peter Gidal a documentarist because he filmed clouds, aeroplanes, rooms and a hallway. Nevertheless, these are the intricacies of terminology. But more importantly, despite the fact that these filmmakers collectively produced a significant amount of films throughout the 1970s, O'Pray is still insistent that a 'return to image' occurred at the end of the 1970s. While he clearly demonstrated recognition of Larcher, Keen, Tait and Jarman's work, he still continued with this fall-back position, claiming that a 'return to image' occurred at the end of the decade. He did, however, make a thought-provoking comment, identifying that 'perhaps the return to the image as an avant-garde component had never been that far away', possibly suggesting an awareness of these contrived temporal distinctions.[53]

In an account written 25 years later, O'Pray continued to identify the alleged shift of focus at the end of the 1970s, with filmmakers 'returning' to different types of production – as if in defiance of their elders – to embrace the world of myth, dream, symbolism, sexuality or the subconscious:

> More broadly, it may be argued that there was a shift from asceticism to aestheticism. In an Oedipal reaction, the young film-makers embraced what had been anathema to their elders – subject matter. The 1980s in Britain can be seen as a rejection of modernism in its more rationalist formalist forms, and a return to the repressed tradition of modernism – one which embraced the oneiric (Ron Rice, Cocteau), the symbolist (Deren) and the documentary (Vertov, Jennings) [...] Decadence, with its emphasis on the body, opened up a sexual politics evaded by rationalistic machine-based early modernism. The New Romantics can be seen as a later example of this trait. Among the various strands of the

1980s there was a common return to subject matter outside film's own material and ontological concerns.[54]

Interestingly, O'Pray made these claims at a time when Jarman's extensive output of 1970s films had influenced the 'New Romantic' filmmakers Maybury and Wyn Evans. Jarman was without doubt not informed by formal, structural or theoretical filmmaking and was short-listed for the Turner Prize in 1986 'in recognition of the outstanding visual quality of his films'.[55] Additionally, by the time O'Pray wrote his critique (2003) a collection of Jarman's Super-8 films had been screened on BBC 2's *Arena* and edited into the 60-minute compilation *Glitterbug*, which included footage from *Studio Bankside* (1972), *Sloane Square* (1974–1976) and *Ulla's Fete* (1976), indicating that austerity and asceticism were certainly not the only order of the day.[56] The original video cover described the films as 'a stimulating, joyous and evocative self portrait of Jarman the artist and his milieu, showing times of fun and pleasure with friends, together with moments of high camp in the early 70s and frivolity on the sets of his films'.[57] Moreover, O'Pray was a firm supporter of Jarman's work, acknowledging that he 'had been making Super-8 films throughout the 1970s in a style which was visu-ally rich and sensuous and often used constructed and highly theatrical tableaux', yet his statement, signalling the shift from asceticism to aes-theticism at the end of the decade, does not appear to adequately take this into account.[58]

More to the point, O'Pray identified the alleged return at the end of the decade to a filmmaking of representational visual excess as being complemented by a renewed interest in earlier literary and film texts:

> Literature replaced theory – especially Lautréamont, Burroughs with Bataille. For its influences and inspiration the film-makers leapfrogged a generation – back to the 1950s and 1960s of Andy Warhol, Jean Cocteau, Kenneth Anger, Jack Smith, Ron Rice, Jean-Luc Godard, Rainer Werner Fassbinder and Japanese cinema. In its aesthetic it cel-ebrated artifice and images pillaged from both high art and popular culture. It emphasized the body, performance and sexuality, notably gay. This meant a shift from the materialist-realism of the Le Gricean formalists, to montage and collaging techniques in which the assem-bling of images took precedence over the shot of reality.[59]

Interests in more expressionistic and subversive literature and film from earlier decades thereby also purportedly signalled a marked rejection of the theoretically formalist and politically informed Marxist position prevailing at the LFMC in the 1970s. While this may have been the case for *certain* (mostly) LFMC filmmakers, an air of caution should be adopted when recounting this as the definitive history of the decade. Not all filmmakers were involved with the LFMC, and some that were – such as Larcher – didn't necessarily follow the hardline theoretical position on film form, structure and material. Moreover, filmmakers such as Jarman had sustained interests in Romanticism, ('I think William Morris is wonderful and I like Blake'), poetry (citing Rimbaud and Shakespeare as inspiration), and in the archetypical psychology of Carl Jung; and all these were continuous influences on his work.[60] Margaret Tait called her works 'film-poems', saying 'I think that film is essentially a poetic medium', and was inspired by the poet Frederico Lorca's approach to 'stalking the image'.[61] These were consistent interests throughout Tait's life as she took a sociological and personal interest in recording her surroundings. Larcher, who worked on his films at the LFMC during the 1970s, had never taken the extreme, formal, theoretical line in filmmaking and had an interest in mysticism and psychoanalysis, citing the mystic Gurdjieff in *Monkey's Birthday* (1975).

If a 'return to image' did occur anywhere, this was perhaps evident in the work of younger filmmakers affiliated with the LFMC and influenced by Gidal and Le Grice's theoretical positions. These included filmmakers such as Lucy Panteli (*Across the Field of Vision*, 1982), Michael Mazière (*Untitled*, 1980), Rob Gawtrop (*Distancing*, 1979), Will Milne (*Fattendre*, 1978) and Nicky Hamlyn (*Guesswork*, 1979). Gidal's uncompromising theoretical position and continued influence in subsequent decades almost certainly consolidated the view on the dominance of formal experimentation during the 1970s, potentially also consolidating the alleged 'return to image' thesis. Gidal's dominance – and continued influence on younger filmmakers – was outlined in Curtis's 'Gidal's Legacy' and Nicky Hamlyn's 'From Structuralism to Imagism: Peter Gidal and his Influence in the 1980s' (1999), which serve as useful references.[62]

While Gidal maintained his more fervent position in later decades, Le Grice turned to more narrative forms of filmmaking in the latter part of the 1970s with *Blackbird Descending: Tense Alignment* (1977), *Emily Third Party Speculation* (1979) and *Finnegan's Chin* (1981), identifying that his 'own film crisis was influenced by feminist theory and French film theory (Mulvey, Metz, psychoanalysis, etc.)'.[63] Many of Le Grice's earlier films, though, also had a strong poetic edge, even if there was a focus on more formal aspects of filmmaking. I would even suggest that films such as Le Grice's earlier *Little Dog for Roger* (1967) and *After Lumière* – *Arroseur Arrosé* (1974) have a poetic, Romantic sensibility – despite also revealing formal aspects of point of view, film materiality, film-stocks and – formats (*Little Dog for Roger* uses 9.5mm home-movie footage with sprocket holes revealed through reprinting). The piano scores in both films are evocative and poetically sentimental, with *After Lumière* also focusing on more formal aspects of the sound/image relation in its four 'parts'. The first three parts show the same scene filmed in black-and-white positive, then negative stock followed by colour negative stock (with the non-diegetic sound of a piano), while the final 'part' reveals the pianist (diegetic sound) playing. While Le Grice's personal crisis may indeed have led to significant shifts in his filmmaking, leading to more narrative engagements with formal filmmaking in his trilogy of films, this may be indicative of a possible 'return to image' of certain filmmakers within the LFMC.

In a further account reinforcing the notion of the 'return to image' thesis Wollen summarised 1970s and 1980s filmmaking for his ICA Biennale catalogue essay:

The dominance of 'structural' film lasted until the early 80s, when it was disturbed by the 'New Romantic' film and video-makers, who broke with the rigorous formalism and asceticism of 'structural film', revelling instead in flamboyance and excess, reviving the suppressed aesthetic of Cocteau and camp. Thus the 70s were marked by the influence of the fine arts, at the moment when they turned away from painting and the galleries, whilst the 80s were influenced by music, fashion and style.[64]

Again, this may well have been the case with *certain* films/filmmakers; however, this generalisation not only fails to account for the diversity in 1970s filmmaking, it also apportions out the history as if only two specific forms of filmmaking were evident in the decades.

Clearly the neat sectioning-off of different types of filmmaking into temporal zones, with the alleged shift of focus – the 'return to image' – has informed (mis)readings relating to experimental film histories. In a more recent observation on 1980s filmmakers Maybury and Wyn Evans, Lucy Reynolds suggested that if 1970s experimental filmmaking was primarily concerned with 'problematising notions of representation, illusion and pleasure, then the beginning of the 80s saw the New Romantics taking what some would inevitably see as a reactionary about-turn by exploring the "*myriad permutations of how beautiful one could make [an] image"'* (Reynolds' emphasis).[65] She further noted that filmmakers screening films in the ICA's 'A Certain Sensibility' (1989) exhibition 'marked a radical turn within British avant-garde film'. This they did, Reynolds continues, by 'embracing aspects of popular culture', thereby allegedly helping to 'reunite two spheres that had been effectively severed' during what Maybury has described as the '"intellectual death" of the 70s'.[66] The severance of the two spheres (high and popular culture), however, is as mythic as the 'return to image' thesis, which does not appear to account for filmmakers such as Keen, for instance, (one of the most prolific working in the decade) whose oeuvre includes numerous films using popular culture imagery (comic strips, Hollywood stars, adverts and advertising slogans). Keen's filmography by 1980 ran to almost 30 films – these had been screened, amongst other places, at the LFMC and in expanded cinema festivals – Maybury's 'intellectual death' and 'severance', therefore, should be recognised as applying to *certain* filmmakers (such as those exploring structural and material film at the LFMC) preoccupied with more formal filmmaking.[67]

The above examples give an indication of the perpetuation of the 'return to image' thesis, but in order to accelerate the nit-picking to a degree it will be useful to examine additional accounts which, on the one hand, reinforce the established 'return to image' position but, on the other, recognise that other forms of filmmaking also occurred. In the first example Rees valuably identified some of the strained links between different forms of filmmaking in the decade:

> [F]ilm-makers like Jeff Keen, David Larcher and Dwoskin himself – *who kept up the anarchic underground tradition* – were for a time marginalised by the Co-op structuralists. It was a clash of spirit as much as of substance, signalled in the switch of name from the liberatory 'underground' to the more theoretical 'avant-garde'. For some the Co-op's turn away from the films of Dwoskin, Larcher and Keen was a sign of new scholasticism. *But celebratory cinema was not much in evidence during the post-euphoric 1970s,* when the major choices for young film-makers lay between the purist avant-garde and the agit-prop collectives like Cinema Action, Politkino, the London Women's Film Group and the Berwick Street Collective. *For much of the decade the visionary film-makers of the first Co-op continued to add to their extensive bodies of work regardless,* often ironically enough using the techniques and tropes of structural film, although these efforts were more often appreciated in France, Germany and Holland than at home.[68] (my emphasis)

While Rees recognised that other forms of filmmaking (besides formal or politically engaged) continued *throughout* the decade, the 'anarchic underground tradition' persisted with 'the visionary film-makers' adding 'to their extensive bodies of work regardless'.[69] Yet he also stated that 'celebratory cinema was *not much in evidence* during the post-euphoric 1970s', therefore setting up some problematic negations (my emphasis). Rees also continued by saying that:

> Broadly the structural tendency won out in those younger film-makers who showed their first films around 1977. It was their immediate legacy and context, although each distanced themselves from it. The underground visionary tradition (in Larcher and Dwoskin, partly in Jeff Keen and later in Derek Jarman) *went further underground*, and was only picked up again in the 1980s by new groups who definitively rejected structural film.[70] (my emphasis)

How could filmmakers go 'further underground'? And where might this mythic place be? While Larcher made only one film in the 1970s, *Monkey's Birthday* (1975), it is an epic work lasting six hours. Dwoskin made over ten films between 1970 and 1980. Jarman and Keen made over 50 films collectively in the 1970s. It would be interesting to know which 'underground' these films were part of? Perhaps this 'underground' is indeed similar to O'Pray's 'far away' mentioned above, i.e. distanced from the main critical spheres of influence (structural and material experimentation). Additionally, other filmmakers such as Margaret Tait, Peter Whitehead and Jane Arden also made image-rich experimental films in the decade. These explicit (but contradictory) accounts of inclusion and exclusion certainly raise some questions about the positioned nature of histories and how historical canons might be created and maintained.

Wollen, interestingly, made a similar reference to the persistence in 'personal' and 'visionary' filmmaking in his aforementioned essay:

> The Co-op film-makers developed a distinctively British variant of American avant-garde film, in which the 'structural' tendency, influenced by minimal and conceptual art, became dominant, rather than the tradition of 'personal' or 'visionary' film-making, although *this did persist*.[71] (my emphasis)

This persistence of 'visionary', 'underground', 'celebratory' and 'personal' film is clearly indicated here, with these types of filmmaking existing throughout the decade, rather than returning as has been mooted. Perhaps the return may rather conveniently mete out the idea of a type of practice which came to fruition and then waned with the changing historical context to provide – as O'Pray suggests above – 'an alibi for its contemporary ideas, strategies and tastes'.[72] Yet, while there is an awareness of the alibi that certain historical positions might take, the dominant idea that a 'return' occurred at the end of the 1970s was still maintained.

This positioned notion of a 'return to image' is again perpetuated (with a title heading reading 'Before the Break') in O'Pray's most recent essay.[73] Citing his earlier review of Holly Warburton's *The Reflections of a Portrait: The Petrification of Transience* (1983), O'Pray stated that 'for those nurtured on the bare minimalism of the 1970s, Warburton's work was an aggressive onslaught'.[74] Interestingly, in reference to the influence of the 1950s and 60s Fluxus and 'intermedia' work of Stan VanDerBeek, O'Pray says '[s]uch an "overload" *never quite went away*, especially in the Dadist mixed-media shows of the British filmmaker Jeff Keen, who had regularly combined film, painting and performance in his work since the 1960s' (my emphasis).[75] O'Pray continued, saying that 'a more poetic-symbolic' and personal cinema developed in the films of Derek Jarman, Jayne Parker, Sandra Lahire and others, and of course the New Romantics themselves'.[76] While he admitted that his 'demarcations are rough and ready' and he is certainly aware of Jarman 1970s poetic, expressive films, he calls him a 'documentarist, filming his friends, social events and his milieu'.[77]

In a final example relating to this alleged 'return' I want to consider film historian Julia Knight's analysis, as she identified some interesting points in her critique of the continued dominance of the 1970s structuralist position laid out in the *Undercut* journals (1980–1990). Although Knight recognised that this was not particularly remarkable as the publication came out of the LFMC and focused on its own history, she indicated that it was also problematically taken 'as an important reference point – a starting point even – and subsequent developments are repeatedly mapped out in relation to it'.[78] Knight identified this 'neat linear history of British avant-garde film' as follows:

- The British structuralist movement grew out of the 1960s US structural film, but developed a distinctive identity to counter the US hegemony.
- Peter Gidal coins the term structural-materialism for the direction taken by British filmmakers during the 1960s and early 1970s.

- The strict 'formalism' of structuralist filmmaking is not totally abandoned but a 'representational' element is reintegrated, as exemplified by the 'landscape films' of the 1970s. In contrast to Gidal's assertion that 'the real content is the form', according to Deke Dusinberre, 'not only does shape determine content, but content determines shape'.[79]
- The early 1980s sees a return to narrative, representation and visual pleasure as a reaction to the strict formalism of earlier practices.[80]

Knight supported her account of the problematic perpetuation of this 'return' with recollections from filmmaker Barbara Meter. Writing in 1990, Meter's account provides some interesting points relating to the alleged influence of structural and formal filmmaking and the apparent 'return to image' at the end of the 1970s:

> [L]ooking again at the British avant-garde after 15 years it is as if I have plunged into an orgy of romantic images, grainy colours, decadent and dark moods and personal evocations. What a reaction against the asceticism of the formal and structural film which reigned at the time I was around. A predictable reaction of course – and one which is *highly indebted to just that formal movement*. I think that *all of British experimental film pays a tribute to the structural movement* (even when being vehemently the opposite, like the work of Cerith Wyn Evans, Derek Jarman, Anna Thew, etc.).[81] (Knight's emphasis)

As Knight also highlighted, it was rather a large claim, on Meter's part, to state that *all* British work was informed by structural filmmaking. Jarman, for one, noted that he found 'all English filmmaking with the exception of social documentaries and David Larcher excruciating', and could hardly be considered highly indebted to the formal or structural movement by paying tribute or challenging it in his filmmaking.[82] While Jarman was aware of the structural movement, his interests lay elsewhere rather than in creatively critiquing it, as Peter Greenaway did in his short film *Vertical Features Remake* (1978), creating a kind of 'mocking documentary' informed by the 'great concern amongst English filmmakers for notions of structuralism'.[83]

Knight recognised the importance of British structuralist work, yet felt that it occupied 'a very privileged position in the history of moving-image work'.[84] In her opinion this rather one-sided history insufficiently accounted for video work, particularly as 'artists' engagement with video started to happen at around the same time'.[85] More problematically, however, I would argue that the prioritisation of structural and formal experimentation as exemplary of the decade's production perpetuated this notion of an alleged 'return to image' at the end of the decade, thereby relegating other forms of filmmaking to the margins. Existing understandings of this history therefore compromise the richness and diversity in experimentation. These examples corroborate the point made in the introduction to this chapter about the weight that written accounts hold in determining this history and relate to the central argument put forward here: namely, that the established 1970s history essentially led to the marginalisation of 1970s filmmakers taking more personal, expressive, representational approaches to filmmaking.

Concluding thoughts

Clearly, the determinants shaping histories are complex and multifarious, and trying to ascertain clear lines of understanding is complicated by a number of things: preceding historical positions that maintain their authority, (un)available sources and the historian's own approaches to make mute sources speak.[86] Certainly, as mooted above, there is no such thing as an unpositioned history – and I do not pretend to deliver one here – but each new approach should bring with it some clarity and new positions to take forward. I wanted to begin by taking Le Grice's bold 'The History we Need' statement, as it appeared in its singular clarity to suggest that there existed a necessary history in no uncertain terms (although, of course, he admitted that his was also a positioned approach). Rhodes' 'Whose History?' specifically peopled this history by asking who it belonged to (challenging the long-established patriarchal position), while Curtis's 'Which History?' also polemically asked what exactly this history was, and where it might be located, as it seemed (almost) wholly absent from national collections. Certainly, history is always temporally located but I felt that framing this chapter within these questions could provide some markers to help identify its location in the past but also to promote awareness of the present moment of its writing. In this way these questions would help in pinning down the history since it appeared sometimes as slippery and evasive as the flickering images, moving too fast to be held firm, which film *is*, giving it its *raison d'etre*, its fluidity, motion and fleetingness.

My final polemic, challenging what I believe is the highly problematic 'return to image' thesis, has sought to tease out the 'thorns' in the side of this history – a history which has continued to uphold the dominance of structural and material experimentation and overshadowed more personal, expressive or visionary forms of 1970s filmmaking.

My apologies again for the necessary pedantry with which I have identified the culpable 'return to image' 'thorns' – this is in no way personal. I believe that the rich diversity in filmmaking demonstrated here and in the chapters to follow provides the necessary evidence to realign this history, and together with the rooting out of the 'return to image' thesis it will allow for the establishing of this new position. What was necessary, taking my cue from filmmaker Lis Rhodes, was the pulling back of the lens to afford a retrospective view and recognising that '[t]he view through the lens may be blurred or defined – focused or unfocused – depending on what you think you know; what you imagine you see; what you learn to look for; what you are told is visible'.[87] It is my hope that these insights have illuminated some new possibilities and paved the way for further research.

2
Institutional Frameworks and Organisational Strategies

This chapter examines how a complex network of institutional frameworks and organisational strategies enabled the fragile cultural development of 1960s experimental filmmaking to become a thriving endeavour by the end of the 1970s. Filmmaker and critic, Michael Mazière identified that filmmaking was 'part of a complex web of support which include[d] education, social context, artists' organisation, access to technology and the possibility of proper exhibition.'[1] Individual funding was also, as we shall see in this chapter, 'linked to technology, social and political context and cultural practice'.[2] With increased filmmaking developments in the decade it was, however, also necessary, particularly for funding bodies, to appreciate this film form as a personal statement made with a camera – 'a world of individual inquiry' – rather than the 'formal world of Hollywood, with its production crews of hundreds'.[3] Film workshops would be central to developments and the Independent Film-makers Association (IFA, 1974) for a time provided a kind of unifying platform for the heterogeneous modes of independent filmmaking practices in Britain. While the LFMC was one of the main workshops for the kind of filmmaking discussed here, not all experimental filmmakers were affiliated to it; and it is useful to understand its location within the wider framework of other oppositional/independent practices, particularly as these all sought financial recognition from government funding bodies.

Complex issues which related to who was responsible for funding experimental film – the ACGB or the BFI – resulted in the Attenborough Report (1973), helping to resolve distinctions between different types of filmmaking. Funding would, however, remain a complex issue throughout the decade, with the overall proportion spent on experimental film being minuscule in comparison with independent and commercial production. Grants for experimental/artists' films, for example, usually ranged between £1,000 and £4,000; while the independent films *Central Bazaar* (Dwoskin, 1972) and *Winstanley* (Brownlow, 1976) received £10,000 and £24,000, respectively. By comparison, the feature *Shout at the Devil* (Peter R. Hunt, 1976) had a £3,000,000 budget. Although funding was vital to support experimental filmmaking, education also played a significant role in training future filmmakers, establishing a critical and cultural framework for contextualising filmmaking practices and, importantly, also inadvertently funding filmmakers as lecturers.

Film workshops

The history of British film workshops, supporting a network of non-professional filmmaking, extends back to small clubs and societies established from the 1930s onwards. With the post-war availability of 16mm newsreel equipment, earlier incarnations included the Institute of Amateur Cinematographers (IAC) and the Federation of Cinematograph Societies (FCS). These, mostly amateur, filmmakers fore-grounded the need for experimentation as an open-ended enterprise liberated from commercial filmmaking. Supporting contexts in the form of publications were also central for sharing information and offering support, as Duncan Reekie outlined:

> Throughout the post-war decades the amateur movement had both a current of experimental practice and an awareness of the experimental tradition as a crucial element of amateur film culture. The pages of the cine magazines were full of experiments, scripts and ideas for films, DIY equipment projects, advice on how to achieve cinematographic effects and letters from filmmakers detailing their own discoveries.[4]

Amateur Cine World, for example, regularly publicised screenings of experimental films, acting as 'a coordinating centre and clearing house for shared information, debate and collective decision-making', much like internet forums today (although less immediate), offering support for diverse amateur/enthusiast activities.

A number of workshops, established from the mid-1960s onwards, would be instrumental for 1970s developments. These tended to have a socio-political focus, tapping into wider post-war, socialist/Marxist debates either in the form of agit-prop, socio-political cinema or, as with the LFMC, with distribution, screening and filmmaking enabled by production facilities (optical and contact printers, processors, etc.). The sharing of ideas, equipment and resources was central to all workshops, as Margaret Dickinson outlined:

> Much of the momentum behind the politicisation of film culture was provided by proto-workshops – small enterprises concerned simultaneously with production, distribution and exhibition of films. Typically, they began with a few like-minded people getting together round shared objectives, and between 1966 and 1970 at least half a dozen such groups began functioning.[5]

The focus of these diverse workshops is provided in Table 2.1, giving some idea of practices, and Margaret Dickinson's *Rogue Reels: Oppositional Film in Britain, 1945–90* can be consulted for more in-depth accounts.[6] Collectively, these independent film practices ensured that debates in opposition to commercial cinema took place, with a platform for discussions importantly formalised with the establishment of the IFA, creating links between the different oppositional practices.

Audience engagement

An engagement with film beyond its consumption as entertainment was central to the political concerns of the workshops, thereby drawing attention to integral relationships between audience and film. A longer history, dating back to 1920s and 1930s state-subsidised Soviet cinema demonstrates film as a useful political tool. And later 1960s developments by Latin American activists equally used socialist, oppositional approaches to filmmaking ('Third Cinema'). The seminal 'Towards a Third Cinema' (1969) essay argued for anti-Hollywood approaches to filmmaking, urging participants to take military action to engage politically with screenings:[7]

> Each showing for militants, middle-level cadres, activists, workers, and university students became [...] a kind of enlarged cell meeting of which the films were part but not the most important factor. We thus discovered a new facet of cinema: the *participation* of people who, until then, were considered *spectators*.[8] (Solanas and Getino's emphasis)

Certainly, the South American context differed significantly – calling for action 'with the camera in one hand and a rock in the other' – but the

Table 2.1 Film workshops: distribution exhibition and/or production

Date	Organisation	Focus/Specialism
1966 1967 (w/shop)	LFMC (London)	Distribution, exhibition artists/experimental film production
1967	Arts Lab (London)	Experimental theatre, gallery and cinema
1968	Amber Films (Newcastle)	Community and campaign films
1968	Cinema Action (London)	Political films screened with mobile cinema, film production
1968	Birmingham Arts Lab	Research into experimental art and performance
1969	IRAT (The Institute Research into Art and Technology)	Umbrella organisation to administrate LFMC, TVX's video theatre, music, gallery and production workshops
1970	Berwick Street Collective (London)	Socio-political campaign films
1970	TVX (London)	Community/art video
1970	The Other Cinema	Distribution: independent/art-house BFI-supported cinema (1976–1977)
1970	Politikino (merged with Other Cinema 1973)	Distribution: independent films
1970	Liberation Films	Socio-political, modelled on American Newsreel
1972	London Women's Film Group	Informed by Women's Movement
1973	Four Corners	Film distribution network informed by Women's Movement
1974	Film Work Group	Experimental filmmaking (RCA students)
1974	Chapter Video Workshop (Cardiff)	Video production
1974	Newsreel	Socio political, modelled on American Newsreel
1975	2B Butlers Wharf	Artists' live/work studios: screenings, installations, performances
1975	Sheffield Co-op	Serviced the Women's Movement
1976	Leeds Animation Workshop	Women's animation workshop Informed by Women's Movement
1976	Artificial Eye	Distribution: independent films
1977	Cow	Distribution: women's films
1979	Circles Distribution	Distribution: feminist focus, historical women's films

anti-American sentiments of many Marxist-informed 1970s British film-makers was not dissimilar, with workshops taking oppositional approaches to protest against class and gender repressions or taking theoretically informed approaches against the conventions of commercial filmmaking.[9]

Theoretical discussions on political filmmaking and spectatorship also became a central preoccupation for many 1970s filmmakers with the first issue of Peter Sainsbury and Simon Field's *Afterimage* (April 1970) including an interview with the Third Cinema revolutionary Glauber Rocha, his seminal 'The Aesthetics of Violence' essay and an article on Dziga Vertov's 'Kino-eye' and 'Kinopravda'. Theoretical concerns around spectatorship became a central focus for numerous filmmaker/theorists, with Gidal and Le Grice focusing on the 'politics of perception' at the LFMC, and Wollen/Mulvey also engaging filmi-cally and theoretically with film semiotics. By the end of the decade the British Film Institute Production Board's (BFIPB) catalogue was also firmly engaged in socio-political debates, with *The New Social Function of Cinema Catalogue* including Archie Tait's essay using the term 'decol-onising the unconscious' taken from Solanas and Getino's polemic.[10] The Berwick Street Collective made visually experimental campaign films such as *Nightcleaners* (1975), and Cinema Action engaged new audiences by taking a van with films and projection equipment (as Soviet filmmakers had done in the 1930s) to working-class communi-ties to discuss films in pubs and factories.[11] Other collectives found measures to politically engage and inform a wider audience with The Angry Arts Group (later Liberation Films), for example, stressing the importance of challenging existing ideologies by 'co-ordinating small-group discussions after each screening to encourage spectators to consider what they had just seen and its significance to their lives'.[12] More participatory and engaged formats thus became central to audi-ence engagement, enabling a wider dissemination of independent and experimental films. For the experimental films related more explicitly with engagements in the arts, regular 1970s screenings took place at, for example, the LFMC, Jarman's Studio Bankside, the B2 Butler's Wharf (video), and touring programmes such as the Film-makers On Tour (FMOT, 1975–1989) scheme. All these generally included formal or informal talks by filmmakers.

Independent Film-maker's Association (IFA)

While the workshops supported diverse filmmaking practices, the formation of the IFA opened up debates between different forms of oppositional filmmaking and situated diverse practices within broader critical contexts.[13] The first meeting took place at the Royal College of Art (RCA) in November 1974 and initial action would provide leverage for an understanding of the broader framework of independent filmmaking, as Sylvia Harvey identified:

> One of the most insistently recurrent ideas to emerge from the debates within the IFA has been the notion of the need to create an *oppositional space* within which the particular social practice of the cinema advocated by the IFA can develop.[14] (Harvey's emphasis)

The IFA's 'First Festival of Independent British Cinema' (1975, Bristol) was a particularly important initiative, and in an introductory paper for their conference held a year later, the organising committee laid out their intentions as follows:

> Our work together forms an aesthetic and political struggle in the field of cinema [...] The ambitiousness of our goals means that these audiences have to be built up more slowly, although we expect this pace to accelerate as the crisis deepens. We have to remain independent of the need to make profits in order to have real artistic independence. Whilst constantly fighting for access to more funds and equipment for its members, the IFA must also defend and develop this political independence and aesthetic independence [...] it is in this respect that we try to use the term independent meaningfully.[15]

Although the IFA indeed provided a welcome platform for debate, the breadth and diversity of interests in filmmaking also proved rather tenuous links, with Rees identifying that it 'was a more fragile and temporary union, strung together by partisans for a "free cinema" from many different and contradictory if overlapping directions: Cinema Action, the Co-op, disaffected media workers, parts of *Screen*, film students, documentarists and artists in loose alliance'.[16] By 1976, however, the IFA were able to elect two representatives onto the BFIPB, thanks to Le Grice's campaigning, and despite some drawbacks it would nevertheless lay the groundwork for an 'intellectual climate in which film was understood, disseminated and discussed', with IFA members being instrumental in the formation of the 'cultural' television Channel 4 (1982).[17]

Funding

Funding was, unquestionably, essential for independent filmmaking, but one of the more pressing concerns lay in defining filmmaking contextualised within such diverse socio-political, theoretical and aesthetic frameworks, as this differed significantly from commercial, industry-led cinema:

> As with the Arts Council, BFI funding was moving into the new aesthetic built on film theory and theorised practice. In these ways, throughout the 1970s, a changing film sector pushed towards new patterns of funding to achieve its core ideas. Increased funding led to increased productivity, generating a constituency of 'independent film-makers' to whom Channel 4 would turn in its mission to encourage 'innovation and experiment'.[18]

It would be some time, however, before filmmakers benefited from Channel 4 commissions, and in the 1970s socio-political or theoretical frameworks contextualising filmmaking formed an integral part in formalising ideas for funding applications.

While funding institutions were central to developments, their roles were also contingent on changes in government legislation. As John Wyver explained, 'the Arts Council's consensual relationship with the government' in the early 1970s, for example, was 'disrupted by the unsympathetic Conservative Arts Minister Lord Eccles'. [19] Yet despite the 'wider economic difficulties, the small corner of the Arts Council's operations responsible for art films enjoyed a productive period in the mid-1970s'.[20] Funding for experimental films, however, consisted of a small proportion of wider Arts Council or BFI budgets, with Wyver noting that the '1969–70 [Arts Council] production expenditure totalled £17,898, which represented just 0.2 per cent of the Council's total budget of £8.2 million'.[21] Despite these small amounts, state support was still instrumental for the growth in experimental filmmaking, and British developments continued throughout the decade as Curtis confirmed:

> A choice between private and public patronage doesn't exist in England although [Curtis recognised Alan Power who funded both David Larcher's films] – simply the question 'what kind of state patronage?' The continuing health of the English avant-garde must rest in the answer that film-makers give to this question – and to their ability to make their collective voice heard. To that end the role of the Film-makers Co-op, the Independent Film-Makers Association and other such film-makers' organisations remain of crucial importance.[22]

Getting their collective voice heard by dissemination through journals, articles and reviews would be instrumental for recognising experimental filmmaking developments, with the LFMC (Gidal and Du Cane) securing space early on (1971/72) in *Time Out* for regular critical (p)reviews and occasional features:

> This brief honeymoon with the media possibly did more to establish a popular appreciation of the concerns of avant-garde cinema than any other single event. It is more than just coincidence that the belated beginnings of a recognition by the BFI and Arts Council of their responsibilities in this field originate precisely during this period.[23]

The point about the interrelation between filmmaking and dissemination is important, particularly where the LFMC's dominance within established experimental film histories is concerned. As the LFMC significantly consolidated their filmmaking and theoretical concerns through regular dissemination (screenings, writing, seminars, etc.) awareness of their activities could naturally reach wider audiences. No such collective voice existed for the other forms of filmmaking I argue for in Chapter 4 (expressive, visionary, diary, etc.) and throughout this book. It is therefore important to understand the importance of the wider 1970s contexts (distribution, dissemination, debate and discussion) shaping progressive interpretations of histories. Despite the importance of these wider contexts, however, funding would be crucial for 1970s experimental film developments.

The Arts Council Great Britain (ACGB) and the British Film Institute (BFI)

The two funding bodies supporting experimental filmmaking, the ACGB (est. 1946) and the BFI (est. 1933), were separate institutions with differing funding remits – the ACGB for the arts in general and the BFI for independent film – but there were points of overlap where co-funding took place or similar types of films were funded. Although the BFI was the first to fund experimental films, the Arts Council would become instrumental in supporting this kind of work as the decade progressed, with Greater London Arts also providing some workshop funding.

By the late 1960s the ACGB had funded very few experimental films, initially funding documentaries *about* the arts as opposed to documentary films *by* artists. However, a scheme developed with the BFI in 1951, whereby documentaries were shown as part of exhibitions of original artworks, and this would sow seeds for future endeavours. By the start of the 1970s the few funded films included David Hall's *Vertical* (1969) and Derek Boshier's *Link* (1970), but changes would occur with the appointment of Fine Art graduate Rodney Wilson, who became an Arts Council film officer in 1970. In his policy paper for art films Wilson urged the committee and executives to support 'new forms of production practice, increasingly working with cheaper, more flexible 16mm cameras and encouraging more assertive ideas of documentary authorship'.[24] These kinds of initiatives were instrumental in shaping developments and, together with Curtis, Wilson advocated for a specialist Artists' Film Subcommittee (formed in 1972) to assist with funding this new artists' medium.[25] Although Curtis retired from the committee to become an Arts Council officer (1977), he would be unwavering in his support for filmmakers throughout his long tenure and the cessation of the committee (1999), as Rees explains:

> David Curtis made an early (1967) case for cultural subsidy, lambasting the then recalcitrant BFI in the pages of the underground magazine *The International Times*. A decade later, as Film Officer at the Arts Council, he was able to set these principles in motion. Along with Rodney Wilson, who revitalised the British art documentary and turned it into an innovative broadcast genre, he made the Arts Council into the lead funding agency for artists' film and video production and exhibition for over twenty-five years.[26]

Thanks to these insightful initiatives, Arts Council support included awards for production and exhibition with the Subcommittee's meagre annual budgets ranging from £6,080 in 1972/73; £14,050 in 1974/75 and £8,078 in 1974/75.[27] By 1977, three fixed-amount bursaries of £300, £750 and £1,250 were available, with Production Awards also providing individually assessed amounts for more specific projects.[28] In 1974 the RCA was the first 'equipment-rich' art school to offer jointly funded Arts Council bursaries, with other schools and polytechnics following suit. By 1980 the ACGB had funded over 250 experimental filmmakers through bursaries and other schemes.[29]

The BFI, on the other hand, was established in 1933 to provide information about all aspects of cinema to the public and educators, with a National Film Library added two years later and a Film Appreciation Unit (est. 1950), headed by Denis Foreman, providing lectures, summer schools and film publications.[30] An Experimental Film Fund (1952–59) with no set policies on supported films 'explore[d] proposals to give the creative artist, such as the painter or composer, much closer control over the design and production stages of a film'.[31] In 1966 the Experimental Film Fund became the British Film Institute

Production Board (BFIPB), intending, according to John Ellis, to support 'films of an experimental nature outside a directly commercial context'.[32] It also 'established a policy of supporting "first films" and "calling-card" shorts by future television, commercials and feature-film directors', with Tony and Ridley Scott, Kevin Brownlow and Stephen Frears in receipt of funding.[33] Despite good intentions, not many experimental films were funded, with Curtis's 1969 review including only two films as possible contenders: Anthony Stern's *San Francisco* (1968) and Don Levy's *Five Short Film Poems* (1967).[34]

New initiatives emerged in 1975 with an influential new head, Peter Sainsbury, at the helm, with BFIPB schemes including the purchase of low-cost film and video equipment for use by practitioners and, importantly, a regular pool of film technicians who 'embraced the political and aesthetic commitments of the independent sector'.[35] They 'proved to be extremely gifted and adaptable', with their 'knowledge and creative use of 16mm filmmaking' proving to be vital to the continuation of an independent sector highly dependent on this gauge.[36] Although this was less applicable for filmmakers working independently or using LFMC facilities, it importantly set up an infrastructure, which included technical support alongside financial backing for filmmakers wanting to take advantage of smaller formats and working in a more hands-on manner, as filmmaker/theorist Laura Mulvey identified: '[t]here was a sense that 16mm was an aesthetic of its own, that it had its own specificity' beyond that of the industry-standard 35mm format.[37] This type of support was important as only two out of 30 independent films were shot on 35mm between 1976 and 1979.

Although Sainsbury helped forge links between different fields of independent filmmaking, the BFIPB was less specifically directed towards artists' experimental filmmaking, with increasingly more well-developed scripts being funded and Sainsbury coming under pressure to produce feature-length films:

> It wasn't that Peter Sainsbury thought that features were the only thing that mattered – not at all. But the Production Board was constantly under the threat of being closed down – within the BFI were constant attempts to erode it. And one of the ways he saw that it could make itself more visible and more indispensable was by achieving this kind of feature level performance.[38]

This led to the production of a number of BFIPB-funded feature-length films, such as Sue Clayton/Jonathan Curling's *The Song of the Shirt* (1979), signalling a 'shift, in a general way, which the Production Board was part of, towards the possibility of a "British Arts Cinema"' inspired by European Art directors such as Jean-Luc Godard and Jean-Marie Straub/Danièlle Huillet.[39] The British new wave, however, never materialised, with some films even excluded from later BFIPB catalogues.

In total the BFIPB funded 43 films between 1970 and 1980, and the ACGB funded 243 filmmakers between 1972 and 1980.[40] For detailed information on funding I would suggest consulting Michael Mazière's in-depth research on institutional support and Christophe Dupin's thesis on BFI support for non-mainstream film.[41] Importantly, Mazière's data shows ACGB funding for individual *filmmakers*, while BFIPB funding indicates individual *films*.

The Attenborough Enquiry

While both funding bodies were instrumental for supporting filmmaking, some complex and irresolvable differences resulted in an important enquiry, seeking ways to move forward. Although the formation of the IFA generated positive events such as the 'First Festival of British Independent Cinema' (1975), differences of opinion between approaches to filmmaking were also exacerbated. Sainsbury, for example, lamented the lack of attention to aesthetics emerging from the film workshops, while Le Grice criticised the socio-politically orientated workshops for their conservative approaches to filmmaking. While attempts were also made to broaden the audience framework, there were difficulties with the widely differing milieux from which many of the independent films emerged. This called for an urgent need to more clearly distinguish different types of filmmaking as funding bodies (Artists' Film Subcommittee and the BFIPB) needed to justify their motivations to their broader funding providers (ACGB and BFI), as Ian Christie explains:

> [I]t seemed very important to get clear how you would define the different spheres – and again there was a kind of common sense-ish [sic] definition to begin with, which was that people who came out of a visual arts background and functioned in a visual arts-ish [sic] sort of way would naturally be aligned to the Arts Council, but that all started to get complicated when you got these distinctly cross-over figures. I mean the most famous, or notable, of the crossover figures were Greenaway, Jarman and Potter.[42]

While defining different spheres was one issue, another difficulty lay in defining the often 'nebulous' nature of the 'product'. Scripted ideas formed a key part of pitches for commercial films while proposals for experimental films usually required more open-ended investigation. As with other visual art practices where ideas were not necessarily explored through predetermined scripts or formulae, this required time, materials (and often equipment) without expectations of a fixed outcome. And judged by commercial or independent feature-film criteria, funding proposals for experimental filmmaking could appear too unformulated to warrant funding, as Mazière identified:

> In the arts, the direct funding of production is like trying to second guess the future. Unlike other models of funding such as commissioning, purchasing works or subsidising distribution, touring and exhibition, it is a form of high risk funding which statistically makes an uneven contribution in output. Funding at the point of creation can also have a distorting effect on the creative process if it is too prescriptive such as in funding works for television. But if the funding support is non-specific (without a specific production or exhibition in sight) then the danger is that the work will not necessarily be widely exhibited.[43]

Filmmakers therefore needed to convince funding bodies to support their projects, and funding bodies in turn needed to trust filmmakers' intentions enough to be willing to support them. This proved to be a steep learning curve.

The support of Arts Council officers such as Curtis and Wilson early on in the decade was therefore vital as they advocated tirelessly for funding without enforcing clear scripted intentions. Curtis pointed out that 'periodically the committee agonised about the folly of expecting artists to be able to fix their ideas on paper before lifting the camera'.[44] Yet, admittedly this was public money being requested and there needed to be some idea of its intended use. This was a dilemma for filmmakers as they needed the (financial) freedom to explore ideas, yet there was a risk that they might fail to produce 'good' film/s. Certainly, taken from a critical viewpoint, this would be a subjective decision, but a visible outcome would generally be expected. Le Grice, one of the first filmmakers to receive funding from the new Artists' Film Subcommittee, recognised this predicament:

> I think I was one of the first people from the Co-op to make an application to the Arts Council's new film and video committee as a film artist. I made *Threshold* and curiously, I looked and thought, 'I'm not sure about this film.' And I'd also made *Whitchurch Down* and

thought it was a more interesting film, so I gave them both because I felt a terrible responsibility as the first person [...] I did feel a terrible weight of having to come up with something [for] which they were going to be able to kind of feel they got their money's worth.[45]

Le Grice's concerns were almost certainly informed by his LFMC involvement and tireless campaigning for funding, but the need to demonstrate a successful outcome was complex for practitioners more familiar with working in exploratory, unscripted ways.

The lack of clear-cut distinctions between experimental film as 'art' or 'cinema' also proved particularly problematic for funding bodies in setting funding criteria and identifying who should fund which types of films. This was made evident early on with James Scott's two Arts Council-funded 'documentaries', *Richard Hamilton* (1969) and *The Great Ice-Cream Robbery* (1971), posing some particular problems due to their experimental nature. Neither of Scott's films conformed to the conventional art documentary format, taking 'complex free-form approach[es]' with 'their culturally confrontational attitude brilliantly encapsulate[ing] much of the excitement and openness of the moment'.[46] These unconventional films, refusing to conform to those typically funded by the ACGB, had the BFI 'alarmed by the extent to which the Arts Council was stretching the definition of "arts documentary"', and disputes eventually led to government intervention in order to clarify terms:[47]

With little or no money available, there were inevitable arguments about where the borderline fell between artists' works (clearly an Arts Council responsibility) and innovative or experimental film and video works (arguably still the responsibility of the BFI). These boundary disputes may be thought of little interest in any other context, but from time to time they managed to engage even government departments, as the Arts Council and the BFI (and later the Film Council) fought over responsibility for this tiny area.[48]

Government involvement in ascertaining who should be responsible for experimental film funding, and how these fitted into the ACGB and BFIPB funding remits, took the form of the Attenborough Enquiry (1971), with one of the central questions, 'Should the Arts Council be making films?', becoming the focus of the Enquiry Committee (chaired by film director Richard Attenborough). The final report (July 1973) drew the following conclusions:

As far as the committee could see, the experimental and non-narrative artists' films, which explored 'the manipulation and use of film as a fine art medium', were not supported by the BFI's Production Board, and this in itself was one important reason why the Council should 'embrace and encourage film-making as a fine art activity'. An initial sum of £25,000 was proposed to support such work. The Council should also purchase video equipment to use for documenting artists' work and with which artists could experiment.[49]

The BFIPB's 'terms of reference' were focused on a 'more traditional view of cinema as an industrially produced dramatic art'.[50] While the Attenborough Enquiry clarified important issues, one of the anticipated outcomes hoping for the establishment of closer working relationships between the two funding bodies never really manifested itself in the decade, with Dupin noting that 'the first real sign of a possible collaboration between the two bodies was the publication by Peter Sainsbury [BFIPB] and Rodney Wilson [Arts Council] [...] of a 1978 joint statement 'to consider areas of future collaboration'.[51] Again, this was never fully realised at the time. The Attenborough Report (1973) clarified matters to some extent with the ACGB becoming the principle funders of experimental films (with a dedicated Art Film Division), and the BFIPB also continuing to provide some funding for experimental filmmaking.

Group funding and other alternatives

While the funding of individual films benefited diverse filmmakers, Le Grice's insistent campaigning on behalf of independent workshops would instrumentally influence the diversity in filmmaking. In 1972 he joined the BFIPB (motivated by the positive outcome of the Attenborough Report), arguing for support of the 'new phenomenon of culturally committed film and video groups'.[52] Le Grice received a small amount of BFIPB funding to visit around 20 film workshops and organisations across Britain to compile a 'report of needs'. While his grant application was refused, the BFIPB conceded by providing £3,000 towards the Group Support Fund, with 12 groups awarded between £400 and £1,000 in equipment grants in 1974.[53] Group funding fulfilled Le Grice's hoped for intentions as it meant freer experimentation without the constraints of first fixing ideas on paper:

Right from the start, I had had a policy, which said, that it was better to fund the workshop facility than it was to fund work, to fund scripts. I started with the view that the best funding system was to fund the production resource which would itself lead to experimental work, so they didn't have to pass opinion on ideas and proposals.[54]

While the LFMC produced many experimental films in the decade, benefiting from an early contribution of £3,000 for printing equipment (from private benefactor and art collector Victor Herbert), it also benefited from a substantial BFIPB workshop grant of £16,020 in 1975. Other film workshops also contributed to film production, with the Attenborough Enquiry (and changes to group funding) also ensuring wider support outside of London:

> There was, for example, an unwritten agreement that made the funding of film and video workshops – which benefited the whole spectrum of independent makers – a responsibility shared by the BFI and the Arts Council-funded Regional Arts Associations, often in partnership with local authorities such as the Labour-controlled Greater London Council (GLC), and, after 1982, Channel 4 Television.[55]

Group funding was central in allowing for freer approaches to experimentation and opening up possibilities for screening and distribution, lending a sense of autonomy that more scripted proposals would deny.

While funding was in many respects essential for encouraging the diversity in filmmaking, it also needs to be pointed out that other alternatives also existed with filmmakers such as Margaret Tait and Derek Jarman funding many of their own films. Funding, according to Curtis, also presented a double-edged reality:

> State involvement in the arts can be a mixed blessing. It can be slow to act and vulnerable to policy changes – and like any intervention designed to influence a natural ecology, almost invariably stimulates the mediocre alongside the good.[56]

Filmmakers, therefore, often chose to forego the frustration of having to fix ideas on paper, wait for funding, and be restricted by funding requisites, despite the best efforts of Arts Council officers supporting the need for open-ended experimentation.

Continental funding in the form of private sponsorship provided some alternatives for filmmakers, with Dwoskin and B. S. Johnson securing funding from German and Belgian sources, while Larcher found support from British art collector Alan Power for his two epic films. Found footage disposed of by film laboratories also provided cheap alternatives for filmmaking, with Anthony Scott's *The Longest Most Meaningless Film in the World* (1968) consisting of 48 hours of found footage. Le Grice also used found and home-movie footage, and Guy Sherwin's *At the Academy* (1974) consisted entirely of academy leader reprinted several times using both positive and negative exposures. Although the initial footage for these films was found material, production facilities and fresh film stock were essential for final prints. While some filmmakers chose to work in this way, most of the films produced in the decade required at least the purchase of a few rolls of film plus processing and printing costs, and if one was fortunate enough to have access to a camera, a tripod and other necessary equipment.

Curtis also recognised that the 'only way in which an artist might make a substantial body of work without funding was to use the amateur gauge of Super-8, as David Dye and Derek Jarman notably did for part or all of their careers'.[57] As a way of maintaining independence, Jarman worked with the smaller format, saying that he

> disliked the subsidized 'avant-garde' cinema. There was a strong official line; but [S]uper-8, which cost next to nothing, allowed one to ignore that. The resources were small enough, so if independence is a form of purity, I had my hands on the philosopher's stone'.[58]

Although experimental film histories tend to highlight Super-8 in relation to 1980s 'New Romantic' filmmakers – mythologised within the problematic 'return to image' thesis – more prevalent 1970s activity also took place, with the 'London Super-8 Film Group' (1975) holding screenings at the ICA as Gray Watson explains:

> The use of Super-8 film by innovatory artists as opposed to essentially imitative amateurs is of course a very new phenomenon, at least outside the United States, but because Super-8 is so practicable and because in many ways it is the natural successor to painting, but with the added dimension of time, more and more people are turning to it as a means of creative expression.[59]

The FMOT programmes also included numerous Super-8 screenings over the years. Many of these are conspicuous by their absence in established 1970s histories, but perhaps unsurprisingly so as most were not in general distribution. The lack of recognition for the format also meant these films were easily overlooked, as O'Pray observed: '[m] any Super 8 films have a rather ill-defined status, and have not been included if they are not in some form of distribution, even if they have been shown in the past.'[60] But significantly this unrecognised body of work is representative of aspects of the decade's production.

Distribution

While dissemination in the form of articles, journals and catalogues was instrumental for spreading the word on film, the screening actually brought a film into existence, as Dwoskin emphasised:

> Like most artists, the serious personal film-maker commits his time, his energies, his emotions and his money to producing a film. But films need to be projected, even to friends; this is one of their distinctive properties. A FINISHED FILM IS A PROJECTED FILM: that is its function.[61] (Dwoskin emphasis)

Dwoskin, however, cautioned that making a non-commercial film could 'put the film-maker into a world foreign to his own, the world of bureaucracy, politics, organization, economics'.[62] This was eased to some extent by collective pursuits as distribution and screening formed an integral part of most workshop operations (although sometimes this also provided space for disagreement), ensuring films were screened, hopefully with opportunities for discussion.

By handling their own distribution, film workshops ensured that films were screened, adding a necessary (while often small) income to filmmakers and organisations. The LFMC was, for example, at the outset a distribution/screening organisation before production facilities enabled filmmaking, with the American Carla Liss bringing a wide selection of US and historical experimental films for distribution (many from the New American Cinema (1968) touring screenings). The LFMC became the sole distributor of these films in Britain and Europe, with an initiative by Gidal ensuring that an equal ratio of British work had to be complemented by the US/historical films hired. The LFMC's democratic distribution policy refused to promote one film over another, posing a problem for some filmmakers, such as Dwoskin, who sought more proactive promotion of his films, leaving the LFMC in 1969 and placing his films with The Other Cinema.

Although distribution was integral to most workshops' operations, the ACGB and the BFIPB also actively promoted wider dissemination of funded films by producing catalogues or publications relating to funded films. Most Arts Council funded screenings included programme notes, either small publications or more substantial ones for larger exhibitions.[63] Curtis's *The Directory of British Film and Video Artists* (1996) is an index of (mostly) ACGB-funded experimental films from 1973–1995 which includes 118 filmmakers. Three BFIPB catalogues (1977, 1978 and 1981), are listings of films for hire, with critical and theoretical essays on film, filmmakers or contemporary political issues preceding each section. These provide useful references which give an idea of funding contexts. The BFIPB catalogues also reveal changing sociopolitical contexts, with increased politicisation by the end of the decade resulting in the editors, Hilary Thompson and Rod Stoneman, for example, taking 'an explicit editorial stance' by subtitling the 1981 catalogue '*The New Social Function in Cinema*' and including polemical essays.[64]

Education

While dissemination was central to raise awareness about films and get them seen, education played an integral part in the growth of 1970s experimental filmmaking, with both formal education (art schools, polytechnics and universities) and informal programmes (workshops, screening events and discussion forums) contributing to expansion. While the former was a longer, more engaged process of learning (mostly) through practice, the latter provided informative aesthetic, critical or theoretical frameworks for films (often presented by filmmakers). Publications and journals were also instrumental for educational purposes, with journals like *Screen* and *Screen Education* disseminated by the Society for Education in Film and Television (SEFT).

Prior to the incorporation of practice-based filmmaking in taught art courses (from the mid-1960s), film director Thorold Dickinson led the first dedicated film course at the Slade School Film Unit (1960). Inspiration came from frequenting Amos Vogel's Cinema 16, whilst living in New York in the 1950s, and discovering US experimental filmmakers such as Kenneth Anger, Maya Deren and Stan Brakhage and also contributing to Jonas Mekas's *Film Culture* magazine.[65] Numerous students emerging from Dickinson's film unit (not practice-based) became central to 1970s experimental film developments. These included the historians, critics and writers David Curtis, Deke Dusinberre, Ray Durgnat, Simon Field and Annette Kuhn, and filmmakers Derek Jarman, Don Levy, Malcolm Le Grice and Peter Whitehead.[66]

At Central Saint Martins, film was taught early on within painting, printmaking or sculpture courses, with Le Grice, Barry Flanagan and John Latham offering diverse approaches:

> With their very different approaches to the medium – one hands-on, the other more detached – Le Grice, Latham and Flanagan's teaching at Saint Martins helped shape some of the most important films by artists of the late 1960s and early 1970s – the so-called structural film-making associated with the London Filmmakers Co-op (Le Grice) and the conceptual and minimal film and video work associated with the emerging small commercial galleries and artist-run spaces of the early 1970s, (Latham/Flanagan).[67]

By 1968 Curtis noted that Le Grice's students had films included in the Young Contemporaries exhibition and that 'the beautifully Heath Robinson developing and printing equipment, designed and largely built by Le Grice, was moved from the Arts Lab to his home in Harrow'. Le Grice's students from Goldsmiths and Saint Martins continued to use the equipment and a specialist unit, The Fine Art Film course (experimental film and video), was introduced in 1972 at Saint Martins.[68]

The RCA included film in their Environmental Media Department (1974–1986), offering interdisciplinary approaches to film and video despite their industry focus, with filmmakers such as Gidal, Dwoskin and Noel Burch influencing more experimental approaches. By the end of the decade film was being taught in universities, art colleges and polytechnics across London and in regional centres. Education therefore became a form of institutional support for filmmakers/lecturers providing initial and later complementary support to a sector which had very few commercial outputs and few other career opportunities.[69] Many of the filmmakers/lecturers were also actively involved at the LFMC, with their names regularly cropping up in 1970s screening programmes or funding applications, with 'The Education Nexus – The Engine of Production', as Mazière referred to it, being instrumental in developing critical and theoretical discourses related to filmmaking.[70] As Le Grice explained:

> The Education system provided an undercurrent, proper debates and a certain degree of protection against the uncertainties of the funding systems outside. As well as facilities, resources, a little bit of production

funding [...] The art schools contributed in a number of ways: One, they stimulated new, young students. Two, the staff could continue to do work as the bread and butter was coming from the art school; and thirdly they became a major part of the circuit [...] It wasn't just like education for the work, it became a context for the work.[71]

While this was not dissimilar to other visual art practices where artists supplemented their incomes through teaching, this also meant that the subversive milieu, motivating 1960/70s underground/experimental filmmaking, became progressively more institutionalised as filmmaking was co-opted into academia and became more reliant on state funding, as Mazière outlined:

From 1973 onwards institutional support played a major and more direct role in the support and definition of artists' film and video. A more stable environment was developed and the underground nature of artists' film and video was eroded.[72]

Curtis had identified this institutionalisation early on in his 1975 *Studio International* article, whereby he concluded that funding and the educational context had in all probability shifted the initial radical nature enveloping experimental filmmaking:

These latest moves confirm the avant-garde's complicity in its own institutionalisation, and a further stage in its integration into the English pattern of education and patronage of the arts. To what extent it can survive this orthodoxy, and preserve its radical position in relation to the (equally uncommercial) 'commercial cinema', is a question likely to be answered during the next ten years.[73]

In spite of progressive institutionalisation, a certain radical, oppositional position about 1970s experimental filmmaking appeared to be maintained, with LUX director Ben Cook identifying that 'there was a kind of a mythology around these organisations [such as the LFMC] and this area of practice, at that time, about a collective scene growing up in response to a kind of perceived exclusion from the institute, or certain institutional structures'.[74] Interestingly, despite acknowledging institutional support perhaps continuing to perceive themselves outside of the institutions' institutionalisation a seemingly more radical and oppositional stance could be maintained.[75]

While art schools contributed to 1970s developments, non-formal education, in the form of workshops, short courses and symposia, also contributed greatly to the education of new audiences and filmmakers. Most events took place in the mid- to late-1970s, also laying the groundwork for increased 1980s regional activity. One of the most successful initiatives taking experimental films to wider audiences was the ACGB-funded Film-makers on Tour FMOT (1975–1989), which encouraged introductory talks by filmmakers with a fee and travel costs subsidised by the scheme, as Curtis outlined:

> Informing the scheme is the belief that an introduction by the artists helps to make the work accessible and opens up a dialogue between the artist and audience. This is particularly important with Artists' Films where the range of ideas and the ways in which they are presented vary considerably and are often unfamiliar. The artist's presence will, it is hoped, contribute to the audience's understanding of the work.[76]

The small hiring fees benefited small cinemas, galleries, regional theatres and art colleges, and also, more broadly, consolidated the 'growing network of screening spaces in artist-run galleries and film workshops'.[77] Importantly opportunities were opened up to further debates on filmmaking with, as Rees outlined, 'strong and interrogative exchange[s] between artist, audience and work. Over 160 artists took part in the scheme from 1975–1989, and personal presentation remains a norm among artist filmmakers today.[78] The steady increase in filmmakers, supporting eight participants in 1976 and around 50 in 1980, brought diverse films, which included single-screen, multi-screen, performance pieces, expanded cinema and Super-8 or 16mm formats.

1970s screenings

While workshop screenings, talks and seminars, distribution catalogues and formal or informal education all led to the spread of experimental filmmaking, (albeit still a small, specialised field), a number of larger 1970s screening festivals and exhibitions were instrumental in further disseminating films. While exhibitions offered stimulating – and sometimes provocative – contexts for engagement due to curatorial decision-making, the bigger film festivals also importantly provided wider international contexts and opportunities for debate, discussion and film viewing.

The broad diversity in 1970s experimentation meant that different types of films required distinctive screening contexts. Where one film might be screened within a specific aesthetically or theoretically informed programme, another might be screened as part of a live performance or, alternatively, be set up as a looped installation within a viewing space. Jarman's Super-8 films, for example, were often screened at a slow projection speed (necessitating the use of special projectors) with sound added through a separate audio system. Larcher's *Monkey's Birthday* (1975) was either screened as a single- or dual-screen projection, with Larcher often providing a running commentary. The performative nature of expanded cinema works (single- or multi-screen) posed other challenges, with filmmakers often screening films themselves and sometimes moving the projector(s) around in the space, as in Dye's *Film onto Film* (1972), and Le Grice's *Matrix* (1973). In Keen's *Rayday Film* (1968–70 and 1976), Nicolson's *Reel Time* (1973) and Le Grice's *Horror Film* (1971) the filmmaker's actual shadowed presence was also integral to the works. Keen's *Final Appearance* (1976), Jarman's *The Art of Mirrors* (1976) and Breakwell's *Growth* (1976) – all shown as part of the ICA's 'Festival of Expanded Cinema' (1976) – were multi-media events, including between them Super-8 and 16mm films, 35mm slide projections and audio tape recordings. Multi-screen works with a site-specific focus – incorporating the architecture of the space into the works – included Nicolson's *Sky for the Bird of the Roof of my Mind* (1975), where a 'bird' in her glass studio roof became part of the work. For Tony Sinden's film and video works for *Another Aspect, Another Time – The Exhibition* (1979, Hayward Gallery), he insisted that all projectors, film loops, plinths and the architecture of the exhibition space be integrally connected.[79] He used mirrors and projections to incorporate his presence into the exhibition space, creating 'a sense of illusion extending itself to the exhibition space', with viewers also seeing their reflections within the works, thereby establishing an illusionary 'displacement of the physical self'.[80] Experiential engagements with film were central to extending the boundaries of the viewing experience, leading to diverse forms of experimentation in the decade alongside the single-screen films taking either personal, expressive approaches or focusing on cinematography, film stocks, printing and processing. All these screening conditions made the diversity in film exhibition as rich and interesting as the films themselves.

Focusing on a number of 1970s festivals and exhibitions gives an indication of activity and significant changes taking place over the decade. While the focus here is on film, video was also included in some multi-disciplinary shows, and certain exhibitions focused specifically on video including 'The Video Show: First Festival of Independent Video' (1975,

Serpentine Gallery) and 'The Video Show' (1976, Tate Britain), disseminated by the newly formed London Video Arts (LVA). London's ACME and Air galleries also presented diverse screenings in the late 1970s, and other video exhibitions took place nationally at venues such as The Third Eye Centre, Glasgow (1976) and the Herbert Art Gallery, Coventry (1978). As mentioned previously, all of these histories (film, video, etc.) need to be recognised for a broader understanding of 1970s moving image production informing contemporary practices.

The long-standing 'Edinburgh Film Festival' (since 1947) provided a vital platform for experimental film screening and debate throughout the 1970s, with close links forged with the LFMC early on. Although the festival also screened more commercial, narrative films, the focus shifted mid-decade under the new directorship of Lynda Miles towards a *Screen*-theory ethos (rather than the auteurist focus from previous years). This was in part influenced by (amongst others) filmmaker/theorist Peter Wollen's influence, recognising 'film as an ideological practice rather than as a predetermined and self-sufficient object of study', with the '30th International Film Festival' (1976) centred on his influential 'The Two Avant-gardes' (1975) essay and the divergent histories he had identified.[81] While film screening was central to the 'Edinburgh Film Festival', the open discussion forums formed a key part in events throughout the decade, generating debates and offering opportunities for international exchanges. This had earlier on also been the case with the 'Knokke Experimental Film Festival' (Belgium) in the 1960s, with festivals held intermittently from 1949 onwards.

The first of three important 1970s festivals held at the National Film Theatre (NFT) was 'The First International Underground Film Festival' (1970). Organised by David Curtis, Simon Field and Albie Thoms, it included a diversity of British and international programmes with over 300 films giving the encouraging impression that a seriously international, alternative film movement was gaining momentum. The eclectic range of films screened (formal, 35mm, 16mm Super-8, expanded cinema, etc.) – including the notorious decapitation of a live chicken in Austrian artist Otto Muehl's 'action' event and his explicit film *Sodoma* (1969) – complemented the debates stimulated by international filmmaking. The second 'Festival of Independent Avant-garde Film' (1973) (again organised by David Curtis and Simon Field) included a two-week programme of films and over 100 filmmakers were present to discuss their films. This included a larger proportion of European and British films than the previous festival, with discussion forums forming a key part of events. 'Official' recognition was received in the form of a *Sight and Sound* review by Tony Rayns, and four reviews by Jonas Mekas in New York's *The Village Voice* alerting US audiences to the level of London activity.[82] In his first review Mekas commented on the title change, signalling some shifting perspectives:

> The first time [a] similar festival was held here, in 1970, it was called the Festival of Underground Films. Times have changed, and the term underground has lost its precision. The organisers of this year's festival needed a double-edged term to at least approximately indicate the kind of film they took upon themselves to gather in one place.[83]

Mekas observed the growing diversity in experimentation with the detailed reviews focused mostly on LFMC filmmakers since close links existed between the LFMC and the New York Co-op. As an adjunct to the NFT festival, the LFMC's 'Expanded Cinema' (ICA) was included, with Rayns full of praise, saying that 'despite the handicap of poor conditions, this section of the festival offered a higher proportion of the most stimulating work than the "normal" NFT screenings'.[84] Again, opportunities for international exchange were of great importance to filmmakers, critics and theorists, with British work now gaining wider recognition on a par – or even surpassing, some would argue – US activity.

The IFA's 'First Festival of Independent British Cinema' (1975) in the middle of the decade was an ambitious event, taking a polemical approach to show the breadth of alternatives to dominant, commercial cinema, with programme notes identifying the main characteristic as being the combination of different 'independent film – the avant-garde on the one side, the overtly political film on the other, plus a lot in the middle'.[85] This diversity included art installations, experimental films by Jarman, Rob Gawthrop and LFMC members, the Berwick Street Collective's *Nightcleaners* (1975) and a first introduction to the Orkadian filmmaker Margaret Tait, whom Le Grice considered to be 'the only genuinely independent, experimental mind in film to precede the current movement which began here in about '66'.[86]

In his review of the event Le Grice raised questions about its eclecticism, wondering whether there could be 'a productive dialogue between the two main axes, the political and the experimental'.[87] He suggested that sufficient points of contact between experimental filmmakers and politically engaged filmmaking groups warranted further dialogues, with experimental filmmakers being exposed to problems of accessibility and co-option into the art-world and political filmmakers being made aware of the 'poverty of sensibility and the reactionary conventionality of much of the film form'.[88] Certainly, he positively concluded that it seemed that the British independent cinema was 'beyond the embryo stage, and in an advanced stage of development'. The initial dialogues opened up between diverse groups was, however, unfortunately never really quite consolidated during the decade.

A number of exhibitions, focused more explicitly on artists'/experimental filmmaking, give further impressions of 1970s activity. A range of eclecticism similar to that in the first two NFT festivals was evident in the Arts Council's 'Perspectives on British Avant-garde Film' (1977, Hayward Gallery), with the exhibition revealing British work within international and historical contexts, as the selection committee curators outlined:

> The survey is not intended to be comprehensive either in terms of films financed by the committee or the historical and critical programmes. Rather, the groups of films and the programme notes about them are intended to demonstrate the changing nature of the films funded by the committee, to show some of the central historical developments and to indicate some of the major aesthetic and ideological concerns that underlie current avant-garde film-making in Britain and abroad.[89]

The success of this exhibition, together with an earlier British Council-sponsored survey of British art in Italy's *'Arte Inglese Oggi'* (1976) resulted in the international touring programme 'A Perspective on English Avant-garde Film' (1978). 'Perspectives' toured internationally to 30 countries and was programmed by Curtis and Dusinberre, presenting a 'series of aesthetic ideas and issues in a coherent fashion' with 24 filmmakers represented in nine diverse programmes including landscape, still life, performance, structural and material experimentation and travelogues. [90]

In contrast to the eclecticism of the festivals and the expanded cinema event, a number of exhibitions with a more specific focus on formal experimentation also took place during the decade. Two smaller, multi-media exhibitions in 1975, 'Structures and Codes' (RCA) and 'Structure and Function in Time' (Sunderland Arts Centre), preceded

Gidal's extensive 18-programme 'Structural Film Retrospective' (1976). The retrospective coincided with the publication of Gidal's *Structural Film Anthology,* containing personal statements and theoretical or critical essays for the almost 100 international films, identifying 'film as a contemporary art which politically needs to share nothing with the cinema', confirming his extreme anti-Hollywood position.[91] While Gidal's retrospective importantly brought a notable amount of work to British audiences, it also provided contextualisation to consolidate his uncompromising position on formal filmmaking.

On a different note, but still focused to an extent on formal experimentation, was Dusinberre's 'Avant-garde British Landscape Films' (1975, Tate which according to Curtis, 'asserted the illusionism of cinema through the sensuality of landscape imagery, and simultaneously asserted the material nature of the representational process which sustains the illusionism'.[92] Curtis further noted that the films combined 'a modernist determination to make visible all the processes involved in the film-making' yet also identified that the 'striking feature of this work was the way it combined a passionate attachment to imagery of mountains, clouds, seascapes, parks and rural pastures', not dissimilar to the work of earlier British Romantic painters, yet 'with a modernist determination to make visible' all the filmmaking processes.[93]

In contrast to these more thematically focused exhibitions, the ICA's 'Festival of Expanded Cinema' (1976) importantly recognised the heterogeneity in experimentation and included a full range of personal, expressive filmmaking alongside more conceptually or theoretically informed investigations. Dusinberre's catalogue introduction reveals the eclectic approach taken to accommodate the rich diversity in experimentation:

[E]xpanded cinema is pre-eminently a discursive and exploratory mode of film-making. And the very qualities which we hope to emphasise through critical selection mitigated against a 'tight' show of such categories, and counselled an openness to unexpected developments, a receptiveness to improvisation, a sympathy to the informality which characterizes much of the work.[94]

True to the festival's intentions the event included a broad range of filmmakers, with LFMC or conceptual filmmakers exploring formal or conceptual aspects of film and others taking more personal approaches. Keen's interests, for example, lay in getting 'beyond the frame' to 'explore the full graphic potential of the medium in the direction of non-linear movement and synthetic vision'.[95] His multi-projection performative events included slides and 8mm and 16mm film, reflecting his interests 'in the art of assemblage and its counter movement destruct-art (collage/de-collage), and in visual poetry'.[96] Jarman screened *The Art of Mirrors* (1973), highlighting the importance of poetic, personal filmmaking over formal investigation, with his letter to ICA committee member Ron Haseldon questioning whether his film would fit 'within the definition of expanded ' as his use of Super-8 was seen more as 'a contraction to the point: the twentieth century hieroglyphic monad and has nothing at its best to do with expansion, more to do with personal perception than any other gauge'.[97] Ian Breakwell's three works included *The Artist's Dream* (1976), involving 'a performance inspired by traditional stage illusions, using 16mm and 8mm film, projection, and 35mm slide projection, lighting effects, taped sounds, and live action by performers. Plus props and costumes'.[98] Raban's account of the event concluded that 'it is important to say that expanded cinema is a dynamic, evolving art form.[99] Ironically, however, while the festival appeared to signal a 'cohesiveness' for diverse expanded forms of filmmaking, it was in fact, as Lucy Reynolds pointed out 'British expanded cinema's swansong' as filmmakers' interests and paths diverged in the latter part of the decade.[100] Interestingly, however, expanded forms of film exhibition – albeit with less of a focus on the performative (although this is still evident with events put on by London-based filmmaker, Sally Golding's Unconscious Archives, for example) – would make a return in the mid-1990s with the 'explosion' into the gallery of the apparently 'new' medium of artists' film and video.

The rich diversity in experimentation and international dialogue which had taken place throughout the 1970s was evident in the third festival, 'Film London: 3rd Avant-garde International Festival' (1979), including expanded cinema events (ICA) and open screenings at the LFMC. Within walking distance, 'Film as Film: Formal Experiment in Film 1910–1975' (1979) presented a historically contextualised exhibition on formal filmmaking, providing a contrast to the NFT's 39 film programmes. Dusinberre noted that 'a more political (if unpublicised) decision by the committee means that fully 50% of the British films at the NFT will be by women.'[101] As with the previous two festivals, the third was initiated by David Curtis and Simon Field, although administration was handed over to filmmakers Tim Bruce, Bob Fearns, Jenny Okun, David Parsons and Penny Webb, noting that:

> British avant-garde film is being produced in various contexts – in film workshops, art schools, and State funding to artists and film-makers [...] The period has seen a proliferation of journals devoted to film criticism and film theory. The attention paid to narrative construction by film theorists has been reflected in the body of work produced from within the avant-gardes.[102]

The richness of the varied programmes, signalling the end-of-decade productivity, was also demonstrated by the collaborative willingness of the NFT, the ICA and the Hayward Gallery to present a diverse range of work simultaneously, with attempts made to ensure that programmes at different venues did not coincide. Dusinberre outlined the miscellane-ous range of work on offer in his (p)review:

> [Events] parallel to the festival do afford a certain depth and his-torical perspective to complement the contemporary overview it offers. On Thursday June 7, Stan Brakhage makes his first British appearance when he presents several parts of his recent work, titled 'Sincerity', at the ICA. Paul Sharits will also introduce new work at the ICA on Tuesday June 19, followed by a retrospective at the Co-op on June 20. Other film-makers will no doubt arrive with extra prints under their arms; keep alert for the ad-hoc screenings in London and elsewhere. In addition the 'Film as Film' exhibition continues at the Hayward Gallery (only 30 paces from the NFT) until June 17.[103]

Again, the numerous opportunities provided space for critical discus-sion on an international level and, in the spirit of experimentation, the *ad hoc* screenings also provided room for improvisation. The dec-ade thus ended with an exposition showcasing a proliferation of film activity, recognising the significant efforts made by 1970s filmmakers, funders, curators and critics, and consolidating film as a unique and versatile medium for experimentation.

Concluding thoughts

Undoubtedly, as funding and teaching opportunities proliferated (as experimental filmmaking took hold in educational institutions) during the decade, the ability to exist outside of the institutional frameworks, if filmmakers were reliant on institutional resources, became increasingly difficult. Yet, some filmmakers maintained a certain amount of independence by working with different film formats, supporting themselves through other forms of work or seeking funding from abroad. Filmmakers working independently also benefited from opportunities made available (often through institutional support) to screen films in the diverse 1970s exhibitions and film festivals, as we have seen. As can be concurred from discussions here, aesthetic, critical or theoretical contexts framing films were central for informing their reading. Large international festivals as well as smaller exhibitions or screening programmes were, therefore, essential for opening up spaces for discussion as attempts were made to appreciate diverse forms of practice. In time, these contexts would also be important for recognising and historicising the diversity in 1970s filmmaking with work produced in subsequent decades.

The issue of historical recognition and inclusion/exclusion is a complex domain, particularly as an understanding of the institutional contexts surrounding filmmaking also reveals why certain works may go unrecognised. As Mazière indicated earlier, there was a complex web of support facilitating 1970s experimental film production, distribution and exhibition. This matrix also included the wider theoretical and political frameworks, shaping and forming *certain* historical readings of the decade – positioned histories – that perhaps fitted more neatly within accepted discourses, but problematically also excluded works deemed unfit for inclusion. Clearly, the lack of a collective voice (which the LFMC had) for filmmakers working independently in more personal, expressive and representational ways or using the 'amateur' 8mm formats and existing (to some extent) outside of the institutional frameworks meant that a considerable proportion of 1970s experimental history fell out of some historical accounts. The fact that some of the personal 1970s films also fitted uncomfortably within dominant socialist and Marxist ideologies, due to their expressive or image-rich representational content, clearly also presented some problems for writers and critics championing the cause of politically or theoretically engaged work. Personal filmmakers such as Tait, Jarman and Keen made no attempts to justify their films through theoretical or critical frameworks like the modernist discourses prevailing at the LFMC or the *Screen*-theory abounding in other independent circles. While many of their films were not in distribution or existed through a single screening, opportunities for screening did exist, as we have seen. Retrospective exhibitions (and related events such as symposia and conferences) would, therefore, also be important not only for the viewing of 1970s films but also in offering opportunities for historical reflection, as they continue to do.

3
Experimental Film and Other Visual Arts

This chapter focuses specifically on relationships between experimental film and visual art practices such as painting, sculpture, photography and drawing, thereby providing a clearer understanding of correlations between the two fields. Close relationships are evident in films used for expressive, personal purposes and in those taking more formal or conceptual approaches to experimentation. Some discussion of the broader visual arts will first be outlined to identify particular aesthetic, theoretical or political preoccupations informing artists and filmmakers. Thereafter, films will be discussed in the context of specific visual disciplines or movements. This categorisation is, however, not to be read as an attempt to fix a taxonomy on the films, but rather to inform the reader where relationships can be drawn between diverse practices. While many experimental filmmakers were informed by the visual arts, there were also prevailing interests in cinematographic recording devices and in taking oppositional approaches to the conventions of narrative, commercial cinema.

The 1960s saw an increased scrutiny of the purpose of art. Diverse questions were raised about its socio-political contexts, how it should be defined, what relationship the concepts informing a work bore to the aesthetic outcome, how exhibition contexts informed viewing and audience interaction, and whether it was possible for art to be political. In surveys relating to 1960s art, some general conclusions emerged identifying, as Daniel Marzona suggested,

> [a]n explicit emphasis on the 'thought' component of art and its perception. In the course of the 1960s, normative definitions of art began to crumble [...] Thus, not only art itself, but also its institutional

context, became the centre of attention, subjected to comprehensive criticism in artistic practice.[1]

This crumbling of the 'normative definitions' played an important role in extending traditional disciplines and developing more experimental practices with film, video, 'happenings' and performance expanding the boundaries of practice. The Fluxus movement, for example, revived Dadaist attitudes by taking iconoclastic approaches to questioning the art 'object' and its cultural status. Fluxus films such as Yoko Ono's *No. 4* ('bottoms' film) (1964) and Nam June Paik's *Zen for Film/No. 1* (1962/64), 'typically tongue-in-cheek explorations of extreme close-up' – often took minimalist and provocative approaches in order to question the meaning of image.[2]

New forms of interrogation emerging in the 1960s also exposed the permeable boundaries between disciplines, with fixed roles traditionally affiliated with artists, writers or curators also becoming more fluid, as Clive Phillpot and Andrea Tarsia identified:

> This formal 'miscegenation' found its echo in the structures of the art world. Lucy Lippard felt able to see her role as that of 'writer-collaborator' with artists [...] Artists meanwhile often reviewed each other's shows, curated exhibitions, published magazines and books, and set up a number of organisations and spaces that operated out-side of institutions.[3]

Openness to experimentation would, therefore, inform 1970s practices which interrogated art's political, theoretical and social purpose to move beyond its historically rarified status as decorative artefact. The visual arts in the 1970s were also dominated by theoretical discourses informed by socio-political concerns, ideology, 1960s counter-culture and May '68 events. Stuart Sillars identified the decade as being 'the years when visual art almost deconstructed itself into theories, ideologies and concepts'.[4] And John A. Walker observed artists' ideological intentions in the 1970s as having 'three objectives: first to change art, second, to use that new art to change society, and third, to challenge and transform their relations of production and artworld institutions'.[5] Fluid parameters between disciplines saw many 1970s experimental filmmakers programming events, writing about their own and each other's work and theorising/philosophising about film or art, thereby ensuring that work was produced, shown, debated and recorded for posterity. While these fluid parameters enabled the dissemination of films, filmmaking was often also approached with a total openness to experimentation, as the filmmaker Steve Dwoskin outlined:

> For the artist even more than for 'professional' film-makers, film meant fluidity, movement, space juxtaposed, illusion, parody, reality, fantasy, twenty-four paintings a second, subtlety, exaggeration, boredom and repetition; it was drawing, photographic scrutiny, scratching, colour, tone, mathematical relationships and patterns. It was all, part or one of these things for each of the individual artists who stepped into film.[6]

This openness to experimentation, unfettered by the historical constraints of more traditional disciplines, brought a richness and diversity to the field. One of the characteristics proving to be singularly important for some filmmakers was the exploration of 'time' or 'duration' as this was central to the unfolding of a piece of work. This differed significantly from static works such as paintings, drawings or sculptures, with Tarsia noting the importance of 'time' as a dominating influence on experimental practices where '[t]ime was introduced as a recurring subject; not as an alternative to space, but as a fourth dimension that (materially and conceptually) re-defined the spatial possibilities of art.'[7] Thus film, requiring the same durational attention, had resonances with music, writing/reading and performance, with all of these providing fertile grounds for engagement with film alongside other static historic practices such as drawing, painting and sculpture.

Conceptualism, modernism and approaches to filmmaking

While not all 1970s experimental filmmakers were preoccupied with theoretical approaches to practice, conceptual and modernist foci informed others in their filmic investigations. Therefore brief considerations of these provide contexts for the discussions to follow. It was specifically the work as 'thought' (or concept), and its relationship to the exhibition context, that proved fundamental in determining future developments related to conceptual art. In his seminal work, gesturing the arrival of 'conceptual' art, Marcel Duchamp submitted his 'readymade' urinal, *Fountain* (1917), to the Society of Independent Artists' New York annual exhibition. In Duchamp's opinion the aesthetic object existed because it had been *chosen* by the artist, asserting that it should be considered within the context of its viewing situation and not purely for its aesthetic qualities.

It would be over 40 years after the exhibition of Duchamp's *Fountain* that these ideas were revisited with renewed vigour, finding more consolidated modes of investigation. The term 'Concept Art' was first used in Henry Flynt's 1961 essay of the same title, and two years later the artist Sol LeWitt's 'Conceptual Art' essay outlined some of the essential maxims:

> Conceptual art is made to engage with the mind of the viewer rather than his eye or emotions. This kind of art, then, should be stated with the most economy of means. Conceptual art is only good when the idea is good.[8]

Conceptual art informed the British artists' group Art & Language, whose artworks took the form of theoretical texts on linguistics. They published the first of their *Art–Language* publications in 1969, and in the same year the artist Joseph Kosuth announced:

> With the unassisted *Readymade*, art changed its focus from the form of the language to what was being said. Which means that it changed the nature of art from a question of morphology to a question of function. This change – one from 'appearance' to 'conception' – was the beginning of 'modern' art and the beginning of 'conceptual' art. All art (after Duchamp) is conceptual (in nature) because art only exists conceptually.[9]

Kosuth went further to state that, 'a work of art is a kind of *proposition* presented within the context of art as a comment on art', therefore calling on the viewer to respond or engage with the work as a question which hopefully provoked an answer or 'thought'[10] (Kosuth's emphasis).

While the 'thought' element was central to conceptual art, artists taking modernist approaches to practice within a particular discipline explored the specificities of their medium. In painting, for example, US painters such as Frank Stella or Jasper Johns investigated attributes inherent to painting such as two-dimensionality, the materiality of paint or the surface of the canvas. These extended the terms of disciplines with a sense of self-referentiality, as Dusinberre outlined:

> The modernist project in the arts might briefly be described as the interrogation of the fundamental representational properties of any medium, and an analysis of the modes of perception offered by that medium.[11]

In analogous modernist investigations, experimentation focused on the interrogation of qualities intrinsic to film (including cinematographic devices and the screening event), such as light, structure, surface, grain, materiality and processes of production, often resulted in a self-referential autonomy.

A focus on viewer activation also formed an important part of 1970s experimentation for many LFMC and conceptual filmmakers, and was outlined by Rees when he recognised that 'the perceiver, rather than the artist, is made responsible for the production of meaning, a specifically modernist tendency'.[12] This shift of emphasis on meaning-making from the filmmaker to the viewer was also elaborated further by Dusinberre:

> Clearly, this formal emphasis is intimately related to the modernist discourse in the other arts, particularly painting and sculpture. So that the quality of literalness which surrounds English avant-garde films is not to be confused with a representational literalness, but to be associated with the presentational literalness of contemporary art. That is, it asserts the primacy of cognition over meaningfulness.[13]

This also extended further into the critique of commercial cinema, seeking to engage the viewer as an active (rather than passive) consumer of film. This became an important preoccupation for many filmmakers in the decade, particularly those affiliated to the LFMC, and filmmakers such as Mulvey/Wollen, informed by discourses around *Screen*-based theories such as semiotics and psychoanalysis, deliberated in the journal.

The screening environment provided a number of different concerns for filmmakers which became integral to the production and dissemination of films. Jonathan Walley identified three preoccupations with cinematic space extending beyond the in-frame image:

> First is the space of the theatre and the activity of viewers within that space. Second is the space of what has been called the 'apparatus' or 'film machine', which extends beyond the screen to the projector and film reel normally behind the audience. Third, and somewhat more abstractly, are the institutional spaces that define avant-garde film and their ramifications for spectatorship.[14]

Thus, filmmakers engaged with these concerns sought ways to raise awareness about viewer-engagement or experiential filmmaking, or merely extended the boundaries of the film-frame by including projector, screen and screening space as integral parts of their work.

In her seminal article, 'Artist as Filmmaker' (1972), Annabel Nicolson discussed the diverse approaches taken by British experimental film-makers to engage with concepts, materiality, structure and form which had international parallels:

> The self-referential nature of much conceptual art provides an interesting philosophical parallel with the materially analytic, self-referential treatment of film evidenced by many independent filmmakers such as the Heins in Germany, Landow and Sharits in the States, Legrice [sic], Gidal, Drummond etc., in England. What may appear didactic concern with the chemistry of the medium is an essential landmark in an overdue, radical re-examination of the nature of film.[15]

Nicolson provided illuminating details on differences taken by 'conceptual' filmmakers (exhibiting in galleries) such as David Dye, John Hilliard and Tony Hill and the formal, modernist approaches to experimentation taken by many LFMC filmmakers. She identified that 'the use of film as an expedient for demonstrating concepts is diametrically opposite from the structural use of film and still more so from perceptual and psychological exploration identified with personal film makers.'[16] She expressed her regret that '[t]he lack of cross reference between artists' and film makers is disheartening since these polarities of conceptual and perceptual emphasis could throw illuminating perspectives on each other'.[17] In a more recent interview, reflecting on the article, Nicolson also revealed how important these different contexts were for shaping the diverse objectives (conceptual and modernist) and outcomes:

> There were a few people from St Martins, mainly from the sculpture department whose work was quite conceptual [...] It wasn't the same as expanded cinema that had grown up with the Co-op [...] [S]ome of them were using film as a vehicle to convey an idea or a concept and so film was quite attractive to them to make these kinds of statements. But this was deeply different to the Co-op where there was a love of the material for its own sake and exploring and seeing where it led and it was a very fluid process. I think those of us who were involved with the Co-op: we were just in love with film. I mean: the light, the radiance, the projection, exploring what the structure meant. Our ideas followed from that.[18]

Nicolson identified these different approaches as distinctive (conceptual and modernist/formal) but with some overlapping concerns, regretting, as she said, that there weren't more opportunities for dialogue.

Although conceptualism and a modernist focus on formalism directed certain aspects of filmmaking in the decade, it must be emphasised that experimentation was, on the whole, extremely eclectic and unconstrained by rigid concepts or systematic directives. In Breakwell's *Nine Jokes* (1971), for example, he mocked the seriousness of conceptual art in nine short film sketches, with titles such as 'The Art World Erupts' playing a significant role (the film is a close-up shot of Breakwell squeezing spots on his nose).

Even at the LFMC, where a significant amount of formal experimentation (modernist 'film as film') took place, approaches were not dictated by ruling decrees. One need only refer to Annabel Nicolson's collection of memories from 'The Early Years of the Film Co-op' to understand that openness to experimentation abounded.[19] Other filmmakers, such as Jarman, Keen, Larcher, Tait and Whitehead, who were certainly aware of developments in the arts, generally took no interest in making films engaged explicitly with conceptualism or modernism in the arts.

'Black box' or 'white cube' and anti-commodification

While production contexts provided opportunities for experimentation, the screening environment also became an important space for investigation. Preoccupations with the space of film exhibition posed questions about the conventions of the 'black box' (cinema) and the possibilities presented by the 'white cube' (art gallery). The former, with its history in early cinema and Edison's Kinetographic Theater or Black Maria (1893), operated as the first production studio and screening theatre, whereas the 'white cube' was typically identified as a white-walled cuboid or rectangular exhibition space for the exhibition of art. By the turn of the century 'black boxes' had spread globally as entertainment venues for film viewing, and the standard design of a blackened room with screen, seating and the projection of films (at specific times) became the convention. While size or décor changed over the decades, the traditional cinema format has generally remained the same, despite screening venues becoming more varied and catering to specialist audiences. Fundamentally, however, these 'black boxes' were spaces where films were screened to a (usually) passive and seated audience.

Although the 'white cube' – a colloquial term for the art gallery formalised in Brian O'Doherty's seminal 1976 essays – was typically identified as a white-walled cuboid exhibition space for the presentation of art, gallery spaces differed significantly in shape, size and design. O'Doherty's 'white cube' identified and critiqued ideologies related to institutional and commercial aspects of gallery exhibition:

> The ideal gallery subtracts from the artwork all cues that interfere with the fact that it is 'art'. The work is isolated from everything that would detract from its own evaluation of itself. This gives the space a presence possessed by other spaces where conventions are preserved through the repetition of a closed system of values. Some of the sanctity of the church, the formality of the courtroom, the mystique of the experimental laboratory joins with chic design to produce a unique chamber of esthetics.[20]

This 'unique chamber of esthetics' presented some real benefits for viewer engagement, differing significantly from the formality of the seated cinema auditorium. Although galleries often conformed to a certain spatial format – square or rectangular room/s – they offered more fluid viewing spaces, enabling viewers to move around the space, taking in work at their own pace and volition. Gallery spaces, therefore, facilitated different forms of audience interaction and were as important for single-screen films, where the display of the projection mechanism might form part of the work, as they were for wider explorations with multiple screens, film installations or performative works, as Gareth Bucknell elucidates:

> Once films were taken out of the cinema – with its darkened room, fixed seating and single screen – numerous possibilities were opened up. Films could have live soundtracks of great complexity, the projectionist could be visible to the audience, and utilise more than one screen – in short, they could become performances, or events, rather than mere screenings.[21]

These possibilities are evident in, for example, Anthony McCall's *Line Describing a Cone* (1973) where viewers could move into the sculptural cone of light between projector and screen; and in multi-screen works such as Lis Rhodes' *Light Music* (1975), Steve Farrer's *The Machine* (1978–88) and David Dye's *Unsigning for 8 Projectors* (1972) where viewers could equally engage with works on an experiential level.

Certain aspects of gallery exhibition were, however, particularly problematic for some ideologically concerned artists and filmmakers, especially where this formed part of the hierarchy of commodification. The commodification of art and its sale was often seen as devaluing or stripping work of its political or ideological intentions, inducing a rationale for 'anti-commodification' informed by disdain for a commercial gallery system often purely interested only in turning a profit:

> There were various views about what radical artists should do but three options recurred: One was to avoid galleries altogether – the artist Peter Dunn baldly stated: 'A socialist cultural practice cannot be gallery-orientated' – and to seek new audiences by employing different means of communication and patronage. A second was to make use of existing galleries but to reform or subvert them; a third was for artists to establish and operate their own 'alternative' spaces.[22]

These considerations invariably led to more productive solutions for screening venues affiliated either to film workshops or artist-run spaces, ensuring flexibility and freedom from the art 'system'. The LFMC and LVA held numerous screenings, and spaces such as 2B Butler's Wharf, for example, showed 80 live events, including 30 film screenings, performances and video installations in its three-year life span. Jarman's 'Studio Bankside' also provided rich opportunities for filming and lively screening events, albeit often to an inside coterie of supporters.

Arts Council galleries such as the Hayward Gallery (London) and Walker Art Gallery (Liverpool) also provided support outside the commercial system, with 1970s exhibitions including film as part of the broader visual arts. Extensive exhibitions such as 'Art Spectrum' (1971, Alexandra Palace) and 'A Survey of the Avant-Garde in Britain' (1972, Gallery House) included film and video. Yet, while inclusion in these kinds of exhibitions was welcome, the uneasy position experimental filmmaking held – neither wholly engaged in the field of the arts nor the cinema – also posed some problems, as Curtis outlined:

> Though historically important as announcements of the arrival of a 'new art', these big mixed-media shows rarely provided a sympathetic physical environment for the showing of film, and the most significant developments in the installation in the 1970s took place in the more familiar contexts of the Co-op's black box and the controllable environment of the gallerist's white cube.[23]

In the 'Art Spectrum' exhibition, for example, experimental films were relegated to a side-aisle in a venue usually used for trade fairs.[24]

Problems concerning the exhibition of work were compounded by the belief that experimental film was not an easily saleable commodity, due to its reproducibility and problems of display (precisely the reasons for anti-commodification welcomed by many filmmakers). Le Grice acknowledged the fairly high level of 1970s art exhibitions many of the filmmakers showed in, yet lamented the fact that they failed to sell work:

> While a dealer might come to another artist in the exhibition and show interest, it would not function like this for the film area. It was seen as a kind of lively entertainment within the exhibition, but it always stayed outside the art market.[25]

He did, however, admit that the fault also lay with filmmakers and their resistance to the commodification of their work:

> I came to the conclusion that some of this is our own fault because we were radically against the commodity world of art as well as we were radically against the world of commercial cinema. We wanted to be in the philosophical context of art, we wanted to show in art spaces, because we were doing multi-projections and installations and what we now call expanded cinema. But actually the work we did was anti-commodity. And so in some senses we made it impossible for the re-incorporation into the art world.[26]

While resistance to commercialisation was problematic for selling work, it also liberated filmmakers from producing durable 'objects' for commercial acquisition. Notably, Nicolson's seminal *Reel Time* (1973) was only performed once as the film was progressively destroyed whilst being fed through a sewing machine and a projector.

Expanded cinema

Although longer-term gallery screenings set certain challenges for filmmakers (particularly with the mechanical breakdowns of projectors or films requiring on-the-spot repair) some particularly innovative ways were sought to extend the boundaries of 1970s film screening through (mostly) one-off live events which came to be known as 'expanded cinema'. The term had been coined in the US by Jonas Mekas' (initially as 'absolute cinema') and later became 'expanded cinema' (1965), with Gene Youngblood's *Expanded Cinema* (1970) publication exploring film within the wider contexts of video, television, computer graphics and holography.[27] The British focus, however, was more preoccupied with European interpretations, as Le Grice outlined:

> [This] was largely characterised by a concern to bring the cinematic experience consciously into the space of the spectator through performed action and installation. Film structures were developed to initiate a positive reflexive role for the spectator, a concern also debated in theory by film-makers at the time.[28]

Expanded cinema often included live-action performances, thereby opening up particularly lively debates about space, duration, experiential viewer experience, the incidental and the unique film event, subject as it was to the moment of time passing in a given space. Le Grice addressed these issues early on in the decade when he 'considered the situation of the audience politically and ethically', focusing on the projection event as an affirmation of the central reality in his seminal 'Real TIME/SPACE' (1972) essay.[29] In his essay he identified 'five interrelated areas of exploration': the relationship of the audience to retrospective filmic reality; the nature of the medium (materials, equipment and processes); the nature of audience experience in relation to a current 'concrete' reality; time or duration as a 'concrete' dimension; and notions of the spatial or TIME/SPACE structuring of the projection event.[30]

British concerns and an opposition to the dominant cinema, particularly in LFMC circles, also saw filmmakers extending the in-frame film content through challenging orthodox projection modes in film installation. Chris Welsby, for example, did this with *Shore Line II* (1979), which consisted of six identical film loops of waves breaking on the shoreline projected in portrait format with projectors lying on their sides. Experimental screenings were enthusiastically encouraged at the LFMC by individuals such as Nicolson, whose interest in incidental occurrences also informed her film programming (1976–77):

> Chance has no relevance for film used as concept but for those exploring the nature of film as film it can be a positive, contributing factor. Legrice [sic] would respond to stray light on the screen and Hollis Frampton confessed himself more interested in the image reflected on the wall behind the projector when he showed *Zorn's Lemma* at the London Film Co-op this year. Since every projection is inevitably influenced by the immediate context and is essentially the

moment when film exists as a fact in time, it is surprising how few artists respond to this basic premise of film.[31]

Nicolson here reveals the openness to chance and liveliness with which film was explored at the LFMC, contrary to some of the drier theoretical reckonings such as Gidal's insistence that the viewer understand duration through enduring some rather tortuously boring films.

Although expanded cinema was explored fairly extensively in the decade, it was by no means a new innovation and a longer history dating back to the early days of cinema and artists' filmmaking draws a line from contemporary '[d]igital video installation go[ing] back to the light-play experiments of the Futurists and the Bauhaus, including Oscar Fischinger's five-screen films (two overlapping the other three) with live percussion, in 1927'.[32] A longer history also includes László Moholy-Nagy's 1922 manifesto, focusing on the effect of Kinetic Art on the spectator, and his *Light-Space Modulator* (1930), a sculpture consisting of metal structures, light bulbs and a mechanism enabling rotation. This was exhibited in a contained space with reflective metal pieces projecting 'images' onto the walls, revealed in Moholy-Nagy's film *Light Display: Black and White and Gray* (1930). In Theo van Doesburg's essay on 'Film as Pure Form' (1925), issued a few years after Moholy-Nagy's manifesto, he advocated for an expanded form of film presentation with an architectural – as opposed to theatrical – setting, whereby '[t]he spectator will no longer observe the film, like a theatrical presentation, but will participate in it optically and acoustically'.[33] This kind of immersion would force an active engagement with the film screening, with the viewer compelled to take the space and their presence in it into consideration. The US artist Stan VanDerBeek took this a step further with his 1966 proposition, imagining an environment 'where it might be possible to re-order the structure of motion pictures as we know them'.[34] In '"Culture: Intercom" and Expanded Cinema: A Proposal and Manifesto' (1966) VanDerBeek charted his visions for creating an immersive environment, the 'Movie-Drome', with thousands of images projected onto the entirety of a domed screen and the audience lying down with feet towards the centre.[35]

Viewer engagement and explorations into film space (in-frame and out-of-frame) were taken up with renewed vigour in 1970s Britain, with artists/filmmakers such as Keen, Dye and Jarman experimenting with multi-screen performative platforms and a group of LFMC filmmakers referred to as 'Filmaktion' (Gill Eatherley, William Raban, Malcolm

Le Grice, Annabel Nicolson and Mike Dunford, and on occasion other filmmakers) focusing on the live projection event. 'Filmaktion' was never a formal group but there was 'a considerable sharing of ideas and thoughts and inter-influence [sic]', with an article about their exhibition 'Filmaktion: New Directions in Film Art' detailing their concerns:[36]

> The Walker Art Gallery's lecture room is a cinema at present, but the programme now showing bears little resemblance to anything happening at the Odeon or ABC. This is film for film's sake, film without the smooth illusion, with its technology laid bare, its techniques used as an end in themselves.[37]

Although the live-action works included reliance on (occasionally) temperamental projection mechanisms and site-specific accommodations to the exhibition space, these 'problems' were instead exploited, with a balance between planned structure and live extemporisation proving to make for dynamic events. The immersive environment and the experiential were integral to conceptualising and perceiving these works, as Moholy-Nagy, Van Doesberg and VanDerBeek had also proposed years before. For an in-depth history and contemporary discussions, the recent book, *Expanded Cinema: Art Performance Film* (2011), by Ball, Curtis, Rees and White provides extensive details and includes a wonderful map of expanded cinema.

Film experimentation

In this section relationships between experimental filmmaking and visual art practices are explored in greater detail, but it needs to be understood that these relationships are not drawn in order to fix set 'genres' onto experimental filmmaking. Instead they provide links and open up understandings of the fluidity between different visual forms of practice. While the films discussed may be related to diverse genres in art, filmmakers also often explicitly interrogated the conventions of the discipline informing them. Where earlier movements such as Cubism informed filmmaking, filmmakers also sought to push the boundaries of Cubist ideas further, extending them through the use of the film medium. Where the landscape genre was investigated, films, for example, expanded the boundaries of the meaning of landscape painting or Land Art, often mediating the viewer's experiences of landscape. In some direct-surface films the celluloid was used as a 'canvas' or 'paper' to literally paint or draw on, in order to see the physical marks transformed in projection.

Painting and its related theoretical discourses offered up particularly interesting areas for investigation beyond the explicit exploration of animation of still images. Shared commonalities between painting and film, such as composition, frame, colour, tone, perception, image construction and space, provided a rich foundation for filmic investigations. Some filmmakers, such as Derek Jarman and Peter Greenaway, were also painters and this would significantly inform their approaches to film experimentation. A number of 1970s filmmakers took a literal approach to painting on the film-strip – also referred to as 'direct animation' – following on from earlier experimentation exemplified in 1930s films by Norman McLaren and Len Lye. Both these artists/filmmakers worked under John Grierson for the General Post Office (GPO) Film Unit, painting or scratching on film acetate to create imagery. In Margaret Tait's *Painted Eightsome* (1970), for example, diverse abstract and figurative shapes were painted directly onto the film-strip to accompany the soundtrack, consisting of an Orkadian eightsome reel. Her *Colour Poems* (1974) also included – alongside filmed footage – abstract and figurative imagery painted onto the film-strip. Larcher also reworked filmed footage for *Mare's Tail* (1969) and *Monkey's Birthday* (1975), painting, scratching or heating the filmed celluloid to transform the imagery. Influential US filmmakers Carolee Schneemann and Stan Brakhage also worked directly on the film-strip to enhance imagery, with Schneemann's *Fuses* (1968) discussed in Chapter 4 and Brakhage dedicating increasing amounts of time to this way of working in later epic, abstract painted films.

Jarman's painting, romanticism and 'sensuous' film

Relationships between painting and film are evident in the painterly quality of many of Jarman's Super-8 films, such as *Garden of Luxor* (1972), *The Art of Mirrors* (1973) and *Jordan's Dance* (1977). These were informed by his diverse practices as painter, set designer, film director and writer, as well as by his interest in mysticism and symbolism, as O'Pray outlines:

> Unlike many of his contemporaries, Jarman made films rather as one makes paintings. To recognize this is to understand films like *In the Shadow of the Sun* (1974–80), *The Angelic Conversation* (1985) and *The Last of England* (1987) whose raw power, fragmentary style, textured images, sprawling narrative and bricolage-like forms suggest a painterly approach to film.[38]

Jarman's initial choice of Super-8 for short and feature-length films was as much for economic independence as it was for the technical ease and possibility for experimentation that the format facilitated. His Nizo camera had a built-in light-meter, easily loadable film cartridge and variable speed button, which were all instrumental in furthering experimentation. While Jarman was dismissive of his technical abilities – in a diary entry revealing: 'I was phased by numbers, I never got a Maths 'O' level, and [was] hopeless with machines' – his very skilful, intuitive approach brought about a rich body of work evident in over 60 short and 11 feature-length films. He recognised the possibilities film offered, saying '[w]hen I received my first film back and it was in focus it seemed like magic, an instrument to bring dreams to life and that was good enough'.[39] His particularly distinctive body of work included re-filming from the screen, using time-lapse photography and experimenting with shooting speeds.

The film critic Chrissie Iles acknowledged the unique, painterly aesthetic of Jarman's films and eloquently described the way that he 'folds painting and film inside each other, blurring the lines between cinematographic and painterly composition'.[40] His working process, resulting in a unique filmic sensibility, was also described by O'Pray as follows:

> Any interest in the films lies in Jarman's ability to compose the shot, but more importantly, in a technique he discovered for himself in the early 1970s and made his own, of shooting at between three to six frames per second, and refilming it projected at the same speeds. The refilming and original shooting speed allowed Jarman a control over the imagery which produced a strong painterly texture and pulsating rhythm. The grainy streaked colour effect is like a strong broad brush-stroke, and assisted by the degeneration effect of re-filming the colours are often softened and suffused. The rhythm is one which Jarman describes, aptly, as like a 'heart-beat' – sensual, dream-like and erotic.[41]

While eschewing formal or structured approaches to filmmaking, the painterly qualities in Jarman's films were, however, not devoid of theoretical or philosophical interests. In personal notebooks and published writings he referred to diverse texts on alchemy, mysticism and the writings of Carl Jung, with Wollen noting that Jarman's 'own work is full of references to magic, alchemy and occult lore'.[42] Gray Watson also identified these influences on Jarman's filmmaking:

> Jarman read widely in the areas of psychology, magic and the occult [...] In addition to Jung, he read James Hillman, notably such books

as *Dream and the Underworld* and *Pan and the Nightmare,* and he was deeply influenced by Frances Yate's writings on the hermetic tradition in the Renaissance: Giordano Bruno and, still more, John Dee were important reference points for him, as was Henry Cornelius Agrippa's *Three Books of Occult Philosophy.*[43]

These mystical and psychological texts informed his broader creative practices, and in his elegy for Jarman, Wollen discussed his final film *Blue* (1993) and the extensive thought that had gone into this work over many years, from Jarman's early admiration of the artist Yves Klein to an engagement with theories on colour and perception by artists, philosophers and theorists such as Johann Wolfgang von Goethe, Ludwig Wittgenstein and William Blake. Therefore, while his Super-8 films were born out of intuitive experimentation rather than scripted forms of filmmaking or engagements with theory, his output cannot be separated from his extensive read knowledge and work as a painter, film director and designer which all infused his unique oeuvre. While *Blue* operated like a Colour Field painting with an emotive voiceover, detailing Jarman's diminishing eyesight and slow demise from AIDS, Wollen saw it as a 'magical act of resurrection through love', with the film reaching 'far beyond minimalism or colour, into the realms of poetry, symbolic discourse and yes, politics'.[44] In this way, the painterly, symbolic and mystical were carried through from the earlier Super-8 films to Jarman's final work.

Colour Field painting and Cubism

References to Colour Field painters, such as Mark Rothko and Clyfford Still, are also evident in Le Grice's *Matrix* (1973), which consists of six looped films of optically printed solid blocks of colour. Each film has two blocks of colour divided horizontally by a black line, and the films are projected simultaneously by six projectors lying on their sides. The quiet stillness of a Colour Field painting is subverted in this expanded cinema piece, presenting a dynamic exploration of coloured fields, with projectors moved around by Le Grice mid-performance to ensure an active space of projection as Deke Dusinberre explains:

The superimposition of the colour loops yields complex compositions of colour as well as of rhythm, and the screen space is not accepted as given but is exploited as needed. There is a strong sense of shifting lines of horizontality and verticality as the screen shape shifts. In this way, Le Grice effectively activates what is normally passive screen space.[45]

Le Grice's interest in 'the politics of perception', viewer engagement and film materiality informed his practice, with no two presentations of *Matrix* being the same, due to the live-action projection situation. These rendered the colour fields into active explorations of colour, space, light and film apparatus, ensuring that each event was a singular, unrepeatable work.

While the dynamism of Le Grice's *Matrix* materialises through the expanded projection event, Jenny Okun's *Still Life* (1976) – a dynamic film informed by the historic 'still live' genre – is enigmatically brought to life by the in-frame recording of the painting process. The short film reveals a progressive change in palette as a tableau of fruits and vegetables is portrayed in negative colour film-stock. Here Okun elucidates:

> [The film] attempts to reinstate some sort of representation of reality by painting the fruit in front of the camera its negative colours: but the burnt-out shadows and black highlights consistently prevent any illusionistic interpretation of the space within the frame while also asserting the processes involved.[46]

Okun's hands, frequently visible as the painting process takes place, create an idiosyncratic rendering of these edible objects with direct references to the still-life genre and the act of painting. *Still Life* also comments on film materiality as Okun chose to screen the film as a negative print, rather than the more conventional positive film print.

Still life in painting and drawing provided rich material for engagement with this historic genre, with 1970s films including Mike Dunford's *Still Life with Pear* (1974) and works from Guy Sherwin's 'Short Film Series' (1975–1998), such as *Vermeer Still Life*, *Metronome* and *Candle and Clock*. The genre also gave Le Grice the opportunity to engage with Cubism in *Academic Still Life* (1976), where specific reference is made to Paul Cézanne's still-life paintings and Cubist-inspired *Basket of Apples* (1890), where different viewpoints disrupt conventional perspectives found in historic 'still-life' paintings. Le Grice's film includes the same objects – apples, plate, wine bottle – as Cezanne's earlier painting, but film movement brings an idiosyncratic dynamic to the concept 'still life', with perception explored through the multiple viewpoints produced by moving around the objects. The use of time-lapse photography and timed exposures with a hand-held camera present dynamic fast-moving multiple viewpoints, operating to activate the viewer, who is forced to become conscious of the act of looking (of perception) and film content. This ensured viewer reflexivity – a key theoretical concern for Le Grice – unlike the intended viewer absorption which seamless editing in dominant, narrative cinema provides.

In this way, *Academic Still Life* operates as an investigation into the act of looking. Both Okun and Le Grice's films provide critiques of, and investigations into, the still-life painting genre, yet represent a kind of oxymoron, in that they are, in effect, moving 'still lifes'.

Engaging with Cubism provided fertile ground for interrogating its historic antecedents and theories of perception, as well as for extending the parameters of painting through film. Wollen, in his 'Two Avant-Gardes' essay, noted that Cubism (the innovations of Picasso and Braque) had 'an implication beyond the history of painting itself', representing 'a critical semiotic shift, a changed concept and practice of sign and signification, which we can now see to have been the opening-up of a space, a disjunction between signifier and signified'.[47] An exploration of Cubism through film was, however, not a new practice, with films investigating perception, vision and multiple viewpoints documented in Standish D. Lawder's *The Cubist Cinema* (1975). Lawder, asking whether 'the Cubists use[d] the medium to release the implied movement of their paintings into an actual passage through space and time', revealed relationships between Cubism and film already existent in early films by Walter Ruttman, Viking Eggeling, Hans Richter, Germaine Dulac and Fernand Léger.[48] He also cited evidence of two unrealised film ideas by Cubist painters Picasso and Léopold Survage.[49] Lawder discussed Léger's *Ballet Méchanique* (1924) in great depth as it exemplified relationships between Cubism and filmmaking for him. Cubist periods of innovation, assimilation and consolidation therefore provided rich terrain for filmic investigations.

In William Raban's *Angles of Incidence* (1973) the 'Axis of Camera Rotation' and shifting minor changes in viewpoint were explored by fixing a rope between a camera (fixed to a tripod) separated by a few metres from the central point in a window. With the camera moved in an arc, shooting took place at particular 'broad angles of incidence', with a repetition of patterns of movement occurring at regular intervals.[50] The film followed written and sketched plans 'to see if I could transliterate a cubist approach to film' and took 30 hours to complete, also allowing for incidental occurrences such as changes in light.[51] *Angles of Incidence*, screened as a dual-screen projection with one of the films flipped, sees the films progressively moving out of sync, thus extending Raban's interests in the Cubist focus on perception and by '[i]ncorporating the composition into the shooting period allows for a greater degree of flexibility: chance occurrences may be more easily incorporated, and it is less mechanistic than copying from a prescribed score or model'.[52] In Le Grice's review he identified the film's importance in the way 'the spatial construct of the film is a product of the relationship of the space of the camera to the space which it observes'.[53] This was similarly revealed in Ron Haseldon's *Tracking Cycles* (1975), with the camera documenting a living room within a 'densely coloured, almost cubist representation' of space.[54] Haseldon achieved this through a rigorous filming procedure using a tracking device for the camera recording two cycles of movement. John Du Cane's *Zoomlapse* (1975) and Roger Hammond's *Window Box* (1972) equally reveal preoccupations with perception, film space, light and camera operations. Both films are shot looking out of a window, with *Zoomlapse* focusing onto the buildings opposite and *Window Box* focused on the box and window of the title. Through the representation of fast-paced fragmented views Du Cane wanted the viewer to be conscious of the way film and space are manufactured, and with *Window Box* Hammond attempted to address focus in an epistemological manner, additionally making the viewer aware of the film medium.

Optical painting/optical film

Similar modes of interest in extending the film medium also informed Sherwin's *Optical Sound Films* (1971–2007), although these were focused on optics and 'perception of vision' (theory whereby an after-image is thought to persist for a fraction of a second on the retina). Interesting parallels can be drawn with the Op Art paintings of Bridget Riley as she explored the illusory effects of vision and the picture plane in works such as *Movement in Squares* (1961), where the painting appears to have a restlessly moving surface. Op Art was part of a 1960s movement concerned primarily with optics and perception, with Le Grice observing that 'as with the more serious areas of Op Art, film work in this area exposes rather than exploits perceptual phenomena'.[55] Sherwin's interest in retinal after-effects produced in film echoed the retinal effects produced by Riley's optical paintings, although his interests also extended into the soundtrack which he created by working directly onto the optical sound-strip. This resulted in the projector 'reading' the soundtrack and producing an abstract rhythmic score.

In *Cycles* (1972/77), for example, Sherwin produced sound and image by working directly onto the film-strip, with paper dots stuck on or holes punched into the film-strip. Sherwin explored equivalences between sound and the 'persistence of vision', identifying differences between units of time in film (24 frames per second) and sound (72 beats per second), thereby creating interesting dialogues between visual and aural perception. During projection, as the dots increase on the film-strip, they eventually become 'a pulsating ball of light', and together with the sound 'the film highlights the different sensitivities in our visual and aural senses'.[56] While Riley's paintings are silent, the visual resonances create similar pulsating 'moving' images, with both films and paintings operating on the act of seeing and perceptual modes of reception.

Film and photography

Interests in human optics and perception were also exploited through investigating the mechanics of the recording 'camera-eye'. The relationship between photography and film is self-evident as both are lens-based media sharing commonalities relating to camera-based image-making, such as light, frame, composition, film-stock, processing and printing. Parallels are also evident in the physical film-strip, where one can observe the thousands of still frames making up a film sequence and becoming animated through projection. A number of 1970s films explicitly reveal these interrelationships, drawing on historical antecedents or taking a modernist turn to explicitly explore properties inherent to photography.

The early pioneer in photography and motion Eadweard Muybridge (1830–1904), provided fertile ground for exploring relationships between still and moving image, with Fred Drummond's *Photo Film* (1967) consisting of sequential Muybridge photographs and still shots of an animated subject. Anne Rees-Mogg's *Muybridge Film* (1973) captured the filmmaker Renny Croft performing a cartwheel, with Croft's action first shown in accelerated motion then gradually slowed down. Production shots were also included within the film and in this way Rees-Mogg 'took a simple action, took it apart, shuffled its order, and then reprojected it as a mime of its ancestor', thus revealing the still moments of recorded photographic action becoming motion.[57]

In a number of films from Sherwin's 'Short Film Series' (1975–1998), such as *Tree Reflection, Metronome, Bicycle, Eye* and *Bowl*, a single scene is focused on, showing the image of the title like a beautifully composed photograph with subtle changes in light, movement, tonal range or focus made evident. Sherwin's enduring interests in light and time also reveal how a simple planned structure allowed for unexpected revelations in *Metronome*:

> What happens at some point is that you have these two clockwork mechanisms and there are slight variations in that, and I didn't expect that and the arm starts to kind of struggle. And this sort of reveals something about the mechanism that you use to record it.[58]

Sherwin's comment also reveals the importance of the incidental when working within a planned structure, therefore allowing for chance 'happenings' to occur.

Revealing the mechanism of the cinematographic process was also central to a number of conceptual filmmakers' approaches. John Blake's *Arrest* (1970) is a short film recording Blake's head (filmed by Gidal) moving in and out of frame. Dialogues between still and moving image were explicitly emphasised through the exhibition of the printed film-strip (resembling a wave-formation from a distance), a written theoretical statement and the looped film installation in the space. David Lamelas similarly included a visual synopsis in sets of contact strips exhibited alongside his film *Cumulative Script* (1971), which recorded fellow filmmakers Mike Dunford and Roger Hammond playing about on Primrose Hill.[59] A few years later, Anthony McCall would similarly include nine printed film frames from *Landscape for Fire* (1973) with his screening of *16mm Film in Three Parts from Two Points* (1973). Similarities in the three films were evident in the way direct links were made between the photographic/cinematographic by revealing film's historical antecedent photography, relationships between still and moving image, and showing conceptual investigations into the 'thought' elements in film form.

Drawing on film

Steve Farrer's *Ten Drawings* (1976) drew direct references from drawing and the mechanics of projection, with the film screening often accompanied, like the three films mentioned above, with an exhibition of actual film-strips (as in Blake's *Arrest*) and related drawings. Farrer literally drew/painted on 50 strips of clear, 16mm film leader laid side-by-side in rectangular formation. The strips were joined together end-to-end, with the projected film operating as a compilation of abstract images offering an equivalence of the whole surface of a drawing, satisfying Farrer's intention to 'deal with a film in one stroke; to say, well – slash – I've dealt with beginning, middle and end in one go'.[60] In exhibiting both film and drawings in the same space, the transitory nature of film (the moving 'drawing') and the physical drawing were juxtaposed, creating an idiosyncratic dialogue between film physicality and the ephemeral existence of drawings projected in fragmented form. This exposed the relationships between drawing/film and still/moving image still further, with Dusinberre identifying the film as a:

radical departure from the technology and codes of cinematic representation, its adoption of a visual abstraction related to painting (and related to the abstract, dynamic 'universal language' envisaged by the neo-plasticists in the '20s), the transformation of a static drawing apprehended instantaneously into a projected strip apprehended temporally (with the complementary subversion of 'beginning, middle, and end' through the 'all over' nature of the original drawings), the congruent/divergent sensory impressions produced by the marks as sound and as image (distribution prints have been adjusted to account for projection sync), the serial order and differentiation which accompanies minimal imagery.[61]

As in Sherwin's *Optical Sound Films*, the soundtrack of *Ten Drawings* is produced through 'drawing' on the film's optical sound-strip, with Rees comparing Farrer's self-referential film conceptually to Robert Morris' seminal minimalist work, *Box with the Sound of its Own Making* (1961), consisting of a tape recorder, hidden inside a wooden box, playing the soundtrack of its construction.[62]

Ten Drawings is not a chronologically sequential work and can be shown with film-strips in any order, leading Dusinberre to suggest that the work needed to be read beyond its apparently formalist organisation for its immediacy and spontaneity and 'the lucid (game-playing) quality of the film'.[63] With serial film works not requiring a fixed screening order, like *Ten Drawings* and Sherwin's *Short Film Series*, the works in effect become renewed with each screening, lending vitality to their existence, not unlike the live-action expanded cinema works.

Land Art and landscape in film

The landscape tradition with its histories in drawing, painting and photography also provided rich terrain for exploration in film. Landscape, either being the central focus or playing a more peripheral part, informed newer disciplines emerging in the 1960s and 1970s such as film, video, performance and Land Art. In some films cinematographic recording devices, procedural approaches or concepts about space directed experimentation, while in others more personal resonances connected with the British Romantic landscape traditions of painters such as J. M. W. Turner or John Constable. In Larcher's *Monkey's Birthday* (1975), for example, he combined romantic engagements with the landscapes, through which he travelled on an epic road-trip, with his interests in mysticism, his skills as a photographer/cinematographer (capturing light on film) and hands-on processes of working directing with the filmed material in the LFMC workshop. Rees noted that '[t]he romantic vein in this tradition continues with Larcher's epic scale films, which celebrate the same interaction of the eye and the machine to expand sight'.[64]

Romantic affiliations with landscape also featured regularly in Jarman's films, with his unique style seeking not to impose a certain 'view of the countryside but rather encapsulat[ing] and explor[ing] the nature and experience of a particular place'.[65] In *A Journey to Avebury* (1971), painterly shots through the Wiltshire countryside reveal details of Neolithic landmarks with details of trees and grass infused with a warm, golden luminosity. Wollen noted that Jarman's 1960s paintings often revealed 'a dreamlike, surreal aspect, which is also explored in many of the films [...] not a familiar geographical landscape but an eternal celestial one'.[66]

For other filmmakers more romantic affiliations with landscape were also evident, with Margaret Tait's *Aerial* (1974) including poetic shots of nature (birds, trees, earthworms, grass) in her familiar Orkney surroundings. For B. S. Johnson the landscape around Port Ceiriad in north Wales – the location of *Fat Man on the Beach* (1974) – held equally personal, but more mystical and spiritual significance, in this 'place charged with memories for Johnson, memories of a strange, emotionally unsettled, superstitious phase of his life.'[67] And a poetic spirituality is resonant in Yoko Ono and John Lennon's *Apotheosis* (1970), displaying the receding landscape as the camera rises progressively from a village at ground level to reveal a pristine snowy landscape, and Lennon's idea for *Apotheosis* ('a release from earthly life') as the passage of life from physicality to spirit.[68]

While romantically infused landscapes informed some filmmakers, others took more conceptual or cinematographically informed approaches to landscape, with relationships explored between the landscape (natural or urban), recording processes and figures in the landscape used to exploit these relationships. Rees, describing urban and rural landscape films made by LFMC filmmakers, such as Le Grice's *Whitchurch Down (Duration)* (1972) and Halford and Raban's *Time Stepping* (1974), saw these linking

> back to the story of British art and to its fusion of the empirical gaze with the new scientific meteorology in the nineteenth century. Just as in that earlier meeting of Constable's eye with scientific topography, so in the 1970s a painterly understanding of light and form met up with the mechanical apparatus of camera and printer.[69]

In John Hilliard's *From and To* (1971), for example, two cameramen simultaneously recorded each other's movements in an urban environment including nature and buildings. While one filmmaker turned on the spot recording at eye level, the other filmmaker moved in a circle around him, recording the first cameraman's actions. The film was screened as a dual-screen projection, revealing different viewpoints simultaneously.[70] In a similar vein, Mike Duckworth's *Body Arcs* (1973) revealed the landscape recorded from a fixed, but rotating, position in 'four self-filmed movements', while contrary to this, Martin Hearn filmed a small, remotely positioned immobile person in *Central Figure* (1976) and *Figure Spiral* (1978) as the camera moved around the landscape.[71]

While more 'scientific' (structural/procedural) approaches to the landscape were used in Raban and Welsby's collaborative *River Yar* (1971–72), filmmaking also allowed for incidental occurrences to enter the work. A tidal estuary was filmed over three weeks during the spring and autumn equinoxes, referencing the landscape tradition but offering insights into duration, light and cinematographic recording devices. Welsby acknowledged the influence of Systems painters, appreciating this systematic approach to working, but confirmed that he 'was always tempered by his desire to oppose "what is structured, measured, systematic and predictable, [with] what in nature is quite the opposite"'.[72] The two-screen film consists of real-time footage of sunrise and sunset and time-compression sequences where the swift rush of time is evident in the changing patterns of light, nature, day and night, thereby compressing the time of the seasonal equinoxes and revealing dialogues between film content and cinematographic recording.

Welsby also made a number of landscape films revealing structuring devices within the filmed content and showing evidence of weather conditions taking a central role in determining the final filmed outcome. In *Windmill II* (1973), for example, Welsby attached eight mirrored blades onto the front of the camera and filmed on a windy day, with the filmed images determined by the direction and speed of the wind, as in his earlier film *Wind Vane* (1972). The resulting film consists of alternate views of either the park landscape, or a reflection of the camera and the landscape behind it. In a similar manner, *Seven Days* (1974) (made with Jenny Okun) was given over to the elements, with the sun determining the filmic content. Filming took place in the Welsh countryside, with the camera placed on an equatorial mount (commonly used in astronomy) and a single frame shot every ten seconds for a week, recording the sun's arc across the sky. The shot direction was governed by the swivelling camera mount recording either sky (when the sun was behind a cloud) or landscape (when the sun was out). In both films the natural elements directly determined the final outcome, as Wollen identified:

> The techniques developed by Welsby made it possible for there to be a direct registration of natural phenomena on film. Natural processes were no longer simply recorded from the outside, as objects of observation; they could be made to participate in the scheme of observation itself.[73]

This formed a kind of collaborative work between the natural and the scientific/technological.

Relationships between nature and structured approaches to filmmaking was the focus of the Tate Gallery's 'Avant-garde British Landscape Films' (1975), with curator Deke Dusinberre identifying the films as asserting 'the illusionism of cinema through the sensuality of landscape imagery, and simultaneously assert[ing] the material nature of the representational process which sustains that illusionism'.[74] Interestingly, despite Dusinberre's selected films focusing on conceptual and procedural approaches to landscape, Curtis also described the way this was combined with 'a passionate attachment to imagery of mountains, clouds, seascapes, parks and rural pastures', suggestive of more romantic, pastoral traditions in art.[75] Furthermore, Curtis remarked that 'perhaps its greatest relevance in this context is the reminder it represented that alternatives existed to the materialist (anti-illusionistic) school'.[76] Dusinberre's exhibition also made explicit links to landscape in other art forms:

> In his notes for the exhibition Dusinberre commented on the link between the kind of measured progress through the landscape found in many landscape films (Renny Croft's *Attermire* [1976] is a good example) and the photographs of the English artists Richard Long, Hamish Fulton and John Hilliard; and here perhaps some cross-fertilization did take place.[77]

While landscape films drew on either historic Romantic traditions or were informed by cinematographic procedures, walking as art also formed part of the conceptually informed Land Art movement emerging in the 1960s. This newer experimental art form (taking a stance against the commodification of art) literally transported art out of the gallery, as exemplified by the US artist Robert Smithson's *Spiral Jetty* (1969). The focus of British land artists Richard Long and Hamish Fulton became their walks, which they documented using photography, drawings, maps and notes, with Long's *Walking a Straight 10 Mile Line Forward and Back Shooting Every Half Mile (Dartmoor, England, January, 1969)* existing as a filmed record of a walk.

While Long and Fulton's walks share the common feature of landscape with the other films discussed here, the work of LFMC filmmaker Annabel Nicolson provides an interesting case for discussion due to the diversity of her practice. While Nicolson has been recognised for films such as *Shapes*, (1970), *Slides* (1971), *Frames* (1973) and her seminal expanded cinema piece, *Reel Time* (1973), her works falling within the Land Art tradition have received scant recognition. In *Redefining the Contours of Britain: Survey of Rural Circumstance* (1974) Nicolson carried out a walking tour around parts of southern England and the Midlands, with documentation included in local newspaper reports and later published in her artists book *Escaping Notice*.[78] In Nicolson's enigmatically poetic performance piece *Sweeping the Sea* (1975), she literally swept the sea at the edge of the shoreline – '[h]er sweeping was slow and careful. Her movement was with the brush, towards rather than against it [...] Perhaps it was deliberate this trick of making herself part of the background of being just slightly out of focus'.[79] The sensitive nature of Nicolson's engagement with the land was also documented in two tongue-in-cheek photographic pieces, *Combing the Fields* (1976) and *Sleeping Like a Log* (1976). The former is a photographic record of the artist in an early morning field 'combing' knee-high plants full of frost with an oversized comb.[80] The latter, *Sleeping Like a Log*, consists of six photographs depicting Nicolson (as a log of wood) either lying in a field or 'sleeping' on a tree trunk horizontally placed on the ground. While Nicolson's walking/performative works did not include film, the actions through space and the durational nature of the events, arguably, bear relations to film and certainly relate to Long and Fulton's Land Art works.

Two films by Anthony McCall, relating specifically to Land Art and also existing as records of performances, demonstrate similar interrelationships of practice. *Landscape for White Squares* (1972) and *Landscape for Fire* (1972) are records of large-scale performances taking place in rural landscapes (fields), with the former documenting an event with participants moving across a frozen field out of a dense fog, holding large, white, square sheets. The event was performed specifically for camera, with the original intention being to distribute the 'filmed, photographed, or audiotaped records'.[81] *Landscape for Fire* (1972) relates to a performance consisting of 36 fires laid out in grid formation in a field, with fires intermittently lit by performers attending to McCall's instructions. Although McCall's conceptual interest in serial structures and mathematical formation initially informed the editing process, he became frustrated with the attempt to reconfigure the event on film, instead following a multiplicity of approaches to foreground the film-making process, as Branden W. Joseph reveals:

> [H]e spliced in bits of film upside down, backward, and both upside down and backward (indeed in all of the ways that he described as evidently 'wrong') [...] In *Landscape for Fire*, each of these 'incorrect' orientations serves to produce a visual analogue between film record and recorded event [...] Completing his decision to feature the means of documentation prominently, McCall's editing empha-sized the filmstrip's materiality, continuing his questioning of the disembodied transparency of the facilely consumable commercial reproduction.[82]

Diverse material, structural and cinematographic processes were held together with the soundtrack of foghorns – inaudible at first, then gradually moving 'closer' and louder – providing continuity between sound, landscape image and film material. While McCall's interests lay in film construction – no doubt also informed by his involvement with the LFMC – clear links could be seen with McCall's monumental landscape performances and the Land Art works explored by Fulton, Long and Nicolson. In McCall's reflections on his earlier filmmaking, he acknowledged the anti-Hollywood position taken by many 1970s filmmakers and Gidal's more militant theoretical approaches to film-making, but affirmed that his interests lay fundamentally in process as this 'was part of the air we were breathing, and I was far more inspired by conceptual originality as far as form was concerned, than by ideo-logical analysis'.[83] While landscape formed a common denominator for the many approaches to filmmaking and engagements with the land-scape – whether procedural, systematic, conceptual or romantic – the breadth of filmmaking also reveals the openness to experimentation in the decade.

Sculpting space

While rural or urban landscapes provided rich frameworks for engage-ment with wide-open spaces, more confined interior spaces also provided opportunities for interaction. Conceptual artists like McCall, David Dye, John Hilliard and Tony Hill used film to engage with physical aspects of space either in-frame or in the projection context, creating experiential engagements for the viewer. In, arguably, the seminal sculptural film of the decade, McCall's *Line Describing a Cone* (1973) follows a 'solid' light cone appearing to take on physical, sculptural form. The film begins with a white dot on screen, slowly progressing into a circular line and concluding with a completed cone of light, with the white line on the black background taking on an increasingly sculptural form as the darkened space gradually lightens. Emissions from a smoke machine (or 1970s smoking audience) increase the 'solidity' of the light beam, with viewers encouraged to move around and interact with the light-cone.

In Hill's films more specific physical engagements were required as viewers literally had to walk on the screened image or climb through physical spaces to engage with the films. In *Untitled/1st Floor Film* (1971), for example, the film was projected onto the floor of a cubicle, creating a dynamic viewer situation, whereby '[o]ne is physically confined and in contact with the screen/image, walking on clouds, water, fire. One's own sense of scale and weight is transformed in this intensely physical situation'.[84] Mona Hatoum's later projection of *Corps Étranger* (1994) similarly echoed this screening context as viewers looked down (or walked on) the endoscopic journey filmed from the inside of her body.

For Hill's *2nd Floor Film* (1972), the audience had to crawl through a tunnel and onto a glass floor where the film was projected from below onto tracing paper stretched beneath the glass. The film content consisted of people crawling and clinging onto the lower side of the glass. These works therefore created very specific viewer situations whereby '[t]he image content dictates the spectator experience as much as the environmental framework, but the nature of the controlled spaces for two and three people at a time keeps the experience particularly immediate'.[85] These site-specific films directly engaged with the architectural space, thus also determining the shape of the work.

While Dye didn't impose such active engagements with the viewing space, he was interested in creating a dialectic between film content and viewing context and sought to reveal the essence of the film 'by stripping away almost everything: seeing what you've got left'.[86] Dye's works ranged from single-screen films to installations and performative expanded cinema pieces, with the architectural space often becoming an integral part of the work. In *Film onto Film* (1972), for example, the installation included the projected image on the wall with the actual

looped film passing in front of the projected image: literally presenting 'film onto film' as the title suggested. In *Screen* (1971) Dye painted
a circle onto the gallery wall, covered it up and projected a film of the
circle over this. Dye wanted to reveal the paradox in the word 'screen'
as it simultaneously meant 'to screen onto something, to reveal something, or, to hide something'.[87] This conceptual playfulness is also
evident in *Unsigning for 8 Projectors* (1972) where eight film loops simultaneously screened the same action – Dye's hand signing his name in
reverse – onto a screen suspended from the ceiling. The signatures were
fragmented on the hanging (and moving) screen and on the surrounding walls, with Dye conceptualising the work 'very much as a piece of
sculpture. Though it involved film it was one of the most sculptural
things I've done, it was a very static piece in a way, that people walked
around it'.[88] Thus, experiential viewer engagement, with the mechanics
of the film revealed and projector and screen visible within the space,
opened up further sculptural considerations for the works.

'No-film' film

The conceptual idea of film was pushed to its limit in a number of films
which in fact included no actual film or projection mechanism. Walley
used the term 'paracinema' to describe works tangentially related to
film but refusing to adhere to conventional modes of production and
screening practice:

> Paracinema identifies an array of phenomena that are considered
> 'cinematic' but that are not embodied in the materials of film as tra-
> ditionally defined. That is, the film works I am addressing recognize
> cinematic properties outside the standard film apparatus, and there-
> fore reject the medium-specific premise of most essentialist theory
> and practice that the art form of cinema is defined by the specific
> medium of film. Instead, paracinema is based on a different version
> of essentialism, which locates cinema's essence elsewhere.[89]

Walley drew on essays by André Bazin and Sergei Eisenstein, as they
both located film within the imaginary sphere of culture prior to the
invention of the cinema, providing particularly interesting analyses for
works referencing the pre-cinematic. Eisenstein suggested that the concept of montage existed 'everywhere outside film' including our everyday perception of visual experience.[90] Bazin was interested in the idea
of film unconstrained by its physical properties and, like Eisenstein,

he considered it a 'conceptual phenomenon – a dream, a fantasy' preceding its technological and material invention.[91] Both related this to memory and the capacity for imaginative visual invention, with film as a concept manifesting itself temporarily in a particular physical form. These insights are useful to consider for forms of experimentation preoccupying a number of 1970s filmmakers opening up parameters between practices, particularly where conceptual and sculptural concerns prevailed.

In a work investigating the essence of film and its apparatus, McCall pared the concept of film down to its barest essentials in *Long Film for Ambient Light* (1975). Interactions between space and time were explicitly revealed in this minimal work, consisting of a large room with a single light bulb hanging from the middle of the ceiling. Windows were covered with white paper, allowing light to enter during the day and forming a screen at night. Typed text, exhibited within the installation space, formed an integral part in contextualising the work, with McCall providing a critique of the 'conventional distinction between static and temporal events', underpinning the principle distinction between art and film.[92] The text, 'Notes on Duration', outlined his intentions:

> This film sits deliberately as a threshold, between being considered a work of movement and being considered a static condition. Formalist art criticism has continued to maintain a stern, emphatic distinction between these two states, a division that I consider absurd. Everything that occurs, including the (electro-chemical) process of thinking, occurs in time.[93]

Thus, duration (the passage of time) was central as viewers moved within the space, devoid of film and projector, and as they became aware of the presence of the rudiments of the film medium: light, space and time. The title of McCall's conceptual critique was a key factor in determining his intentions and directing the viewers' comprehension of the work, with this paradoxical 'no-film' film described by Dusinberre as 'the very emphasis on the material nature of the cinema and of cinematic representation [which] leads to immateriality'.[94]

Nicolson similarly referenced the cinematic through immateriality in her performance piece *Matches* (1975), whereby two actors, standing in front of two screens, read identical copies of the same text by light emitted from matches repeatedly struck by the two readers. The slow, staggered progress of the intermittent light determined the progression of the work, with Nicolson dealing with very basic elements, namely light, shadow, time and space, and the duration of the piece referencing film's progression through time. In works such as this, the conceptual was combined with experimental approaches, allowing for incidental occurrences to determine the final outcome of the work. This formed a key aspect of Nicolson's approach to her practice, which she outlined as follows:

> Since 1973, I have been working away from film, towards more circumstantial situations. The aspects of projection which interest me have always been the transient, fragile qualities of light beaming through space. The accidental, the inadvertent light sources which crept into projection situations give me a point of departure. These performances change shape depending on who helps perform them.[95]

Concerns reflecting Nicolson's were also evident in Tony Hill's *Point Source* (1973), with the pre-cinematic engaging the viewer as Hill performed with a small, bright light (the projector) throwing light onto a screen or wall. Hill held small cage-like objects such as baskets or sieves between the screen/wall and 'projector', creating a shadow-play as he alternately moved objects closer or further away. A loud soundtrack complimented the shadow-play, forming an unnerving yet melodious score, and transfixing the audience though these simplest of means. Simon Field described Hill's expanded cinema works as being 'unpretentious, justly popular, they captivate and intrigue with a "hall of mirrors" astonishment, engendering the sort of child-like wonder that still surely underlies our enduring fascination with the experience of cinema'.[96] Field's comment therefore also interestingly relates to Eisenstein's and Bazin's concepts, relating to the pre-cinematic existence of 'cinema', which Walley identified. Walley also cited examples of films by the US structuralist filmmakers Paul Sharits and McCall in his article, identifying that 'this initial gesture of disintegrating the medium, literally piece by piece, was the first step in a larger process of locating the cinematic outside of film'.[97] Thus, he draws pertinent parallels with *Long Film for Ambient Light, Matches* and *Point Source*, where film, stripped down to its basic components, such as light, shadow, space, sound and duration, reconfigures the meaning of film and the mechanics of projection that bring it into existence.

Concluding thoughts

The diverse intersections between experimental filmmaking and the visual arts are evident from the film examples and contextual discourses presented above. Notably, it is revealed how other visual practices could inform filmmaking, but simultaneously also extend the boundaries of the film medium. Although the influence of diverse visual practices is evident in either film content or in the screening context, essentially the motivation behind the works was in the personal approaches for film 'thought' to occur, whether through poetic interactions with light, colour or subject matter, or through more planned approaches, sometimes using cinematographic devices, determining filmmaking processes or procedures. In this way the medium of film offered opportunities for a wide range of experimentation with ideas (where more conceptual approaches could be taken) or with the application of material processes used in other media onto film in an exploratory manner, through engaging with the camera as a tool for drawing/painting, with the film-strip or the exhibition context as a medium of exploration. The following chapter extends some of these investigations to explore films taking personal, often expressive routes informed by aspects of the counterculture: mysticism, popular culture, psychoanalysis or diaristic approaches to filmmaking. For all of these artists and filmmakers it was clearly the joy of stepping into the possibilities of film, as Dwoskin earlier outlined, which offered so many opportunities for enquiry and engagement.

4
Visionary, Mythopoeia and Diary Films

In this chapter, personal, expressive films informed by aspects of the countercultural movement, psychoanalysis, mysticism, the occult, popular culture, literature and diaristic approaches to filmmaking are discussed. Although relationships with the visual arts are also evident, the personal, symbolic or metaphoric use of image tends to be central to many of the films under discussion here. For some filmmakers, such as Margaret Tait, it was merely the joy of 'stalking' and capturing images, offering unique records of individual lives, that drew her to film. For others, connecting these to greater personal mythologies or psychological narratives was also central to developments. Many of the filmmakers discussed here trained in art schools, with others informed by their work as avant-garde writers (B. S. Johnson), poets (Tait) or playwrights (Jane Arden). Some had affiliations with the LFMC, although others were oblivious to its existence; and while cinematographic recording and structuring devices also informed aspects of filmmaking, these would generally not form the overriding focus of these films. At the outset of this chapter a number of key issues relating to the counterculture, psychoanalysis and personal approaches to filmmaking are discussed, as they provide contexts informing filmmaking. Thereafter, films are considered in greater detail, referring (where applicable) to P. Adams Sitney's taxonomical definitions of 'psycho-dramatic trance', 'lyrical', 'mythopoeia' and 'diary'.[1] While Sitney's definitions act as useful guidelines, this is not to suggest that all British films should explicitly be read through his analyses.

Contexts for filmmaking

In the Introduction to this book the underlying disquiet about the conservatism of post-war Britain and the influence of counterculture contexts was briefly discussed, with Peter Whitehead identifying the frivolous media term the 'Swinging Sixties' as belying the underlying societal conflicts driven by the Vietnam War, CND, movements for racial and gender equality and the crisis in Western culture arising from recent decolonisation. Alongside (and often driving) the urgent 1960s socio-political protests was a trans-Atlantic flow of information related to diverse scientific, theoretical, literary, anthropological and religious/mystical texts. Many of these investigations were informed by research into non-Western cultures and societies, seeking increased understandings of the human mind and Western society. Significant countercultural influences, dating as far back as the 1880s, came out of scientific research into aspects of the human psyche, such as the unconscious mind and dreams, in order to understand neuroses and psychoses. Sigmund Freud's psychoanalytic theories and Carl Jung's analytical psychology proved particularly groundbreaking in the early years of the twentieth century, with alternative approaches to psychiatric and psychological scientific research also being taken by philosophers and medical professionals investigating individual and cosmic consciousness from the early 1900s onwards.[2]

Aldous Huxley's influential countercultural text *The Doors of Perception* (1961), for example, – informed by his earlier research into Eastern mysticism, primitive ritual and folklore – included research into consciousness and states of psychosis after taking mescaline. His findings, considered a fundamental breakthrough in understanding the 'reservoir of untapped vision and inspiration' held within the unconscious, informed further research into psychotropic drugs and particularly inspired Harvard psychologist Timothy Leary's research into the effects of psilocybin and lysergic acid (LSD).[3] Leary, convinced of the therapeutic effects of LSD in consciousness expansion, became an ardent campaigner for its widespread use and (naïvely) hoped for an international transformation of consciousness. His adage, 'tune in, turn on and drop out' – first delivered at a press conference in 1966 – has since become inexorably linked with countercultural attitudes.

A seminal Albert Hall poetry event (1965), presided over by US Beat poet Allen Ginsberg, had marked a significant point in London's counterculture movement, offering a sense of hope against the socio-political malaise, with Jeff Nuttall claiming:

After the Albert Hall I wrote to Klaus Lea crying: 'London is in flames. The spirit of William Blake walks on the water of Thames [...] Come and drink the dew.' [...] After the sick capitulation of CND it did look as though we were once again winning. The Philadelphia Foundation had procured Kingsley Hall for their regenerative madness. Leary had set up and established the Alte House at Millbrook. We were all suddenly in touch with one another, thrown out by the termination of our loneliness.[4]

Nuttall admitted, however, that the renewed optimism in the possibility of a more agreeable, humane society was to a large extent attributed to one factor: 'It seems fastidious to pretend that the overriding agent which produced this new bizarrity, the new relaxation and colourful contrast to previous earnest tight-lipped attitudes, was not Lysergic Acid'.[5] The 'Alte House' Nuttall referred to was Leary's establishment outside New York, and Leary had ties to the influential anti-psychiatry movement in London led by R. D. Laing and housed at Kingsley Hall from 1965.

Preceding and continuing in parallel to Leary's quest to 'liberalise humanity' through the use of LSD, was an important group of literary individuals known as the 'Beat Generation' or 'Beatniks', exemplified by key texts such as Jack Kerouac's *On the Road* (1957), Allen Ginsberg's *Howl* (1956) and William S. Burroughs' *The Naked Lunch* (1959). The Beats were notorious for their association with drug-taking, sexual permissiveness, Eastern mysticism and a rejection of US values as they sought to throw off the conventions of US conservatism as Reekie explains:

> Like European bohemianism, beat developed as a zone of relative transgression in square society. They shunned the nine-to-five corporate existence and lived desperate lives of voluntary poverty. They experimented with drugs, magic, Zen, popular montage, sex and psychoanalysis. Instead of cabaret they had the jazz club, bebop and poetry readings at the coffee shop. Mostly they were middle-class, male and white but there were working class Beats, female Beats, black Beats, and the saints of the movement were queer or bisexual: Jack Kerouac, William Burroughs, Allen Ginsberg, Neal Cassady.[6]

The influence of Beat culture in US experimental filmmaking was evident in films such as Robert Frank and Alfred Leslie's *Pull My Daisy* (1959) and others by Jack Smith, John Cassavettes and Ken Jacobs. A number of them formed part of the New American Cinema films screened in Britain in 1964/68 and were included in the first LFMC distribution catalogue.

Some of the more explicit connections between US and British countercultural circles were also made through the presence of the

US filmmaker Kenneth Anger and the writer William Burroughs in England. Burroughs lived in England for six years from 1966, collaborating with British film distributor/director Anthony Balch and artist Brion Gysin on the films *Towers Open Fire* (1962–3), *Cut-ups* (1966) and *Bill and Tony (aka: Who's Who)* (1972). *Towers Open Fire* was screened at the *International Times* launch (October 1966), and *Cut-ups* opened at the Cinephone Cinema in London's Oxford Street. *Bill and Tony* features Burroughs and Balch as two talking heads with mismatched voices and a Godardian disjunction between sound and image. The heady mix of psychoanalysis, drug use, meditation and occult ritual also informed certain British filmmakers, with influences evident in Jane Arden and Jack Bond's *The Other Side of Underneath* (1972), *Vibration* (1975) and *Anti-Clock* (1979), in Anger's *Invocation of my Demon Brother* (1969) and in Dwoskin's *Central Bazaar* (1976).

Yet, while the countercultural milieu influenced certain aspects of 1970s British experimental filmmaking, the wider framework of personal, expressive filmmaking also included poetic renderings of individual observations, reflections or memories which can collectively be considered British 'diary' films. These include discussions below on Tait's *Tailpiece* (1975) and *Place of Work* (1975), documenting the move from a long-term family home, and David Larcher's epic travelogue *Monkey's Birthday* (1975), which 'must be appreciated in the simplicity and beauty of its diary format, in the intensity of its personal quest, and in the ambitiousness of its representation as universal odyssey'.[7] Johnson paid homage to Carl Jung and Robert Graves' *The White Goddess* in his enigmatic self-parodying *Fat Man on a Beach* (1973), and Anne Rees-Mogg's autobiographical diaristic trilogy drew on US sources to document her family history: 'I was trying not to be within the conventions of the English avant-garde. I felt much more related to American films like Jonas Mekas, and diary film'.[8] Ian Breakwell, one of Britain's most tireless diary artists, observed the minutia of daily life with acute observations of the absurd-in-the-ordinary in written, drawn, painted and filmed accounts. Collectively, these autobiographically informed (often poetic) filmed recordings of the everyday and ordinary (sometimes extraordinary) life form a substantial body of 'diary' works, adding to the rich diversity in 1970s filmmaking.

New considerations for 1970s British films

Criteria used in Sitney's descriptions of US experimental filmmaking – 'psycho-dramatic trance', 'lyrical', 'mythopoeia' and 'diary/diaristic' – provide useful tools for examining the personal, expressive forms of 1970s British filmmaking too often overshadowed by structural and material experimentation in the majority of 1970s historical accounts. It will be useful to consider more closely Sitney's distinctions on these types of filmmaking to provide illumination for their British counterparts.

'Psycho-dramatic trance' was used to describe US films holding aspects of psychoanalysis, transcendental states of dream, hallucination or imaginary states-of-being in dramatic tension. Sitney's examples included films by Deren and Anger's *Fireworks* (1947), where a fast-paced editing style was used to depict the trance state, revealing a disorientated sense of time and geography. The influence of 1920s and 1930s German Expressionist and French Surrealist films was also evident in the dislocated narratives, rapid editing style and depiction of surreal experiences. Sitney outlined these films as dealing with 'visionary experience':

> Its protagonists are somnambulists, priests, initiates of rituals, and the possessed, whose stylized movements the camera, with its slow and fast motions, can re-create so aptly. The protagonist wanders through a potent environment toward a climactic scene of self-realization. The stages of his progress are often marked by what he sees along his path rather than what he does. The landscapes, both natural and architectural, through which he passes are usually chosen with naïve aesthetic considerations, and they often intensify the texture of the film to the point of emphasizing a specific point of symbolism.[9]

In contrast to the 'psycho-dramatic' films, Sitney's 'lyrical' film (discussed in relation to the early films of Brakhage) differed in its approaches to consciousness, as 'the filmmaker could compress his thoughts and feelings while recording his direct confrontation with intense experiences of birth, death, sexuality, and the terror of nature'.[10] With superimpositions, rapid editing, hand-painting and scratching on the film-strip, these films created a lyrical, poetic sensibility, embodying a personal vision and an 'uneasy inwardness'.[11] Brakhage was also the topic of Sitney's 'mythopoeia', with *Dog Star Man* (1964) recognised as stationing 'itself within the rhetoric of Romanticism, describing the birth of consciousness, the cycle of the seasons, man's struggle with nature, and sexual balance in the visual evocation of a fallen titan bearing the name of the Dog Star Man'.[12] Although Sitney's description was specific to Brakhage's film, the general preoccupation of mythopoeic filmmaking identified filmmakers drawing inspiration from a range of sources firmly bound up within their visions of dream, nightmare, religion or symbol, thereby creating a kind of personal mythology. It signalled a type of filmmaking drawing heavily on a self-referential poetic sense of mythology and invention, including classical mythologies (Greek, Roman or Egyptian), earth cults or the supernatural.

In contrast to the above distinctions, Sitney's 'diary' films – while also including self-referential approaches to filmmaking – did not include the extent of invention and personal mythology revealed in the lyrical or mythopoeic films. The relationship between the individual and their place in the world was the focus of many of these diary films, although they rarely followed a didactic, narrative style. While approaches to 1970s British diary filmmaking varied greatly, generally films revealed no chronological account of events and were more akin to Sitney's description:

> Unlike the literary diary, the diary film does not follow a day-by-day chronology. Structurally, it corresponds more to a notebook, but in its drive towards a schematic or fragmented expression of the totality of the film-maker's life, it is more like a diary, perhaps one in which the entry dates have been lost and the pages scrambled.[13]

Sitney discussed the films of the prolific US film diarist, poet, archivist, writer and filmmaker Jonas Mekas, who has spent the past 50 years recording his life events and reflections. Mekas documented his life as an exile in New York, attempting 'in a period of desperation' to 'grow roots into the new ground, to create memories'.[14] Although the British diary filmmakers discussed here had no need to find a sense of connection to their surroundings informed by experiences of exile, relationships between themselves and the world they inhabited were key to their ruminations. The films of these diarists thus form a rich seam of work contributing to the diversity in filmmaking.

The overall productivity in 1970s British experimentation is revealed in the range of personal, visionary and expressive films discussed below, adding to the already acknowledged filmmaking histories. It may be prescient to be reminded of questions posed earlier on, asking how much Marxist ideological positions potentially militated against forms of personal expression; and how the absence of a collective voice for more expressive, personal forms of filmmaking also resulted in the lack of adequate recognition in 1970s historical accounts. In Pam Cook's essay on expression in 'avant-garde' film (published in 1978) she identified some important issues about personal forms of filmmaking, providing clues in answer to my questions:

> The idea of 'self-expression' suggesting as it does the creation of a private language to convey the personal fantasies and obsessions of a single individual, has come under attack from 'structural' film-makers in America and Europe with their formalist concerns, and from Marxists for whom it is a concept based on bourgeois individualism which asserts an independence from the dominant system that can only be illusory, thus relegating itself to a politically marginal position from which it can never radically change the dominant ideology.[15]

This type of filmmaking therefore sat in stark contrast to 1970s collectivist Marxist ideals, seeking to dispel any sense of 'bourgeois' individualism and personal expression. Cook identified personal expression as being particularly important for the Women's Movement, as 'it is a concept', she said, 'with its emphasis on the personal, the intimate, and the domestic'. '[T]he personal diary form', she continued, 'has always been a means of self-expression for women to whom other avenues were closed'.[16] I would suggest, however, that these personal, more expressive forms of filmmaking – overshadowed as they were by dominant Marxist ideologies holding sway in the 1970s – were not gender-specific, as can be seen in the examples here. Instead, they offered filmmakers opportunities for observation and engagement with the world around them through the keen eye of the camera.

Psycho-dramatic trance, lyrical and mythopoeia in British films

Fire in the Water (1977)

Peter Whitehead's *Fire in the Water* is arguably one of the most informative 1970s films documenting the socio-political and cultural milieu. Operating simultaneously as a diary of sorts and as Sitney's definition of a 'lyrical' film, Whitehead's final work functions as a kind of somnambulant leave-taking from filmmaking. It includes clips from many of his previous films and an aural repertoire of 1960s and 70s musicians, including The Doors, The Rolling Stones, Pink Floyd and Bob Dylan. The 80-minute film is divided into seven parts, with intertitles such as 'Requiem for the '60s', 'The Inner Self', 'Assassination: the Other Self', 'The Collective Self' and the 'Divided Self' demonstrating

clear references to Carl Jung's 'collective unconscious' in the penulti-
mate title mentioned, as well as references to Laing's influential *The
Divided Self: An Existential Study in Sanity and Madness* (1960) in the final
part. Brief biographical notes provide some background contexts to
Whitehead's interests – he graduated from Cambridge with a degree in
physics and crystallography, but at an early age developed an interest
in the occult, Ancient Egypt and ancient systems of mysticism. He later
studied at the Slade, attending Thorald Dickenson's Film Studies course
and taking up a style of filmmaking personifying 'the *nouvelle vague*
concept of *le caméra stylo* (camera-pen); camera-on-shoulder'.[17] His last
two films, *Daddy* (1973) and *Fire in the Water* (1977), made before he
gave up filmmaking to become a falconer, reveal Whitehead's long-term
interests in mysticism, psychology, mythology and the inner quest for
self-actualisation.

In the opening scene of *Fire in the Water* a young couple drive through
isolated, mountainous terrain to a cottage in the Scottish Highlands.
The film then cuts between footage of the couple watching clips of
Whitehead's films on a Steenbeck editing table, accompanied by the
musical soundtrack, and scenes of the woman walking in the mountains,
surrounded by the sounds of nature: bird calls, brooding thunder, a running river, wind blowing or, alternatively, silence. The countercultural-
infused pop songs set the mood for the viewing of the film clips,
reinforcing a nostalgic atmosphere. This contrasts with the scenes depicting the woman's slight figure in the wilderness, giving the impression of
her being both at one with nature, yet also engulfed by it. In these latter
scenes a sense of foreboding prevails – as if predicting some unpleasant
event – compounded by the progressively ominous soundtrack of rolling thunder, rushing water or strong wind, seemingly exacerbating the
woman's danger, which is revealed in the film's denouement as she is
surrounded by writhing snakes and disappears into the watery depths.

The earlier film, *Daddy*, reads as an uncomfortable 'bedtime story'
taking place on a country estate and chronicling bizarre events occurring between a little girl/woman and her military-clad father. Initially
intended as a semi-documentary film about the artist Niki de Saint
Phalle (credited as co-director), it ended up as a surreal, Freudian
account of a woman attempting to deal with the memories of a preda-
tory father. *Daddy* operates as an interesting case for feminist deploy-
ment, engaging with Saint Phalle's work and biography, and taking a
psychoanalytic route to wrest revenge on an evil father-figure.

Whitehead has dismissed both *Daddy* and *Fire in the Water* as being
unimportant films, yet they interestingly stand as significant historical

texts, imbued as they are with a countercultural patina of introspection, turning to psychology, mysticism or the arcane in the search for self-realisation. The film clips shown on the editing table in *Fire in the Water* also form a unique countercultural narrative, providing significant visual and spoken accounts of historical events. These include an interview with David Hockney, Michael Caine discussing the loss of the British Empire, Allen Ginsberg and Ernst Jandl's readings from the 1965 Albert Hall event, Peter Brook and Glenda Jackson protesting about the Vietnam War, Martin Luther King's memorial service (1968), the W. B. Yeats poem 'Things Fall Apart', the Columbia University student rebellion (1968) and Ralph Ortiz's performance where he 'dusts' the audience with a bird and proceeds to smash both bird and piano to pieces, to the strains of The Doors' song 'The End'. For these cultural references alone, it *is* an important film, being the cultural indicator that it is.

Vibration (1975) and *Anti-Clock* (1979)

Three films by feminist filmmaker, writer and actress Jane Arden reveal countercultural influences related to the anti-psychiatry movement, mysticism and meditation. Arden collaborated with Jack Bond on the short film *Vibration* (1975) and the feature-length films *The Other Side of the Underneath* (1977) and *Anti-Clock* (1979), with all three demonstrating a broad range of stylistic and formal approaches. Although *The Other Side of the Underneath* is less aesthetically experimental, it draws interesting parallels with Dwoskin's *Central Bazaar*, discussed below, with both films revealing countercultural influences. The influence of psychoanalysis and the anti-psychiatry movement is evident in Arden's work, and she was a close friend of R. D. Laing. She and Bond were also interested in Sufi meditation, which forms the central focus of *Vibration* (1975). Arden's interests in consciousness, madness, women's oppression and the anti-psychiatry movement also inform all her work as a radical feminist, poet, writer and actress.

Vibration operates as a non-linear exploration into altered states of consciousness – Sitney's 'psycho-dramatic trance' – reached through Sufi mysticism and meditation, which Arden identified in her film notes as follows:

> A scientific, therapeutic investigation through an audio-video unification. Hypnagogic technique – to release the restricted life pulse from our paralysing rationale. *Vibration* anticipates video as a device for self-actualisation. Man and woman are their own laboratories. During this healing process video-film is a powerful tool for

demonstrating both the traps of our own mechanical behaviour –
and revealing the pulsating heart within.[18]

Vibration was filmed on Super-8 and converted to video, facilitating the
special effects and editing which play a key role in the film's structure.
Therefore, content (the search for self-actualisation) and technology
(audio, film/video) were integrally combined in this search for self-
realisation, with its protagonists often operating as Sitney's 'somnam-
bulists, priests [or] initiates of rituals'.[19]

Arden's voice opens the film with the words 'a Sufi meditation' and
ends it with the word 'rabbit' uttered repeatedly in a heightened state
of agitation. She presides over events as Sitney's 'initiat[or] of rituals'
with a recurring, questioning voice, articulating the different states of
consciousness of the two main performers, Sebastian Saville (Arden's son)
and actress Penny Slinger. They are led in their visualisations as Arden
instructs and questions, all the while deconstructing images, words and
experiences in an attempt at providing illumination on states of being,
informed by 'the new gestalt initiated by Jung and [Wilhelm] Reich
and Frederick Perles'.[20] As in *The Other Side of the Underneath* and *Anti-
Clock*, the interrogation is always uncompromising, with destruction –
perhaps in the hope of illumination – prevailing. Arden's instructions
are interspersed by the voice of Sufi mystic Cherif Abderahmane Jah
explaining, in mystical terms, what occurs during meditation. In other
parts of the film the sound forms a kind of abstract score, at times
jarring, bubbling or crackling.

No coherent linear narrative exists in *Vibration*. Instead, diverse film
fragments are repeated or shown singly. These include images of Saville,
Slinger and Bond, documentary footage of local Moroccan people, 'cosmic' images of planetary movements and serene shots of the sun setting
over the sea. These are intercut with abstracted images of objects, such
as a reel-to-reel tape recorder or buildings, with the latter video-edited
in bright, 'hot' colours, not unlike the colours in Le Grice's *Berlin Horse*
(1970). The film culminates with Arden receiving instructions on meditation, with scenes progressing at a frenetic charge as the deep chanting
of the Sufi mystic and Arden's voice (repeating 'mindful is mindless')
increases to finally become a kind of barking verbal score, until it
abruptly cuts to an image of abstract computer glyphs and Arden's
final 'rabbit' resonation. The progression of the film between gentle,
meditative enquiry and fragmented, unnerving interrogation into the
inner workings of the mind make the final repetitive uttering of 'rabbit'
appear as a call to 'run-rabbit-run'.

Bond and Arden's experience of working with video on *Vibration* informed *Anti-Clock,* as did the subject of altered states of consciousness. *Anti-Clock* follows the experiences of a young man as he undergoes the interrogation of his unconscious mind, prompted by himself and a group of scientists leading the inquiry. Both the main protagonist, Joseph Sapha, and the therapist, Professor J. D. Zanof, are acted by Sebastian Saville, and although there is a thread of narrative in the main protagonist's attempts at self-illumination – through the self as he is both subject and object of the investigation – the film is essentially a nonlinear exploration of memory and experience. The experimental nature of *Anti-Clock* was groundbreaking for its time, with footage captured on 50 surveillance cameras installed in the Portman Hotel, sections shot on black-and-white and colour film stock, and editing often resonating with the interior spaces of a mind, revealing the disordered and fragmented ways in which memory or dreams operate. This sense of fragmentation was enhanced further by parts of the film having the screen divided into four frames and fast-paced editing between disconnected shots. The use of mostly monochromatic images – with blue filter – and the 'reframing' of Sapha's memory and recollections are offset by seemingly arbitrary clips of archival footage of Hitler, a firing squad and documentary footage of baboons. What could have amounted to a highly contrived montage of disparate images was salvaged through the editing process and the use of video manipulations such as static disruption, freeze-framing, the abstraction of images and scenes including multiple-frames.

Anti-Clock has resonances with Chris Marker's *La Jetée* (1962) with its attempts to cut across time to bring past and future into the present, and where the trip down memory lane is full of uncertainty. Both films deal with memory and precognition, where illumination ultimately only leads to the protagonist's future death (*La Jetée*) or nowhere (*Anti-Clock*). The critic, Chris Darke considered the way *Anti-Clock* and Arden's poetry collection represented a personal belief system, suggesting that the hermetically sealed text was of its time, yet also revealing in its historical influences:

[T]hey could also be said to represent the last gasp of one of the great historical adventures of the counter-culture. From Romanticism and Symbolism, Baudelaire and Rimbaud, and via Surrealism all the way to the Dionysian abandonment of rock and drug culture, the systematic disordering of the senses was part of the programme for the authentic liberation of the self.[21]

Darke drew comparisons with Jean-Luc Godard's *Numéro Deux* (1975) and David Cronenberg's *Videodrome* (1983) in the innovative use of video, suggesting that the film's lack of critical recognition was due to the 'perennially conservative and formally timid British cinema'.[22] Yet, I would suggest that it was also due to Arden's suicide (1983), the film's withdrawal from distribution and its uneasy assimilation into the fields of commercial, independent or experimental filmmaking.

The Other Side of the Underneath (1972) and *Central Bazaar* (1976)

Although Arden's earlier *The Other Side of the Underneath* is not as aesthetically innovative as *Vibration* and *Anti-Clock*, it draws some interesting parallels with Stephen Dwoskin's *Central Bazaar* (1976). Both films, redolent with 1960s and 70s countercultural influences relating to self-actualisation, psychotropic intoxication and sexual permissiveness, focus on unfolding events as participants unselfconsciously express their inner feelings, desires or bewilderment for the camera. There is a visceral sense of exposure, with the films appearing to take their inspiration from 1960s 'encounter groups' – a type of group therapy popularised by Eric Berne and Carl R. Rogers whereby individuals explored 'repressed emotion and improve[d] interpersonal communication'.[23]

The Other Side centres on a group of women living in a semi-derelict Welsh asylum who explore their anguish, anxieties and madness. It was 'underpinned by Laing's view of madness or "schizophrenia" as a political response to conditions in society and the family' and has Arden presiding over events as the (simultaneously) interrogative, yet supportive therapist.[24] The film cuts between scenes of the women's frenzied antics in the madhouse (dressed in Victorian nightgowns) and pastoral scenes taking place in the small Welsh mining village where the asylum is located. Most of the actors and crew lived collectively for the duration of filming, as they did for the filming of *Central Bazaar* when Dwoskin invited a group of people to live in his house for five weeks as a kind of human experiment in personal interaction.

The Other Side develops at an uneven pace, vacillating between serious therapy sessions and absurd, surreal scenarios. In one such scene an inmate reclines on a bed with a live sheep lying next to her and a mad, bald clown verbally attacking her. In another scene – reminiscent of a bad Hammer-horror film replete with fake blood – two girls attack a rock band with axes. In contrast, a later, more evocative scene shows a woman's face superimposed with war footage, creating poetic tensions between memory, dream and reality. *Central Bazaar* opens with a man and woman repeatedly setting a table and slowly develops into a progressively bacchanalian state-of-play. In the second scene, a woman recounts the story of The Three Little Pigs to camera, with film critic William Fowler suggesting that it sets an unnerving claustrophobic tone with the question of the 'wolf at the door' ever present throughout the film.[25] After a Labour Party canvasser makes a chance call to the house – and Dwoskin records this for what becomes the companion piece to *Central Bazaar's* recent DVD release, *Laboured Party* (1974) – the question of the wolf as the outsider, coming into a hermetically sealed world, is once again raised. Fowler suggests that it is not the Three Little Pigs fairytale, the Labour canvasser or the filmmaker who constitutes any threat, but that 'if anything, the wolf represents the threat of context and location – the entire world outside – hanging in the wings ready to break the spell'.[26] Yet, I would suggest that the wolf also represents the 'dangers' inherent as a group of individuals subject themselves to a social experiment of sorts – as they do in Arden's *The Other Side* – where they are invited 'to act out their fantasies on and about each other, asking whoever was involved to give their active support'.[27]

Reality and theatricality are at odds throughout *The Other Side* and there are times when it is difficult to tell the two apart, particularly in the therapy sessions which appear realistic and were bolstered by the use of drugs. The actress Penny Slinger described how the morning workshops were often followed by 'a puff of marijuana to help us go deeper' and as the therapy advanced 'a number of us took a prescribed dose of psychedelics'.[28] Although the film makes for an uneven reading, with some badly executed horror scenes and incidents of unselfconscious, flamboyant acting, the 'real' encounter sessions, revealing the dismantling of the self – as in Dwoskin's film – are illuminating, albeit disturbing.

In *Central Bazaar*, as the scenes unfold in progressive states of undress and fancy dress, the sexualised antics are captured in wide- to medium-shot and – particularly with an anorexic-looking child/woman – in close-up. Allegations of Dwoskin's voyeuristic eye were assuaged by his own, and film critics' such as Paul Willeman's, justification that the intention is to implicate the viewer in feelings of discomfort when watching intensely private moments. Willeman called this the fourth look: 'the look at the viewer' as he/she 'has to confront his/her sadistic voyeurism', following on from Laura Mulvey's three looks (camera, viewer and looks between actors) outlined in her seminal 'Visual

Pleasure and Narrative Cinema' (1975) essay.[29] Rees's observations about Dwoskin's *Dyn Amo* (1972) might also equally be relevant for *Central Bazaar* (and *The Other Side*):

> By taking private acts and making them public, the film elicits the viewer's uneasy participation. 'To use the camera as a character', he said in 1978, 'to use the camera so as the viewer is within the action'. The voyeurism of cinema is made visible. Absorption becomes theatricality.[30]

While Dwoskin suggested that this was a bazaar – '[t]he miscellaneous collection looks splendid and full of expectations'[31] – where manifold things are on offer, Mekas (in his review) suggested that *Central Bazaar* was 'a bazaar for voyeurs'.[32] And this indeed is what both films feel like for the viewer as they prefigure the now (in)famous *Big Brother* television series and the viewer is left feeling as if he/she has been privy to the private moments of individuals falling apart at the seams. The sense of voyeurism is unavoidable with the camera observing private moments and the individuals losing themselves – perhaps the longed-for loss of ego – in both films.

While the films of Whitehead, Dwoskin and Arden discussed here differ significantly from one another, one could agree that they stand very much as documents of their time (the 1970s), revealing countercultural influences in their content and in their modes of articulation. They share some common traits by drawing influences from psychoanalysis, the unconscious or dreams, as depicted in the unfolding of events and in the unselfconscious questioning of the self in relation to others and the surrounding world.

'Psycho-dramatic trance'

A number of films by Kenneth Anger, Jeff Keen and Derek Jarman have clear correlations with Sitney's 'psycho-dramatic trance' distinction. Anger's *Invocation of my Demon Brother* is first considered in relation to Keen's *Rayday Film* (dated as 1968–70 and 1976); and secondly, *Lucifer Rising* (1970–1981) is discussed in relation to Jarman's *The Art of Mirrors* (1973) and *In the Shadow of the Sun* (1974–81). Although Anger is an American, he lived in (or had links with) Britain throughout the 1970s, and both films have production ties with Britain.[33]

Rees noted that Anger's main British supporter was 'the incisive critic Tony Rayns, [who] had limited time for the earnest structuralists at the

Arts Lab and Camden Town'.[34] Anger's two films also neatly bookend the decade, despite the 11-year gap in their release dates, and were closely connected, as Alice L. Hutchison explains:

> The development and footage of the two films is integrated. *Invocation* as it now stands is based on fragments of a larger-scale unfinished work, a template from which *Lucifer Rising* was produced. Recycling the footage filmed in California from the original *Lucifer Rising* project with the new London material, *Invocation of my Demon Brother* was conceived.[35]

Gary Lachman also elaborated on the relationship between the two films, suggesting that they should be 'viewed back to back', as they provide unique insights into the shifting countercultural milieu:

> The intensity and jagged texture of *Invocation* – it's a film in which, as Tony Rayns remarks, 'every cut hurts' – seems to parallel the intensity and uncertainty of the counterculture at the time, and *Lucifer*, rising more than a decade later, seems to embody the less intense but more 'harmonious' sensibility of the New Age consciousness that emerged from 1960s radicalism.[36]

Both films were influenced by Anger's interest in the occult, and a closer look at them in relation to Keen and Jarman's films will provide insights into these enigmatic works.

Invocation of My Demon Brother (1969) and *Rayday Film* (1968–70 and 1976)

The soundtracks are instrumental in setting the tone in *Invocation of my Demon Brother* and *Rayday Film* since both are aurally abrasive, heightening the tension as progressive frenzy and chaos prevail. The soundtrack of *Invocation* was scored by Mick Jagger on a Moog synthesiser, and begins with a slow, rhythmic drone as the film's opening shots cut between a group of young, naked men sprawled on a sofa and a male albino face. In the ensuing opening scenes a small, skull-shaped hashish pipe is passed around a group of performers dressed in opulent costume. The sound gradually quickens, continuing as an abrasive whirr throughout the film. In the opening scenes of *Rayday* the names of performers are announced before a sonorous, rasping soundtrack ensues and a group of costumed and masked actors are seen occupying an outdoor wasteland filled with car wrecks and detritus. Keen's films are generally – and *Rayday* is no exception here – characterised by an excess of images, often in double or triple superimposition, with short jump-cuts often operating as a barrage of montage. Similarly, although not quite as visually cacophonous and with more of a 'narrative' (if one can go so far to say this) *Invocation* is a stream of images, unfolding in fast-paced montage with some superimpositions and the occasional use of a prismatic lens breaking up the screen.

The filmmakers take the lead in both films as co-ordinators of events, but Anger more resolutely presides over the scene as a Magus, initiating and overseeing the occult ritual unfolding on the screen. Keen's leading role as executor of events is less authoritative than Anger's as he is represented as an inadvertent Mickey Mouse-masked Magus, reeling in the excessive array of tacky plastic toys, junk and consumer goods that are repeatedly burnt, smashed or dismembered. Shots of Keen's comic book illustrations fuel the disarrayed narrative disorder, and in both films an interesting relationship can be drawn between the ritualistic, frenetic rhythm and the use of fire. Fire in Anger's occult ritual has close affiliations with the satanic realm, but for Anger, Lucifer – as the devil – means literally 'bringer of light'. During Anger's ritual he sets a page alight as he 'gyrates widdershins (counter-clockwise) around the "solar swastika" as "Swirling Spiral Force" to enable the Bringer of Light to break through'.[37] The burning flames then fill the screen and in a later scene they are transposed over writhing bodies. In Keen's world, fire is wrought as a destructive mechanism: burning, melting or dismembering the paraphernalia of trash littering his film. Fires also burn in Keen's outdoor wasteland scene as if part of a ritual; at one point a fire burns in a car and at another a burning chair is placed next to the sea. In both films the transformative element of fire operates to elicit change, as the necessary Phoenix-like destruction before resurrection.

Both Keen and Anger drew on images of popular culture and media in their films. Keen used Hollywood icons such as Marilyn Monroe and Mickey Mouse, comic book drawings and clips of newspapers, which are burnt or effaced in *Rayday*. Anger used documentary footage of the Rolling Stones' Hyde Park concert (1969) and newsreel footage of the Vietnam War in *Invocation*. Text is used by Keen in many of his films, and in *Rayday* two key phrases stand out. The one at the beginning, 'How right Motler was to kill the word!', is spray-painted onto a wall, and the other, near the end, shows unspooled film dropped into the sea at the water's edge, followed by the words 'Above the waves beneath the sea!'. In *Invocation,* after a group of masked, costumed actors trail down a spiral flight of stairs, playing musical instruments and holding a gold-fish bowl, the words 'Zap! You're pregnant! That's witchcraft!' appear on the screen. Keen also used 'Zap!' in *Rayday* (and in his other films) as this forms part of his oft-used comic book aesthetic. None of the texts in the two films imbue an understanding of what is going on, or solidify the narrative, but only serve to further discombobulate the viewer.

An element of excitement and mayhem prevails in both films, although the sinister or dark side leaks through, in the fractured and frenzied sense of ritual or dance that the filmmakers present, with Anger's film being slightly more 'directed' through the progression of the occult ritual. Images of sexualised, naked or writhing bodies are seen briefly in both films, representing both the liberation of joyous, hedonistic excess and a brooding eroticism. Anger has referred to *Invocation* as 'an attack on the sensorium' in the way that the film assaults the viewer's perceptive, sensory (visual and auditory) and interpretive modes of comprehension.[38] This could equally and validly be said about *Rayday*, as both films subject the viewer to a salvo of visual and auditory information-overload, providing entry into two manically – but splendidly – deranged worlds.

Lucifer Rising (1970–1981), In the Shadow of the Sun (1974–81) and The Art of Mirrors (1973)

Jarman considered *The Art of Mirrors* as one of his favourite Super-8 films, comparing it in his notebook to Anger's work as 'the most extreme dream film ever made, even more extreme than Kenneth Anger'.[39] Anger, Jung and alchemy were, however, not the only influences informing Jarman's filmmaking; the Beat poets and writers also wielded a significant influence on his young adult life, as he outlined in his memoirs:

> In 1962 I moved to London from home. I was twenty, and out on my own. Things changed quickly. At King's I read my tutor's copy of *Howl*, and learnt of William Burroughs. [...] In late August [1964] I left Ron and took the Greyhound bus to San Francisco to visit the City Lights Bookshop. I'd crossed the world to get to that bookshop, to buy Burroughs' *The Naked Lunch*, banned in England. I bought my copy of it along with Ginsberg's *Howl*, and Kerouac's novels.[40]

Jarman's diverse interests infused his open-minded approach to filmmaking, thereby echoing the Beat's sentiments to break out of systematic or conventional ways of working and living. Burroughs had also agreed with occult 'master', Aleister Crowley's judgement, that 'humanity was held back by conditioning and controls, and once free of their shackles could become gods'.[41] Although Jarman was influenced by Anger's films and shared his interests in magic, alchemy and mystical texts, he remained wary and was 'anxious to distinguish this "virtuous" interest in magic from the more sinister "black arts" dabbled in by figures like Aleister Crowley and his disciple Kenneth Anger'.[42]

Lucifer Rising and *In the Shadow of the Sun* are both scored with rock music soundtracks, focusing the viewer's passage through the numinous landscapes in the films. *Lucifer Rising* was scored by Bobby Beausoleil and *In the Shadow of the Sun* was complemented by Throbbing Gristle's *Hot on the Heels of Love* soundtrack (although the soundtrack was only added in 1980 with James Mackay's assistance). Both films have a quieter visual and auditory tone than *Invocation* and *Rayday*, which sets the mood for unfolding events. Although there is a less cacophonous barrage of images than in the previous two films, one could not go so far as to suggest that a linear narrative exists in either *Lucifer Rising* or *In the Shadow of the Sun*, and they differ significantly from one another.

Anger's *Lucifer Rising* offers a kind of cohesive scenario focusing on ritual, with an implicit narrative depicting the birth of Isis and Osiris's son, Horus. Crowley envisaged the dawning of a new age, characterised by Horus and the overthrowing of 'all restraint ("the word of sin is restriction", Crowley counselled) and a plunge into the holy delights of what Freud called "polymorphous perversity"'.[43] Jarman's *In the Shadow of the Sun* submerges the viewer in a world of dream or memory and includes a strange ritual, the purpose of which is rather more diffuse than in Anger's film.

Both films were influenced by mythology and mysticism, with the symbolic use of light and shadow informed by alchemical texts, the Tarot or occult symbolism. However, they differ significantly in their visual style and mythological focus, with *Lucifer Rising* consisting of mostly crisp, single-shot images and *In the Shadow of the Sun* being made up of superimposed, re-filmed or single shots filmed at slow speeds. Anger's film was inspired by a poem by his revered Crowley, and celebrated Lucifer as the 'beautiful and rebellious angel of light: Lucifer not the devil, but Venus, the morning star'.[44] Jarman was similarly interested in light, but more specifically in the dual integration of light and dark with the idea of 'the shadow of the sun' – synonymous with the

Philosopher's Stone – enabling a continuous interplay of images high-lighting light and darkness. In his personal notebook Jarman described the influences on this film:

> In 1974 I bought Jung's *Alchemical Studies and Seven Sermons to the Dead*, and this provided the key to the imagery that I had created quite unconsciously in the preceding months, and also gave me the confidence to allow these dream images to drift and collide at random.[45]

Oranges and pinks tinge the imagery *In the Shadow of the Sun*, with deg-radation caused by re-filming lending a 'shimmering mystery/energy like Monet's "Nympheas" or haystacks in the sunset'.[46] Jarman was insistent that viewers should not wrack 'their brains for a meaning', as there was no explicit narrative to the film, and should rather just relax 'into the ambient tapestry of *random* images' (Jarman's emphasis).[47] John Wywer, however, was more dubious about this approach:

> The lure and promise of a deeper meaning, of something beneath the surface, is always present in his work, demanding a closer level of attention than the invitation to treat the film as wallpaper unfor-tunately implies.[48]

While the film may hold deeper meanings, Jarman's intention to allow for the drifting and collision of dream images demonstrates his desire for the film not to be interpreted with too much fixity of mean-ing, presumably in the hope that the viewer could equally enter the dreamscape.

Links can be seen between Anger's interests in the occult, ritual and mystical transformation and in Jarman's filmed locations. Jarman notes that *In the Shadow of the Sun* is divided into four sections: the standing stones at Avebury (Wiltshire) and two fire mazes in the first part; an invoca-tion which includes masked figures walking through flames and a couple dancing in flames devouring the landscape in the second part; evanescent images with typewritten text and 'pyramids burn[ing] to a candlelit req-uiem' in the third; and the images fading into blank footage and a figure 'listening' to a message from a shell: 'SLNC IS GLDN' in the final part.[49]

Gesturing, as part of an apparent ritual, occurs in both *Lucifer Rising* and *The Art of Mirrors*, with the viewer appearing to be momentarily implicated in an arcane ritual. Isis and Osiris raise their wands repeat-edly to signal the birth of their son Horus in *Lucifer Rising*, and in *The*

Art of Mirrors a mirror, held by a performer gesturing to the viewer, is used not to reflect an image but to refract the light into the camera, darkening the whole scene as the inbuilt light-meter (set at automatic) reacts to it. The multiple landscapes also differ significantly in the two films. In *Lucifer Rising* the landscapes were filmed in Egypt, Germany and England, with each location having ancient, occult connections with sun-worship, thereby providing a context for the actions. In *The Art of Mirrors*, meanwhile, landscape provides less of a precise location, the action appearing to take place largely in a vast outdoor courtyard area (in all likelihood the 1,000-ft terrace on the Thames where Jarman lived at Butler's Wharf), with mountainous terrain appearing occasionally in superimposition.[50]

A few words need to be said about Jarman's use of the Super-8 medium, enabling the cheap production of films and lending the distinctive aesthetic to his films. In Jarman's journal he noted the cost of making *In the Shadow of the Sun* (aside from the later funding to convert it to 16mm and add the soundtrack) as being around £120.[51] On receiving the footage for *The Art of Mirrors* in the post, he identified it as the most unusual film he had ever seen. 'It will be impossible to edit', he said, 'as there is not a moment I'll want to lose – each reel is more surprising than the last'.[52] He noted that '[t]his is the first film we've made on Super 8 with which there is nothing to compare. The other Super 8's of the last few months are still too close to 16mm work; whereas this is something which could only be done on a Super 8 camera, with its built-in meters and effects. At last we have something completely new'.[53] This (alongside the economic reasons) would also undoubtedly be the reason why he would continue to use Super-8 for later feature-length productions such as *The Garden* (1989).

Technical and economic aspects informed Anger, Keen and Jarman's filmmaking (choice of format, superimposition, re-use of older footage, etc.) alongside their interests in metaphysical, occult or popular culture contexts, but it was their sheer openness to invention which would also lead to their particularly distinctive styles of personal filmmaking. In Dwoskin and Arden's films the countercultural infusions relating to psychoanalysis (and particularly self-actualisation through the self/others) provide insights into these 1960/70s preoccupations; and Whitehead's *Fire in the Water* (with its use of historically specific archival footage) is probably one of the key experimental films, providing a snapshot of the socio-political and cultural contexts framing the decade. Having therefore closely considered films informed by and broadly fulfilling the criteria identified in Sitney's terms 'psycho-dramatic trance', 'lyrical' and 'mythopoeia', it will be useful to now turn to a number of British 'diary' films which reveal the diverse personal approaches taken by film-makers to recount life experiences and inscribe the world around them.

British 'diary' films

The British diary films discussed here are varied, taking diverse routes to mark certain occasions or moments of personal significance yet Margaret Tait's exposition on her working process could equally apply to the other diarists' approaches:

> I found this expression about 'stalking the image'. That's Lorca in a tercentenary lecture about Don Luis de Gongora. And he also says 'for Gongora, an apple is no less intense than the sea, a bee is no less astonishing than a forest.' 'He takes all materials in the same scale', and 'the Poet must know this,' Lorca says.[54]

This in no way suggests that the diarists discussed here should be considered under Tait's all-seeing captivated eye, but affirms that the most minor of details could lure the diarists in to etch their thoughts or sights onto film. As Sitney suggests above, the diary format does not follow a day-by-day chronology, but offers events or fragments, often in scrambled format.[55]

Ian Breakwell

Ian Breakwell's work in film, video, painting, drawing and writing was informed by his observations of mundane and ordinary life events. Observations were recorded in notebooks, often focusing on life's absurdities and attempts to come to terms with them. His work was intensely political, although not in an overt slogan-carrying manner, with Nick Kimberley observing that 'this is William Burroughs naked lunch [sic], forcing us for the first time to confront what we consume. We don't like what we see'.[56] Humour lay at the centre of Breakwell's work:

> For all the grime, for all that this life is no more lastingly substantial than the hunks of meat carted about Smithfield Market, for all that suppressed violence threatens to erupt from almost every page, the diary finds life constantly marvellous. The monstrous and the tragic exist cheek by jowl with the erotic and the laughable. Breakwell's epiphanies are every bit as enhancing as Joyce's – and less religious. Here, the marvellous is supremely human.[57]

Although humour was central to most of Breakwell's work, he also took a serious interest in the role of institutions and in how institutional discourses shaped people's lives. He was involved with the Artist's Placement Group which facilitated artists' residencies in government or industry-based organisations, with an internship at the Department of Health and his research into mental illness resulting in the film *The Institution* (1978).

Breakwell drew inspiration for the voyeuristic *The Journey* (1975) from observing train passengers on his placement with British Rail. In an earlier observation, documented in his notebook, he concluded that '[p]eople do everything to avoid each other's gaze. They read newspapers on the tube because if everybody stared at the person opposite, it would be intolerable'.[58] *The Journey* takes a prying look at two train passengers in close proximity to one another (with knees almost touching), but who are contained in their own thoughts (probably, as Breakwell discerns, because they daren't stare at each other). They are lost in thought with their isolation echoed in the way the windows seal them off from the world outside. Breakwell parodies the travelogue film convention, with his montage of film clips having an erotic overtone and concluding in a sexual encounter. A diary entry draws parallels with Breakwell's voyeuristic observations of the woman in *The Journey*, revealing his dark humour:

> The face of the woman in the opposite seat has a skin complexion like a sugared almond. She wears a beautifully cut grey tweed jacket and a grey pleated skirt. Her breasts stir under her white silk blouse with the movement of the train. Her eyes are glazed; they keep closing. Sleep overcomes her. Her manicured hands slide off her lap, pulling back her skirt over thighs in white silk stockings. Her face slackens; the little frown disappears. Her lipsticked mouth parts to reveal pearly white teeth on which, for a second, lands a black fly.[59]

While Breakwell's voyeuristic 'camera eye' might draw parallels with Dwoskin's in *Central Bazaar*, the actors in *The Journey* don't perform to camera but are observed from a distance. Although Breakwell's diary entry above reveals rather lascivious observations of the woman, his voyeurism was generally 'social rather than sexual'.[60] His extensive body of work included *The Walking Man Diary* (1978), and *Continuous Diary* (1977) (shown in Bristol and London's ICA) was later commissioned as a Channel 4 series. *Continuous Diary* also prompted 'A Season of Diary Films' (1977) ICA screenings; and programmes of 'Diary Films at the Co-op' (1977) were concurrently screened at the LFMC.

B. S. Johnson

B. S. Johnson was an established writer of avant-garde novels when he made his final film, *Fat Man on a Beach* (1973), for Welsh television, just weeks before his suicide. He had written and directed five films, including the BFI-funded *You're Human Like the Rest of Them* (1967), the ICA-supported *Up Yours Too, Guillaume Apollinaire* (1968) and *Paradigm* (1969), and two films for ACT: *Unfair* (1970) and *March!* (1971). Johnson's work had received scant recognition since his death, but has recently been brought to public attention through Jonathan Coe's comprehensive biography and the BFI reissue of his films on DVD.[61]

Fat Man on a Beach provides further evidence of personal, diaristic types of filmmaking, but also engages with psychoanalysis and the mystical/occult. The film is essentially *about* a fat man on beach. Johnson is the 'fat man' who discusses a diverse range of topics, including the weather, the Welsh peninsula where filming is taking place, some very bad jokes and a detailed recollection of a car crash where dismembered bodies were cut through as if by a 'cheese-cutter'.[62] The soundtrack alternates between Scott Joplin's upbeat *The Entertainer* and Johnson talking to camera. He also reads poetry and cajoles camera and audience to follow him like a dog, (saying things like 'sit' or 'good boy'), with the direct, self-reflexive address to the viewer adding to Johnson's peculiar antics and recollections. James Joyce's *Ulysses* (1922) and the writings of Carl Jung had been a source of inspiration for Johnson, although it was Robert Graves' *The White Goddess* (1948) that wielded the greatest influence on his life:

> [He was] captivated by the more mystical writings of Robert Graves, with their insistence that poetic inspiration comes from the Muse Goddess, a figure bound up with complicated myths of birth and death, the Moon and the all-providing Mother.[63]

In his life Johnson wrestled with the search for integration between the domestic and creative, revealing something of this ongoing search (through mysticism) in his final film.

In a pensive moment near the end of the film, both Johnson and the cameramen are seen reflected in a mirror half-immersed in sand; Johnson says, 'some things can only be said indirectly [...] one can only reflect the truth of what they were. I'm not sure I know the truth about this particular thing that I want to talk about indirectly.'[64] Johnson then recounts a story about a spiritual experience, where he finds himself naked on the top of a mountain in Wales at dawn, gesturing wildly to a female deity. He confesses disbelief in such religious gestures and also his failure to understand how he came to perform these bizarre actions, admitting that he was not there of his own volition. He continues by saying that there is nowhere on earth where he could do this except here in Wales, an area that has transfixed him and been instrumental in allowing this to happen. He justifies his actions through a discussion of Jung's archetypes and how these compel us – even as evolved and civilised beings – to attend to this type of ritual. This near-final scene reveals clues to Johnson's life-long internal search: to find answers to human behaviour and the passage our lives take. Johnson death, two weeks after filming, provides a poignant suggestion that answers were perhaps not forthcoming. I believe the knowledge of Johnson's imminent death also adds a sombre note to the viewing, imbuing it with a patina of loss, particularly in the closing shot as Johnson walks fully clothed into the water; the camera pulls back further and he walks ever deeper into the sea.

Although Johnson regarded himself as an avant-garde writer and filmmaker, he appeared to have no awareness of 1960s or 1970s underground poetry or film activity taking place at Better Books or the LFMC. No mention is made of Johnson attending alternative (to mainstream) film or art events in Jonathan Coe's biography. In correspondence with Coe (who spent seven years working on the book) I asked whether Johnson was in any way involved in the underground or avant-garde scene in London. Coe's response was as follows:

> To the best of my recollection, I found no record in BSJ's [B. S. Johnson] archives of his having attended either the LFMC screenings or Bob Cobbing's Better Books screenings. This is not to say that he never attended them, but he certainly left no trace of it behind. But then he tended to move in a fairly restricted circle, despite his avant-garde leanings.[65]

Coe's comment is discerning as it sheds light not only on Johnson's creative environment, but also on the diverse – and often separate – experimental film circles in which people moved. Interestingly, however, Nuttall did mention 'Brian Johnson' and his publication *Albert Angelo* (1964) in *Bomb Culture* (1968).

Margaret Tait

The 30 films by Scottish filmmaker and poet Margaret Tait, made between 1951 and 1998, form an eclectic collection of work, including direct animation (painting on the film-strip) and filmed works. Tait preferred to describe herself as a film-poet, rather than a documentary or diary filmmaker – '[w]hen a Channel 4 interviewer suggested that her films were "diaristic" because they all document people and places with which she was intimately familiar, she objected' – yet some of her films fall so fittingly into the diary form of filmmaking as she was a keen chronicler of everyday life, that I have taken the liberty of including her here as a 'diarist'.[66] Tait studied film at the 'Centro Sperimentale di Cinematografia' and her 'openness of mind, voice, structure, all come from the Beats and Whitman crossed with MacDiarmid, but then cut their own original (and crucially female) path'.[67] She described her 'technique of "breathing" with the camera', using Federico García Lorca's phrase of 'stalking the image' as she was 'preoccupied with catching the "momentary", the "subtle" gestures' in her films and poems.[68] Tait noted Lorca's lecture about Don Luis de Gongora, who considered an apple as 'no less intense than the sea, a bee [a]s no less astonishing than a forest'.[69] In this way, all things were equal before the camera, with the type of cinema she cared about being on the level of poetry and her life's work consisting essentially of making film poems.

The films *Tailpiece* (1976) and *Place of Work* (1976) focus on the emptying of Tait's family home in the Orkney Islands. They were filmed between June and November in Kirkwall, where Tait grew up and lived intermittently as an adult. *Tailpiece* opens with a shot of a garden and continues with the hand-held camera moving, like an observant camera-eye, towards the house. Diverse shots of interior nooks, crannies and windows reveal ordinary spaces clearly permeated with memory for Tait. As two removal men carry furniture away, the empty spaces suggest a sense of loss heightened by the knowledge that these spaces will never again be occupied in the same way. Tait said she wanted to capture the secret places one gets to know through living in a house for many years, and the film appears to reveal these unfolding memories. The soundtrack includes a recording of Tait's young nieces learning a song Tait remembered learning in the house as a child. The children's voices and music resonate, bringing a melancholic atmosphere to the film. Catherine Russell's observations on Mekas's diary films could equally be used in relation to Tait's *Tailpiece*:

> The longing for the past that Mekas expresses constructs memory as a means of splitting oneself across a number of different axes: child and adult, old world and new, pastoral and metropolitan, natural and cultural.[70]

Tait attempts to restore this division between past and present as she captures 'the time of finally emptying a long-time family home, with its personal memories and connection with some of my own work'.[71] *Tailpiece* was described by Jo Comino as 'a diary film which logs shifts in time and space so that they seem almost imperceptible', with sound used 'in a way which emphasizes scale' rather than as synced-sound or as a commentary of events.[72] Comino provides the example of bells tolling some time after a church is seen so that 'seasonal or elemental changes are recorded as if coincidentally, and the actual presence of the film-maker remains elusive, a shadow, a reflection in the mirror, a disembodied voice.'[73]

While a sense of loss is elicited in *Tailpiece,* the longer film *Place of Work* operates more as a documentary account, without the distillation of poetic reflection revealed in the shorter film. In *Place of Work* Tait wished to take the viewer 'from the work table, out the front door, and round the house in an east, south, west and north circling'.[74] This circle was repeated by focusing on aspects of the garden – flowers, cats and people – and the interior and exterior of the house. In this way Tait walked the viewer around her journey of saying goodbye to her house. Tait's films cover a wide range of subject matter – portraiture, landscape, abstract drawings/paintings on film – but they are united by her poetic vision of 'stalking' image and are often accompanied by poetic voiceovers. Le Grice wrote favourably about Tait's films in his 1975 festival review, soon after she had been 'discovered' in England, suggesting that she was one of the true originals. This can be evidenced in the detailed account *The Margaret Tait Reader: Subjects and Sequences* (2004) provides.

Anne Rees-Mogg

Anne Rees-Mogg's trilogy, *Real Time* (1971–74), *Sentimental Journey* (1977) and *Living Memory* (1980), share some common themes with Tait's two films as they are autobiographical reminiscences on the childhood home, the surrounding countryside and events related to filmmaking. *Real Time* records a journey to Rees-Mogg's home, including footage of her driving along the motorway, intermittent shots of red poppies along the roadside, family photographs and re-enacted events from Rees-Mogg's childhood acted by her niece. Nick Wadley described it as 'the most densely autobiographical' of her films, revealing an 'obsessive delving through the family looking-glass'.[75] A conversation with her mother and an evocative scratched record repeating the same lines accompany the disparate visual recollections, forming a kind of memory-documentary without linear narrative.

Sentimental Journey reads as an instruction manual of sorts, detailing the techniques or processes involved in filmmaking, through sound and image. (Rees-Mogg taught at Chelsea School of Art and also worked at the LFMC.) The film includes animated drawings, paintings on film, repeated shots, single frames, colour separation, the use of filters, portraits of students and teachers, a picnic in a garden and a group portrait amidst the ruins of a building. They reveal the LFMC's structural and material influences, but the precarious nature of working with film also has a sense of ironic self-questioning, evident, too, in the jerky, repeated phrases of instruction and discussion on filmmaking.

In *Living Memory* Rees-Mogg reflects on her childhood home and the surrounding environment. Footage of her flying overhead in a plane and walking across fields with her two nephews are edited with earlier photographs of the boys (manipulated on the LFMC printer). The soundtrack further supports this dialogue between past and present, articulating problems of time, memory and place through quotations by philosophers and poets. Wadley made the following observation:

> The pervasive strain of memory throughout her work contrives to outwit time through the act of documentation – as if the process of recording and re-enacting of people and places, changing and unchanging, rescues their passing from any sense of loss and regret [...] The subject of her films is both filmmaking and autobiography.[76]

Rees-Mogg's trilogy thus operates as a personal reflection, not dissimilar to Tait's two films, collapsing time and space to create a memoir imbued with recollections of events but also revealing the processes of filmmaking. Although the influence of the LFMC's structural and material experimentation is evident in the trilogy, Rees-Mogg was insistent that she was not trying to work 'within the conventions of an English avant-garde' but felt 'much more related to American films like Jonas Mekas, and diary films'.[77]

David Larcher

David Larcher is possibly one of the most enigmatic of the 1970s filmmakers, having close relationships with the LFMC, yet following his own unique path. He studied anthropology and archaeology, completed a post-graduate degree at the RCA and worked as a professional photographer before taking up filmmaking. He attended early LFMC meetings at Better Books and literally lived at the LFMC for weeks to edit his films. While he made only two films – *Mare's Tail* (1969) and *Monkey's*

Birthday (1975) during the decade (I take the liberty of including the former here) – these together amounted to over eight hours of footage, with Henrik Hendrikson describing them as being 'firmly in the visionary strain of avant-garde film-making'.[78]

Monkey's Birthday was filmed on a journey across Europe and Asia, recording the people and places in the guise of the Rimbaudian wanderer (albeit with family and friends), 'experiencing the romantic artist's life of poverty and visionary experience'.[79] Described by Hendrikson as 'at once a diary of that voyage, a romanticisation of the quest [...] and a universalization of that quest beyond the individual protagonist', the film is imbued with archaeological and psychological observation and enquiry, as experiences are recorded and edited to form an epic, interior journey.[80]

For the editing of *Monkey's Birthday* Larcher spent the best part of a year at the LFMC, working on the filmed footage by tinting, toning, scratching into the celluloid, adding newly printed material to create repetitions and with 'almost every frame of this six hours [...] subjected to a practically alchemical barrage of procedures and treatments'.[81] The soundtrack mirrors the eclecticism of the imagery, consisting of music, found-sound recordings, and recordings of Larcher discussing the filmed image and quoting the mystic Gurdjieff, (who also informed Arden's *Vibration* discussed above). Although it is almost six hours long, Hendrikson suggested that the multi-layered film 'must be appreciated in the simplicity and beauty of its diary format, in the intensity of its personal quest, and in the ambitiousness of its representation as universal odyssey'.[82]

Although Larcher worked at the LFMC intermittently in the 1970s, his work certainly didn't follow the more rigorous formalism of experimentation with structure and material. Instead, his work took a more personal, mythopoeic approach to filmmaking, incorporating poetry and myth into his art of visionary filmmaking, with Dwoskin's description providing useful insights into Larcher's working processes:

> Larcher, who is also one of the few subjectively responsive and free photographers, has no theories. If any influences seem evidently exerted it is the 'I Ching', hypnagogic imagery and some of John Cage [...] The real influence however is still Larcher, who roves and discovers in his own world without the constriction of ours [...] It is freedom that is desired by many, feared by most and intellectualised out by others.[83]

Larcher's practice – unharnessed by theoretical or conceptual concerns – was similarly shared by other filmmakers such as Jarman, Keen and Anger, finding inspiration in poetry, myth or dream, thus imbuing their filmmaking with a personal vision of the world. Such unharnessed approaches to filmmaking would also influence younger filmmakers, taking on board the liberal approaches to practice: with re-filming, double exposing or reworking filmed footage. The British/Ghanaian filmmaker, John Akomfrah, for example, referred to these filmmakers as 'the magick tradition' (referring to Anger's term), saying that while he was not immersed enough to note direct influences, they definitely legitimised possibilities for experimentation.[84] Poetic resonances are also evident in the contemporary documentary/fiction films of Ben Rivers, with hand-processing and close observations also creating dialogues between film materiality and content.

Although British diary filmmakers took diverse approaches to filmmaking, what united them was the way that personal experience, memory and poetic, philosophical or mystical inspiration were combined to create subjective experiences of reality on film. Jarman, for example, saw art and film as 'archaeology of the soul', revealing:

> My world is in fragments, smashed in pieces so fine I doubt I will ever reassemble them. So I scrabble in the rubbish, an archaeologist who stumbles across a buried film. An archaeologist who projects his private world along a beam of light into the arena, till all goes dark at the end of the performance, and we go home.[85]

Filmmaking was for Jarman, therefore, a way to excavate and resurrect memories, infusing filmmaking with poetic or philosophical reflection or simply presenting fragmentary experiences for consideration, with Chrissie Iles also noting that '[h]e considered the little-known but important body of Super-8 films at the heart of his film-making'.[86] Rees-Mogg, suggested that she felt 'a little bit more at ease with American films on the whole', compared with the more rigorous formalism of LFMC experimentation, as '[t]here's an acceptance of the home-movie, the diary, personal experience, as being perfectly valid'.[87] Hamid Naficy's description of Mekas's working methods as a film diarist also provides some useful insights into these British diarists:

> Each squeeze of the camera shutter-release button produced one random epistolary film note, one postcard, to be added to the stack of visual notes and cards that would one day become a film. This mode of production wove the fragmented biographical life of the filmmaker into its cinematic representation, exilically accenting the

resulting films, which Mekas characterised as 'small films, films that do not force anything upon you'. But these little, unpretentious films are expansive, celebrating the ordinary moments of life by paring them down to such essential simplicity that they achieve poetic eloquence.[88]

Although Naficy explicitly referred to Mekas's process in relation to his experiences as an exile, the fusion of past and present through film was also evident in these British diary filmmakers, as a way of determining their presence in relation to their surroundings and life experiences. Mekas's 'small films, films that do not force anything upon you' are also congruent with the way Jarman considered his a 'cinema of small gestures' – small films and small gestures that speak large.

Breakwell's life-long 'continuous diaries' were recorded in written form and permeated his film diaries. Johnson's recollections, infused by his mystical experiences brought him back to the beach in Wales to recount a number of absurd events and memories, which may best be read alongside his avant-garde novels and Coe's biography. Tait and Rees-Mogg visually reflected on their childhood homes and landscapes to record diaries of interwoven events moving from past to present; and Larcher's poetic odyssey recounted his free-spirited global wanderings. Like Jarman, they all took an archaeological approach to mine their life experiences and project their 'private world along a beam of light into the arena'.[89]

Concluding thoughts

Clearly, the films discussed under the terms 'psycho-dramatic trance', 'lyrical', 'mythopoeia' and 'diary' filmmaking covered diverse approaches to filmmaking. While the range of films discussed here may not form a cohesive body of work driven by a single overarching theoretical, philosophical or aesthetic premise, they are united by their individual styles, and their personal, image-rich approaches (informed by literary, scientific and mystical texts or simply in recording the world). Thus they support my premise that that there was no *return* to personal, visionary and more expressive forms of filmmaking at the *end* of the 1970s – as mooted in diverse histories – but rather that image existed *throughout* the decade. These films are image rich, using superimposition as in Jarman and Keen's films, or are richly textured through physical work on the film-strip, as in Larcher's *Monkey's Birthday*. Subjects have been 'stalked' as in Tait's films and voyeuristically stared at (by camera and viewer) as in *Central Bazaar* and *The Other Side of the Underneath*. Actors have performed bizarre rites and rituals for Anger, Keen and Jarman, and have been the subject of psychological investigation in *Anti-Clock*. Filmmakers have reflected on themselves and their lives in attempts to uncover possible connections between past and present that may shape a hidden narrative, as in Rees-Mogg's trilogy and Johnson's *Fat Man on the Beach*. They have also wandered without restraint, as Larcher did in *Monkey's Birthday*, merely looking and recording what is observed in pure wonderment, with no predetermined purpose.

The films discussed in this chapter form an important aspect of 1970s experimentation, despite sometimes sitting uneasily within any predetermined classification. I believe that they require full recognition as part of 1970s experimental film history. Perhaps it is the case, as Dwoskin says about Larcher, that these filmmakers desired to rove and discover 'without constriction', with a freedom 'desired by many'; a freedom which these filmmakers have pursued without restraint.[90] In the following chapter, filmmaking seemingly following a more rigorous agenda – structural and material experimentation – will be discussed. While questions will be raised about its continued dominance in established histories, the analyses will also reveal that these forms of experimentation were also more diverse than has previously been recognised.

5
Experiments with Structure and Material

While dominant, commercial cinema was about the compression of the time/space continuum and the illusion of the passage of time through narrative, the intention of structural and material film was to raise awareness of duration, film material and process, to encourage viewer-reflexivity and demystify the filmmaking process. A focus on the relationships between film content and film form identified that structural filmmaking was 'often theorised as a cinematic relation – and disjunction – between signifiers and signified.'[1] A.L. Rees additionally noted that '[d]uration became the hallmark of British structural film, a "road not taken" by the mainstream cinema or by the lyric direction in avant-garde film'.[2] This type of film experimentation explored film medium and structure, revealed processes and procedures in filmmaking and took an anti-Hollywood stance to counter symbolic image use and narrative structure. While initially there were considerable US influences fuelling debate and filmmaking – notably in the form of New American Cinema screenings (1964/68) and close contacts with the New York Co-operative – British experimentation was boosted by a number of active and influential individuals, including filmmakers/theorists Malcolm Le Grice and Peter Gidal and activist/film programmer, and later Arts Council officer, David Curtis. Production facilities at the LFMC would also significantly enable and define distinctively British forms of experimentation, with Le Grice identifying film materiality as offering a breadth of possibilities for experimentation:

In its simplest sense, the question of materiality is seen in relationship to the: *physical substances* of the film medium, the film strip itself as material and object. Work in this area drawing, and paying attention to the physical base (acetate), emulsion surface, sprockets, joins etc., easily shades over into an awareness of: *mechanical and physico-chemical processes*. In this case attention is drawn to the photo chemical response and its chemical development, the transfer of image through printing, the transformation of image through these processes and the mechanical systems of film transport in camera, printer, or projector.[3] (Le Grice italics)

While most structural and material experimentation emerged from filmmakers working at – or affiliated to – the LFMC, filmmakers such as Peter Greenaway also produced structural films, and Laura Mulvey and Peter Wollen – influenced by European art-house filmmakers such as Jean-Luc Godard – took more instructive approaches, using pro-filmic structuring devices and feminist discourses to underpin films. Deke Dusinberre, identifying directions taken by (mostly) LFMC filmmakers to counter Romantically infused, emotionally driven filmmaking, described the 'ascetic task' taken by filmmakers as follows:

[T]wo related pursuits: to relentlessly efface the representational aspect of the cinematic image (thus engaging the discourse of the other arts by interrogating the very qualities of film as a specific medium) and the rigorous elimination of a transcendent goal or shape (to forestall an analogic critique which would lead to the 'pathetic fallacy' which undermines the literally reflexive strategies of structural film-making). The positive results of these tactics of negation is to challenge the dominant system of signification and to intensify the spectator's awareness of her/his own capacities for meaning-making.[4]

The films, therefore, focused on the specifics of the film medium or structuring and procedural aspects of filmmaking, seeking to encourage a greater sense of viewer reflexivity (ideally) without eliciting emotive responses to images. Dusinberre also defined this as 'an aesthetics of process, which was based on the very equipment and process inherent to its use'.[5] Discussions on the LFMC below provide further details on its formation and the diverse locations informing filmmaking, and the LFMC needs to be understood as operating within a Marxist framework with an open policy for accepting any film for distribution (like the New York Co-op) without promoting individual films/filmmakers.

The increasing expansion and diversity in British experimentation from the mid-1960s onwards was also driven by the progressive increase in artists/filmmakers coming out of art schools. The education system, therefore, also added to the consolidation of film practices, particularly those affiliated with the LFMC, as many filmmakers such as Gidal, Le Grice, Dwoskin and Rees-Mogg, also taught in art schools such as the Royal College of Art (RCA), Central Saint Martins or Goldsmiths. Mazière noted that the continued output of 1970s filmmakers expanded in that '[t]his "family tree" grew – students would become tutors and spawn new students themselves becoming tutors'.[6] The open policy at the LFMC, where students often worked alongside tutors and had access to filmmaking facilities on leaving their studies, also contributed greatly to the continued growth in 1970s filmmaking.

Although Le Grice and particularly Gidal (as discussed below) to a large extent dominated theoretical developments, there was no one homogenous 'house-style' within the Co-op, with an extensive range of films emerging through an environment conducive to experimentation, revealing the broad range of approaches with film form, materiality and structure, as Rees identified:

[T]he camera's iconic image, single or double, was not in itself the central concern of the early Co-op which – with Mike Dunford, John Du Cane, Roger Hammond, David Parsons and Annabel Nicolson – took film-making further into live events, the handmade film print, procedural systems and expanded cinema (or 'making films with projectors') to question the given definition of film as a representation rather than, as the Co-op saw it, an investigation of its identity as a performance in which viewers as well as makers were engaged. Such films seek film equivalents for light and motion. They aim to renew perception by using the whole register of film language, underlining its normally invisible aspects – frame, surface, print stock – and its 'mistakes' (flare, slippage, double-exposure).[7]

Access to processing and printing facilities, the LFMC's policy of changing workshop operators and programmers every two years, and a generally supportive setting where filmmakers assisted each other on projects created a productive environment for experimentation. Certainly this was not without its challenges – financial, organisational and personal – but the existence of these facilities, and a co-operative working environment, was instrumental in shaping a significant, distinctive amount of 1970s British experimentation.

Other filmmakers, taking conceptual approaches to experimentation, explored relationships between still and moving image, focused on the projection context, proposed film as a concept and often exhibited films in galleries alongside related drawings or photographs. Most of these 'conceptual' filmmakers (also discussed in Chapter 3), such as David Dye, John Hilliard, David Lamelas, John Blake and Anthony McCall, tended to show in galleries and had little or no contact with the LFMC. While there were overlaps with certain aspects of filmmaking, the conceptualists had less interest in exploring film materiality through production processes. Curtis importantly identified how 'the intellectual common cause' between the conceptualists and LFMC filmmakers (particularly the friendship between Gidal and Blake) was in 'dissolving tidy definitions of what belonged in [the] gallery and what belonged in the cinema'.[8] The 'boundary between white cube and black box that has characterised the moving image since the late 1990s' thus already began to be eroded in the mid-1970s.[9]

While theoretical positions informed certain aspects of 1970s experimentation, they also problematically subordinated more personal and visionary forms of filmmaking (discussed in the previous chapter) as these used more representational symbolic/metaphoric imagery. The important question, asking how far the Marxist critique went in terms of undermining the individual authorial voice, needs to be asked. Gidal expressed his distaste for 'the mystic romanticism of higher sensibility individualism'.[10] He was also vehemently against all forms of narrative filmmaking, particularly if this was expressed 'through any form of anthropomorphic, individualist identification with the film-maker'.[11] According to Reekie, Gidal's 1975 'manifesto', outlining his uncompromising position, considered film 'as a necessary element of an advanced revolutionary Marxist struggle'.[12] This allows us to pose some further questions. Did the Marxist collectivist spirit and the LFMC co-operative ethos undermine the equal recognition of more personal, individualistic forms of 1970s filmmaking? Or was it simply the fact that the latter forms of filmmaking had no collective voice? These questions should be kept in mind as discussions unfold in this chapter and as the dominance of structural and material discourses are made evident, ultimately leading to the mythic 'return to image' thesis which allegedly occurred at the end of the decade. It must be understood, however, that by questioning the dominance of structural and material experimentation, there is no intention to undermine the important theoretical and film work produced, as these investigations were substantially important in opening up discourses which are still relevant for filmmakers working today.

At the outset of this chapter international exchanges and theoretical frameworks informing film experimentation are outlined. This is followed by a discussion of films focusing on materiality, structural or procedural approaches, and relationships between sound/image, narrative and humour. The intention is to reveal commonalities in filmmaking but also to demonstrate the diverse range and complexity of films that fall under the rubric 'experimentation with structure and material'. The terms 'experiments with structure and material' or 'structural and material experimentation' will be used here to avoid alignment with more specific terms such as Gidal's 'structural/materialist'.

International exchanges

An international exchange of ideas formed an important part in 1960/70s British film developments, with experimentation evident in countries such as Germany, Austria, the US, Australia and Japan. While a distinctively British type of experimentation would establish itself firmly in the 1970s – primarily due to production facilities at the LFMC – the crosscultural influences were extremely important for British developments. The 'Edinburgh Film Festival' (operating since 1947) provided an invaluable platform for screening and debate throughout the 1970s, with close links forged with the LFMC early on and the 1969 festival, for example, including numerous films held in LFMC distribution. Further afield, in Belgium, the 'Knokke Experimental Film Festival' (held intermittently at Knokke-Le-Zout from 1949 onwards) was also important for building international networks, with British-based filmmakers taking part in screenings and discussion forums. At some point in the 1960s it was mooted that a European Co-op should be formed, but this never materialised. International dialogues, however, were importantly kept alive through festival networks and by either showing work abroad or inviting filmmakers to show/discuss films in Britain.[13] LFMC screenings abroad, for example, included Annabel Nicolson's visit to Canada, documented in her 'Canadada Fragments' (1973), and screenings of films by Gidal and Mike Leggett at an 'Avant-Garde Cinema' (1976) event in Colorado; debates between Le Grice and Sitney (1977) and Le Grice and Brakhage (1978) also provided informative insights into cross-Atlantic exchanges.[14] William Raban's 22-issue *Filmmakers Europe* (1977–81) provided information about screenings, workshops and film courses, and generally opened up further opportunities for European exchanges. Le Grice had also developed a close working relationship with the German filmmakers, Birgit and Wilhelm Hein, after seeing their *Roh Film* (1968), and Austrian filmmakers Peter Kubelka and Kurt Kren also wielded an influence on British structural and material experimentation. Kubelka was, for example, present at an ICA event in 1967, with his minimalist structural films including *Arnulf Rainer* (1958–60) – black and white frames edited alternately using a diagrammatic score – and two advertising commissions, *Adebar* (1957) and *Schwechater* (1958), which both used minimal imagery and repetition in an abstracted, structural form.[15] Significantly, Le Grice first visited the LFMC to attend a screening of Kurt Kren's films in September 1967, with Kren's films making a deep impression on him.[16] While Le Grice resisted the temptation to present Kren 'as some kind of father of European avant-garde film', he acknowledged that his 'work is certainly held in very high regard by almost all the film-makers this side of the Atlantic involved in so-called structuralist film'.[17] Le Grice cited *3/60 – Baüme im Herbst* (1960), with its time-lapse images of trees in autumn, as 'the first structural film'.[18] Kren's influences are also evident in films such as Guy Sherwin's *Tree Reflection* (from 'Short Film Series') and Fred Drummond's *Kurt Kren Portrait* (1976).

The issue of US influence on British experimentation was deliberated with some regularity, as the formation of the LFMC was initially inspired by the New York Film Co-op (1962) and included Americans, Stephen Dwoskin and Simon Hartog, in its earliest formation, with Peter Gidal and Deke Dusinberre becoming involved in the early 1970s. A large proportion of the early LFMC films consisted of New American Cinema works. In Mark Webber's LFMC chronology he noted that of the 60 titles in distribution by November 1967 'few are home-grown', therefore the early influence could readily be assumed.[19] In Curtis's 'Early Chronology' he asserted that 'international' for the first few years of this chronology' was 'virtually synonymous with "American"'.[20] However, in research gathered for Deke Dusinberre's (unpublished) thesis on English avant-garde film, he suggested that US influence tended 'to be greatly overestimated', with Curtis also proposing that British developments endured from 'original and distinctly English impulses', citing filmmakers such as Keen and Le Grice, and possibly also referring to 1930s filmmakers Len Lye and Norman McLaren.[21] But clearly the early US infusion and continued dialogues throughout the decade were important for British developments.

Theoretical perspectives for filmmaking: Sitney, Le Grice and Gidal

While filmmaking was central to developments, a number of key theoretical texts significantly informed British structural and material experimentation. It will be useful to turn to these to see how they provided a framework and came to underpin some of the dominant theoretical positions on the decade's filmmaking. P. Adams Sitney's seminal 'Structural Film' (1969) in the first instance opened up important new directions in US experimental filmmaking informed by minimalism, conceptualism and modernism in the arts, differing from his earlier focus on mythopoeic, lyrical or psycho-dramatic films.[22]

Sitney posited four characteristics defining a 'structural' film: unchanging camera position, flicker effect, looped printing and re-filming from the screen, with films prioritising form over content, investigating structural and procedural filmmaking devices and often referencing the medium itself.[23] He asserted that 'the structural film insists on its shape, and what content it has is minimal and subsidiary to the outline'.[24] This contrasted noticeably with approaches taken by filmmakers such as Stan Brakhage, where the personal 'camera eye' was of prime importance, or the films of Maya Deren, where a shot-by-shot consideration marked her tightly choreographed works.

Sitney's points were addressed specifically in relation to films such as Michael Snow's *Wavelength* (1967) and Andy Warhol's *Sleep* (1963) and *Empire* (1964). *Wavelength*, consisting of a 45-minute zoom filmed across the length of a loft room, begins with a wide shot and ends with a close-up of a framed photograph of a wave. The soundtrack consists of a slowly increasing sine-wave, hence there is a play on the sound and image of the title. While *Wavelength* wielded a significant influence – taught in experimental film programmes and one of the seminal films referred to in historical analyses – Warhol's films would prove especially important for opening up discourses on duration and the time/space manipulation in dominant, narrative cinema. *Sleep* significantly countered earlier experimental films focused on dreams and the unconscious by literally showing someone sleeping. Although Warhol initially intended to produce an eight-hour film, equipment limitations resulted in a heavily edited *Sleep* appearing 'meditative, beautiful, yet complexly structured, achronological and endlessly repetitious'.[25] His eight-hour 'real-time' ambitions were, however, realised with *Empire*, a stationary shot of the Empire State Building filmed in one night. Warhol discredited the myth of the personal, visionary filmmaker – and 'Hollywood' filmmaking – as he 'made the profligacy of footage the central fact of all of his early films, and he advertised his indifference to direction, photography, and lighting. He simply turned the camera on and walked away'.[26] He also insisted that films were projected at silent speed (16fps), thus slightly slowing down the motion and creating a disjunction between filming at sound speed (18fps).[27]

Sitney identified how Warhol's confrontation with duration opened up new possibilities by challenging the meaning of temporality and film-time:

> Warhol broke the most severe theoretical taboo when he made films that challenged the viewer's ability to endure emptiness or sameness [...] The great challenge, then, of the structural film became how to orchestrate duration; how to permit the wandering attention that triggered ontological awareness while watching Warhol films and at the same time guide that awareness to a goal.[28]

In Curtis's early history of experimental cinema he noted that 'Warhol had at least one highly original contribution to make – his rediscovery of the static one-shot movie (the 'actuality' of Lumière brought to life)', further identifying the effects on the audience:

> The formal statement in these silent films is everything: the confrontation of the audience with an image that changed in conventional terms only marginally and only over a long period of time; once again, audiences were outraged.[29]

Warhol's films were first shown in Britain as part of Sitney's 'New American Cinema' tour, with his approaches – particularly to duration – wielding a significant influence on filmmakers.

While Sitney's 'Structural Film' was important for identifying certain tendencies and opening up discourses, it also elicited a number of critical responses. Fluxus artist George Maciunas's one-page commentary (1969), for example, derided Sitney for his '3 Errors: (wrong terminology, wrong examples-chronology and wrong source for original)'.[30] Maciunas's ironic critique presented a table with causes of error, proposed corrections including a list of over 40 films for Sitney's limited examples and accused Sitney of plagiarism for films such as Warhol's *Sleep* (1963–64) and *Empire* (1964), which in his opinion derived respectively from Jackson Mac Low's *Tree Movie* (1961) and Nam June Paik's *Empire State Building* (1964).

Sitney's 'Structural Film' also prompted a number of urgent responses from British filmmakers/theorists, with Le Grice responding to Sitney's essay with 'Thoughts on Recent Underground Film' (1972), taking Sitney to task on his simplistic definition and categorisation. Le Grice argued the futility of trying to find simple commonalities in films that differed so completely – 'a film by Sharits and one by Frampton are different enough to keep a critic busy for a few weeks without including others'.[31] Le Grice also identified that there had been 'a new formal tendency among filmmakers who have a base in the "underground"' and provided eight characterisations – instead of Sitney's four – with a range of specific concerns, rather than strict categories, identifying approaches to filmmaking.[32] These included a number of concerns (summarised here):

1. derived from camera limitations and extensions, such as lens and frame limits or camera movement and time-lapse
2. occurring through editing processes
3. with the eye mechanism and perception
4. derived from printing, processing and re-filming procedures
5. focusing on the physical nature of film and its material reality, such as dirt, scratches or sprocket holes
6. relating to film projection and projection apparatus, such as lens, shutter or screen
7. with duration as a concrete dimension
8. with meaning construction through 'language' systems or the semantics of image.[33]

Le Grice believed these broader and more clearly defined criteria accommodated the diversity in filmmaking practices and encouraged wider critical debate. Most criticisms of Sitney's terminology also censured the fact that continental theories related to linguistics and the social sciences in France had not been acknowledged when Sitney coined the term 'Structural Film'. In his 1977 debate with Le Grice, Sitney also admitted that it was not an ideal term, suggesting that 'the mistake of associating structuralism with structural film was not in the text of mine'.[34]

Gidal also responded to Sitney's essay, defining his critical position and approaches to filmmaking in his singular position on 'non-illusionistic' filmmaking in his manifesto 'Theory and Definition of Structural/ Materialist Film' (1975).[35] The addition of 'materialist' – to Sitney's 'virtually formalist theory' – also identified Gidal's Marxist position.[36] Gidal's firm anti-Hollywood, anti-narrative and anti-representational stance identified that '[i]n Structural/Materialist film, the in/film (not in/frame) and film/viewer material relations, and the relations of the film's structure, are primary to any representational content', with Rees describing Gidal's manifesto as follows: [37]

Gidal's introductory essay opens mildly enough by claiming that 'it attempts to be non-illusionist', but he unpacks this ambition in strongly didactic terms to successively attack all the major forms of cinema, including classic films, documentaries, dramas, political films and even experimental films in the 'visionary' mode of Brakhage. For him film is very clearly a 'modernist art', defined by 'flatness, grain, light, movement', in a state of tension with its representational content and with the viewer.[38]

Although Le Grice and Gidal questioned Sitney's term 'structural', the term 'material' or 'materiality' would also lead to some confusion, and clarifications were needed to ensure that it referred to more than just film material; 'material' also accommodated other processes related to filmmaking, as Rees noted:

> Instead of the primacy of form or shape, as in P. Adams Sitney's famous or notorious definition of the goals of US structural film, the UK filmmakers substituted duration and process – which had more to do with the spectator's experience in time than with the work's objecthood.[39]

Distinctively British experimentation and the LFMC

The history of the LFMC is already well documented (Curtis 1971 and 2007, Dwoskin 1975, Webber 2001, LUX website, etc.), with *The Undercut Reader* and the twentieth anniversary recollections providing reflections from the ensuing decade, but a brief consideration here reveals its divergent and eclectic beginnings.[40] The LFMC was inspired by Jonas Mekas's New York Co-op (1962), as he sought a European base for the distribution of experimental films. It emerged from screenings held at Better Books from 1965 onwards (run by concrete poet Bob Cobbing), and included early members Steve Dwoskin, Jeff Keen, John Latham and Simon Hartog. Concurrent to this, the Drury Lane Arts Laboratory – an artist-run experimental film, theatre and performance space founded by Jim Haynes in 1967 – ran regular screenings programmed by Curtis and had Le Grice's *ad hoc* film workshop *in situ*. The convergence of both groups – as the LFMC – found them housed together at the Robert Streets Arts Laboratory in 1969 (the first of numerous 'homes'), thereby consolidating initial intentions. Increasingly, new members, such as Fred Drummond, Roger Ackling, Gidal and later Annabel Nicolson, Gill Eatherley, William Raban, John Du Cane, Mike Dunford and Deke Dusinberre (writer/critic) joined. Curtis's continued involvement included programming screenings of historic films alongside screenings of new works programmed by one of the filmmakers (usually in post for two years). To return to its beginnings, however, a reminder by Le Grice provides the contexts and motivations surrounding its formation:

> The concepts for the Co-op drew variously for their formation and sustenance on a range of diverse influences as wide as that of the hippy movement, Marx, Marcuse, and May '68. It drew heavily on the precedent of the New York Film-makers Co-operative, but, through the merger with the Arts Laboratory group took on a much wider set of objectives. Though it was not fully appreciated at the time, even by those of us most involved, as well as having more ambitious aims, it always had a more strongly developed set of social and political objectives than had motivated the New York Co-op.[41]

Although the LFMC's survival was plagued by a lack of finances, having an itinerant existence in various sites across north London, it survived for almost 40 years with the longer-term 'home' (20 years) in Gloucester Avenue (1977) no doubt providing necessary consolidation. Rees noted that '[e]ach location stamped its shape on the films that were made there, from the meltdown of media in 'expanded cinema' of the two Arts Labs, to a more purist climate at Fitzroy Road'.[42] Significantly, the LFMC continued operating, despite financial and personal struggles, merging with LEA (London Electronic Arts, previously LVA) under one Lottery-funded roof in 1997 as the LUX, until its unfortunate dissolution in 2001. The LUX has continued distribution of artists'/experimental film, and 'no.w.here', an experimental film 'lab' housing some of the original printing equipment, continues to offer an open-access space for working with film.

Consolidating structural and material filmmaking: Le Grice and Gidal

As Le Grice and Gidal were the two most important filmmaker/theorists forwarding structural and material experimentation in Britain, I would like to look more closely at their roles to understand the continued influence and dominance of this type of filmmaking. The purpose is to recognise its significance as an important strain of filmmaking but also to examine how it came to be problematically representative of 1970s filmmaking to the marginalisation of other forms of filmmaking. Both filmmakers' involvement extended beyond filmmaking/theorising as they also campaigned for greater recognition of experimental filmmaking, sat on boards/committees such as the BFIPB and the IFA and were involved in the LFMC in the early stages of development (Le Grice from 1967 and Gidal from 1968), maintaining a dominant presence throughout the 1970s and to the present. Besides their critical responses to Sitney's 'Structural Film', they wrote extensively on film, with Gidal securing column inches related to LFMC activity in *Time Out* (1972–75) through John du Cane, and Le Grice providing regular film reviews for 'Vision' in *Studio International* (1972–1977), as well as writing for other publications. Their influential monographs, supporting their filmmaking positions – Gidal's *Structural Film Anthology* (1976) and *Materialist Film* (1989), and Le Grice's *Abstract Film and Beyond* (1977) and *Experimental Cinema in the Digital Age* (2001) – remain seminal historical references. (Le Grice's later work, especially in the context of digital moving image, is particularly relevant for contemporary practices.)

Both Gidal and Le Grice have maintained active involvement since the 1970s and their dual roles as filmmakers/theorists invariably brought in-depth understandings to their theorisation and filmmaking. Paul Arthur's commentary on Gidal is equally applicable to Le Grice and identified that '[a]n important distinction for the thrust (and impact) of Gidal's work is that it has evolved alongside an active filmmaking practice'.[43] Theory seemingly followed practice, with Rees noting that despite Gidal and Le Grice being 'associated with "theory-building" throughout the 1970s, Le Grice maintained that LFMC filmmakers applied theory after practice as an analysis of production'.[44]

In attempting to understand their continued dominance in established histories, Constance Penley identified that Gidal and Le Grice's theorisation of filmmaking is 'highly complementary, one often citing the work of the other to help support an argument', but asserted that '[t]hey differ, however, in that Le Grice speaks from within a concerned historical reconstruction of the same movement for which Gidal polemically agitates'.[45] Although they were in agreement on certain theoretical issues, they also differed on others, as Le Grice identified:

> There is probably a greater justification for this link at the level of theory than there is in any specific aspects of the film work. As a theorist, Gidal offers a far more secure scholarship and breadth of contemporary reference than I have ever pretended, but I find more points of agreement in the concepts than I find in disagreements.[46]

Le Grice confirmed that Gidal's position was more extreme (a position Gidal has continued to uphold), and clarified his position independently from Gidal's by stating that 'in using the term "material", I've been very unwilling to put the "ist" on the end and turn it into "materialist"'.[47]

Le Grice's filmography currently runs to over 50 films, including a number of films revealing a poetic attention to reveal film materiality, structuring devices and process – each with lyrical musical scores – for example, *Little Dog for Roger* (1967), *Berlin Horse* (1970) and *After Lumière – Arroseur Arrosé* (1974). His involvement with the LFMC's (unofficial group) Filmaktion produced numerous expanded cinema works, with a turn to longer, more narrative films at the end of the 1970s and continued engagements with film and digital moving image to the present day. Le Grice created a historical trajectory to support his theoretical position, identified by the curatorial choices made (albeit with the committee) for the Hayward Gallery's controversial 'Film as Film' (1979) exhibition (see Chapter 1). He justified his choices in his 'History We Need' catalogue essay and thereby also consolidated the structural and material emphasis on 1970s experimentation.

Gidal similarly supported his position as filmmaker/theorist in the extensive 18-programme 'Structural Film Retrospective' (1976, BFI) coinciding with the publication of his *Structural Film Anthology*, containing personal statements, theoretical and critical essays of the nearly 100 British, European and US films screened. Only filmmakers producing 'relevant work before 1971' were included, with the retrospective intending to contextualise works and 'recognise alliances and misalliances between films'.[48] Gidal's own films and theoretical position interrogated properties intrinsic to the film medium, creating a dialectic 'established in that space of tension between material flatness, grain, light, movement (two dimensionality) and the supposed real reality that is represented (three dimensionality; figurativeness)'.[49] Films such as *Clouds* (1969), *C/ON/S/T/R/U/C/T* (1974) and numerous 'room' films (one discussed below) are informed by Gidal's theoretical concerns. The influence of Warhol's *Screen Tests* (1964–66) is unmistakable in *Heads* (1969) – importantly providing an intriguing historical document of 1960s art/film-world who's-who – and his ardent stance against narrative and representation identified 'film as a contemporary art which politically needs to share nothing with the cinema', confirming his extreme anti-Hollywood position.[50] Gidal has been criticised, however, for the lack of equivalence between his theoretical position and the film. This is discussed further below.

Gidal and Le Grice were uncompromising about recognising films that clearly fitted or did not fit within their historical distinctions, with

Constance Penley making some useful observations about their dominant positions:

> [A]s theoretical writings, the work of Le Grice and Gidal offers an
> already secondarized and rationalized version of their own activ-
> ity, thus making very apparent their way of thinking about film.
> Le Grice's writings, moreover, offer an account of both his and his
> contemporaries' film-making practice across a history of the abstract,
> formal avant-garde, thus opening the way for a discussion of the his-
> torical placement of this avant-garde, of its *historical imaginary*, that
> is, its own conception of its origins and influences, its relation to the
> other arts and to the history of art.[51] (Penley's italics)

The 'historical imaginaries' that Gidal and Le Grice created to support
their positions were not in themselves unusual, and this is often the
way historians, critics, theorists or artists contextualise or theorise
their interests. Commonalities, differences, shifts and radical breaks are
identified to reveal theoretical or aesthetic changes, or to establish new
theoretical or critical positions. The problem, however, with Gidal and
Le Grice's 'historical imaginaries' and the dominant 1970s positions
they defined (governed largely by structural and material film) is that
they have continued to direct accounts of 1970s experimental filmmaking histories, without being adequately challenged. While Gidal and Le
Grice's filmmaking, critical writing, curatorial roles and campaigning
for film importantly brought a notable amount of work to British and
international audiences, their 'historical imaginaries' and the positions
they have defined, have continued to influence dominant readings of
this history. I believe that this has also over-determined the importance
of this type of LFMC activity (and this type of 1970s filmmaking as a
whole) at the expense of overshadowing more expressive, personal,
visionary and diaristic forms of filmmaking in the decade. It will be
useful to look at some of the 1970s films to get a sense of their diversity
and shed some new light on aspects of filmmaking before turning to a
critique about the problematic dominance of 1970s structural and material experimentation.

A brief word on narrative also highlights further complexities on the
structural/material position. Most of the experimental films discussed
in this book – in opposition to dominant commercial cinema – do not
follow a linear narrative structure. Gidal's insistence that '[n]arrative
is an illusionistic procedure, manipulatory, mystificatory, repressive'
informed his theoretical approaches to demystify film by exposing the

structure and material of the medium.[52] The 'manipulatory' aspect of film is, however, rather complex and it could be argued that it relates to *all* forms of film (commercial, independent and experimental), as the viewer is compelled to watch from beginning to end. Thus it differs significantly from the viewing of a painting or sculpture, where the viewer is not manipulated in the same durational manner. In this respect, escaping the 'manipulatory' aspect of narrative (the unfolding of film through time and space) may, arguably, not be possible, except perhaps with conceptual works such as McCall's *Long Film for Ambient Light* (1975) where the viewer takes in the work at his/her own volition. Penley also raised the issue of narrative and the problematic insistence on its elimination:

> As for Le Grice and Gidal's argument that narrative must be eliminated because it constructs and manipulates an unconscious spectator, it is not completely sure that even the least 'montaged' avant-garde films escape the fundamental structures of narrative.[53]

Du Cane similarly recognised how the concept of narrative posed problems for considerations of film's passage through time:

> One of the central facts about film is the fact of its transient duration. The relations between external, objective time consciousness as they exist in the further relation of film time and real time are relations that have only recently been given detailed attention.[54]

These considerations are useful to keep in mind, as film, if it is to be fully appreciated – as opposed to static visual works – is reliant on the viewer's engagement with the whole work, thereby demanding a 'manipulation' of the viewer's attention.

Film experimentation

The films focused on here consider diverse aspects of structural and material experimentation related to film materiality, the objective/subjective 'camera-eye', and questions centred on humour and sound/image relationships, narrative and purposive duration. Many experiments with structure and material were silent or had minimal soundtracks that avoided the use of sound for purposes of narrative formation or 'story-telling'. Although often attributed to financial constraints, 'silent sound' was also used intentionally, forcing closer attendance to visual film content or the mechanics of projection. Sound could therefore also be seen as surplus to requirements, interfering with visual film content, as Brakhage pointed out:

> The sound sense which visual images always evoke and which become integral with the aesthetic experience of the film under creative control, often makes actual sound superfluous. On this premise alone, one could disqualify almost every sound film from consideration as a work of art. There is no definition of a work of art which will admit superfluity. [55]

With the foregrounding of form over content in formal experimentation, Wollen too acknowledged the addition of sound as unnecessarily superfluous for some films:

> Language is still excluded from an enormous number of avant-garde films, which are shown either silent or with electronic or other musical tracks. Again, there are real technical and financial reasons for this, but these practical disincentives coincide with an aesthetic itself founded on concepts of visual form and visual problems that exclude verbal language from their field, and may be actively hostile to it.[56]

Sound, however, also played an important role in shaping narrative, either through the incongruence between sound and image or because the soundtrack offered a narrative structure to the work, as some of the films below will demonstrate. These films have been selected to support the discussions and are in no way definitive of structural and material experimentation; they are best read in conjunction with films discussed in the already well-established histories.

Film materiality

Films such as Le Grice's *Yes No Maybe Maybe Not* (1967) and Gidal's *8mm Notes on 16mm Film* (1971) expose the materiality of the medium by the inclusion of sprockets, frame edges and in revealing film being pulled through the printer. Le Grice identified how the process of exposing film materiality could oppose dominant, commercial cinema construction:

> What Hollywood tried desperately to hide – the material basis of the medium – in order to retain an illusion that the spectator was inside

the scene of the narrative, I, the Heins, Landow, Conrad and others tried to stress. This attention to the material simultaneously disrupted illusion and established a new basis on which artistic experiment in the medium could be built.[57]

Nicolson's films *Shapes* (1970) and *Slides* (1971), equally, would have been impossible to produce without access to production facilities. They are – as their titles suggest – about shapes and slides on-and-in film. *Shapes* was filmed in Nicolson's living space, with the camera moving around objects such as paper and transparent gels hanging in the room. Shots taken from the rooftop of Central Saint Martins School of Art are also included in the seven-minute film, presenting a succession of abstract images, at times grainy and painterly, which David Miller described as being 'exploratory, subtle, humble and thoughtful'.[58] These are as much a record of the external objects observed, as a record of the internal filmmaker's 'receptive eye'.[59] By allowing dust or dirt onto the film-strip, the film also became a physical record of a space, with traces of the minute ephemera held within the space.

Slides is a ten-minute film montage, consisting of, mostly, abstract images including the following as Nicky Hamlyn outlines:

> 35mm slides of a number of Nicolson's paintings, cut into narrow strips and joined together into lengths. There are also some sections and still frames from an earlier film *Anju* and some pieces of celluloid, sewn with dark coloured thread. The imagery consists of landscape footage, still images, abstract colour bands and brush strokes and a sequence of a face which has been cut out from one film and inserted into the material of another. Sprocket holes appear regularly and frequently swop sides as the original film is flipped or alternated.[60]

Nicolson pulled or hand-threaded 8mm, 16mm and 35mm film fragments through a contact printer and by this process also magnified the finest details to reveal dust or dirt, as well as the sprocket holes and light leaking through where the image is smaller than the frame. In discussing Nicolson's working process with the slow-running Debrie printer, Hamlyn singled out how instrumental the machinery was in enabling this type of filmmaking:

> This makes it a good tool for creative/experimental printing, hence its importance for the London Film-maker's Co-op at times when

film-makers have wanted to explore and control those processes normally undertaken by commercial laboratories.[61]

Fleeting images of a bookshelf, a room, or a figure in a landscape are
intermittently visible throughout *Slides*, and through the rich colour
and density of the photographed images, the light flares and the exposure of the physicality of the medium, a dialogue is formed between
film content and film material.

The objective and/or subjective 'camera-eye': Gidal and Brakhage

Gidal's *Room Film 1973* (1973) has some similarities with Nicolson's *Shapes*
in the way the fleeting images from the handheld camera move across a
domestic space – his 'room' of the title – barely alighting or allowing the
eye to identify objects. Gidal's film, focusing on the act of perception,
consists of a 100-ft continuous take edited into five-second units, which
are repeated once in the same sequence. As the camera moves across the
room there are brief moments of repose, giving a sense of recognition to
a plant and its shadow, a light socket, a book and papers, before moving
on, and continuing its restless search across the room. Dusinberre identified Gidal's intended focus on anti-representation:

> The film is almost relentless in its denial of tangible images (that is,
> images which are easily identifiable and spatially locatable) [...] The
> feeling of surface is evoked throughout: surface of object, of film, of
> screen.[62]

This continued search – and denial – draws parallels with Nicolson's
Shapes as both films reveal a kind of navigation through space made by
a personal 'camera-eye'. Gidal, however, with his firm anti-illusionist
and anti-representational stance was entirely opposed to the idea of
subjectivity, and in his statement about the film stated that 'the film
is not a translation of anything, it is not a representation of anything,
not even of consciousness'.[63] The moving camera, however, somewhat
ironically appears to be firmly tied to the filmmaker's roving vision.

In *Room Film 1973*, aspects of the film material and structure, such as
grain, flatness, colour, flare-out and film surface, are revealed in green-
and grey-tinged imagery. Despite Gidal's insistence on an objective,
impersonal reading of the film, the hand-held fleeting images are
(I would insist) subjectively inscribed. Gidal's films have been compared

to some of Brakhage's – to whom he sees himself entirely opposed (in filmmaking terms) – whose personal, visionary filmmaking was heavily steeped in the personal 'camera-eye' and conscious/subconscious processes in filmmaking. Rees suggested that 'like the colour flashes and vivid movement of his later films, they recall Brakhage – a comparison Gidal opposes, since he rejects Brakhage as myth maker and image maker'.[64] Jonas Mekas also made this comparison, identifying that '[b]y the use of early Brakhage techniques, very subtly and very plastically it deals with light, glimpses of light falling in the room, on various objects [...] Gidal's own "Anticipation of the Room"'.[65] Le Grice also noted that despite Gidal wanting it otherwise or 'however much he would like it played down critically', films such as *Room Film 1973* 'are at one level predicated on the sensual lure and the visual pleasure which he derives from the objects looked at'.[66] Hamlyn also identified this connection when he noted that Gidal's films had been 'vulnerable to this kind of [subjective] interpretive reading' that resembled filmmakers such as Brakhage, 'whose work is avowedly poetic and mythopoeic: the expression of personal vision.'[67] Clearly, there is no denying these self-evident connections.

An interesting correlation between Gidal and Brakhage's films was observed by Michael Snow when he said to Gidal: 'I liked your *Room Film 1973* very much. It is very good [...] I felt as if my father had made it, as if it was made by a blind man [...] I feel that searching tentative quality a lot, that quality of trying to see'.[68] This is so close to Brakhage's oft-cited opening line in his seminal 'Metaphors on Vision' essay, in which he stated:

> Imagine an eye unruled by man-made laws of perspective, an eye unprejudiced by compositional logic, an eye which does not respond to the name of everything but which must know each object encountered in life through an adventure of perception.[69]

Certainly Brakhage's essay is written in a visionary or mystical tone of voice, differing significantly to Gidal's theoretical one. Yet there is definitely something about the fleeting journey through *Room Film 1973*, which is equally an 'adventure in perception' in how attempts are made to make sense of space, and where the eye momentarily alights on an object, only to be denied the full shape and form in detail, and is forced to perceive again and again.[70]

More needs to be said about Brakhage's films as these have commonly been considered films of personal vision, mythopoeic or lyrical films, and he has been considered 'too uncritically subjective' by certain critics.[71] Yet, Rees also identified Brakhage's influence on structural filmmakers, particularly the 'modernist montage' of his seminal film *Mothlight* (1963), which includes actual moth's wings, flowers and leaves collaged between clear 16mm film leader and direct-printed onto fresh film stock.[72] Paul Arthur referred to these as 'denatured photographic' images, identifying that *Mothlight* operated as part of the 'strategy of modernist anti-illusionism', not dissimilar to structural and material forms of experimentation.[73]

In Brakhage's later film *The Text of Light* (1974), consisting entirely of shots of sunlight refracted through a crystal ashtray filmed with a macro-lens, the minimalist and spare images capture the materiality of objects as 'the light seems to take on the shapes, textures, movements, even the three-dimensionality, of things'.[74] What is fundamentally important – whether in *Room Film 1973, Mothlight* or *The Text of Light* – is the *way* that these films have been framed in critical or theoretical discourses. This was discussed previously, but it needs to be firmly emphasised as it crucially informs the way these films are read, critically received and historicised. Gidal observed the structural, material or minimal 'unemotional' image (although the critical readings of Gidal's films may not accord with his intentions), whereas Brakhage's films are written about in more mystical language in relation to 'the physical and metaphysical light invoked by Erigena and Grosseteste'.[75]

Anticipation through image construction

David Crosswaite's *Film No 1* (1971) reveals some particularly interesting details on progressive image construction. In Roger Hammond's introduction for Webber's *Shoot Shoot Shoot* 'Structural/Materialist' programme he could not over-emphasise its importance, suggesting that it revealed Wittgenstein's 'anticipation and intentionality, with the imagery exposing the continual correction of thought and fugitiveness'.[76] This is poetically evident in the way the film builds up, beginning monochromatically with one of the four frames flickering and flashing periodically, then gradually changes to reveal single or multiple frames flashing across the screen. Colour is eloquently added, shaping a kind of visual narrative progression, with the monochromatic images at the start of the film complemented part-way through with the select addition of sepia, pale greens, and then gradually more dense yellows and blues and finally some highly saturated hot pinks and reds.

The screen is divided into four frames by using a series of mattes and filming with an 8mm camera without splitting the 16mm film in the processing stage (as is usually done), thus resulting in the four frames within one 16mm frame. Two abstract images dominate the film: one of barely recognisable night-time traffic, occurring periodically with flashing lights of passing cars. The other is a kind of barbed circle, at times 'stationary' and at others spinning and swirling. Both negative and positive image are utilised, with a steady build-up of image occurring from start to finish. A complex series of loops were built up in the printing stage, using a system of masks, with colour added to the original black-and-white footage, creating a dynamic rendition of colourful explosions with the abstract images.

Periodically, a soft whirring, rhythmic sound is heard complementing the whirling and spinning spirals, ensuring continued absorption not unlike the cyclical score (by Brian Eno) and build-up of image in Le Grice's poetic (and much referenced for good reason) *Berlin Horse* (1970), with repetition in both films creating a more lively sense of engagement than some of the more austere structural films seeking to negate the image. Both films begin monochromatically with colour gradually added, the use of negative and positive imagery, reversed images, double-exposures, colour filters and so on. These films are beautifully composed and seductive though their complex simplicity, rhythmic score (visual and auditory) and repetitions, revealing the pleasure of being let loose to experiment in a room full of printing/processing equipment.

Humour, play and sound/image

The disjunction between sound and image in Ian Breakwell's *Repertory* (1973) and John Smith's *Girl Chewing Gum* (1976) raises some interesting questions about film narrative. Humour, little in evidence in most structural and material experimentation, is a crucial factor in both films. *Repertory* consists of a continuous tracking shot around the outside of a closed theatre building, with Breakwell's voiceover detailing a day-by-day account of productions taking place inside. The vibrant descriptions of events, interspersed with random details about the position of the curtains or footlights, stand in marked contrast to the drab, dishevelled exterior of the building. The details, enticing the viewer to imagine the possibility of events taking place in the theatre, are representative of Breakwell's ongoing interest in the mundane. His use of humour transforms the boring aspects of life in a banal manner, whereby, as Mike Sperlinger suggests, the 'unresolved tension between the image on the screen and the voiceover' creates an ambiguity with theatre presented as 'at once as a healthy eruption of the absurd into drab daily life, and at the same time an arbitrary confinement of it'.[77] The soundtrack therefore instrumentally directs the viewer's imagination to construct images and 'see' these theatre productions, bringing imaginary colour and life to the film, despite the fact that the screen only shows dull images of bricks, walls and boarded-up windows of a building in a state of disrepair.

In *Girl Chewing Gum* humour similarly operates by forcing the viewer to question what is being presented in the soundtrack. The voiceover initially appears to be that of a film director instructing the cinematographer and the movements of the actors. Although events initially occur as instructed, the viewer soon realises that the scenes being 'choreographed' are far too complex for such evidently easy cohesion as most of the film consists of a wide shot of a busy street corner with cars, buses and pedestrians moving in and out of frame. The humour becomes evident as 'actors' in the film seemingly obey the directed orders. Before the close of the film a cut to a change of scenery 'ambiguously locates the commentator in a distant field', thus disclosing the 'director's' location.[78]

Girl Chewing Gum established Smith's fondness for creating an illusion through word-play, image and narrative, also evident in *Associations* (1975) and later films such as *Gargantuan* (1992).[79] Breakwell was similarly preoccupied with humour in all areas of his diverse art practice, questioning the roles played by image and word, and asking 'what can you do in words and what can you do in pictures?'[80] Relationships between sound and image were important in defining the political or provocative nature of image (as Godard explored extensively). In his review of structural film theories, Paul Arthur expressed his surprise that Gidal tended to avoid discussions of the sound/image disjunction. Arthur noted that Gidal suggested that 'juxtaposition does not ensure a questioning situation and seemed to reject sound as having a major role'.[81] The disjunctive sound/image, however, played a significant role in opening up spaces for investigation as these two films demonstrate, as they playfully open up questions about narrative construction with 'words and pictures'.

Playfulness – in contrast to more austere theoretical engagements with film – is also key to Marilyn Halford's *Hands Knees and Boompsa Daisy* (1973) and *Footsteps* (1974), with child's play resorted to as Halford used the structure of a game and her background in dance to shape the films. In *Hands Knees and Boompsa Daisy* she performs the game of the title with her on-screen filmed image shown in negative. In *Footsteps* Halford plays the game 'footsteps' with the 'camera' creeping up on her from behind. The first half is silent, with images in negative of Halford standing in front of a high brick wall with her back to the viewer. She periodically turns around quickly, attempting to catch out her 'playmate' (the camera), as the camera moves ever closer, capturing face and upper body in animated action before swinging back across trees and grass to take its position to creep up on Halford once again. The second half of the film is a near-repetition of the first half, although it is complemented by a light-hearted piano score and shown in positive film. Catherine Russell identified that '[c]hildhood was a privileged theme in the avant-garde of the 1960s as the site of a spontaneity and uncorrupted vision that was sought as an ideal of visionary cinema'.[82] Although Halford, Breakwell and Smith's films are not in Sitney's visionary strain of filmmaking, which Russell alludes to here, the combination of child's play (content) and more serious experimentation with structural, formal and material aspects and humour make these engaging films.

Sound as narrative formation

The films discussed here by David Hall, Peter Greenaway and Chris Welsby demonstrate how two films with similar visual imagery can operate on completely different levels due to the content of the soundtrack. Although Greenaway had no involvement with the LFMC, he was aware of wider discourses and practices surrounding formal and structural filmmaking:

> It was the time of structuralism. There was a great desire for the very matter of self-conscious filmmaking. There was a lot of concern for organising film strategies based upon number counts, equations, etc. And I was I suppose a sponge for all that activity. I myself wanted to make a contribution.[83]

Greenaway was critical of the seriousness with which 1970s structural or formal filmmaking was taken up, but his obsession with mathematics, games and structure in his short (and later feature) films led Curtis (somewhat ironically I would suggest) to state that 'in time, the most dedicated structural/formal filmmaker would prove to be Peter Greenaway'.[84]

In the first two films discussed here, Welsby's *Stream Line* (1976) and Greenaway's *Water Wrackets* (1975), some interesting issues are raised relating to sound and narrative. *Stream Line* consists of a single tracking-shot covering approximately nine metres of a stream bed, filmed from above in 'real time'. Welsby constructed a complicated mechanism to hold the camera and track along the stream, enabling him to visually navigate the stream. Sound was recorded synchronously, and the only 'drama', as Welsby called it, was when the close shots of the water became faster as the water burbled over rocks.[85] In many ways *Stream Line* is a simple film, operating as a structured investigation across space and time in landscape, belying the complexity of the filming mechanism used.

The visual images in Greenaway's *Water Wrackets* are comparable to Welsby's *Stream Line*, although there is no single shot (as in *Stream Line*) but multiple, peaceful images of nature – water, trees, insects, grass, fallen trees – with an absence of action. These are quiet, meditative scenes of nature. Greenaway's film is, however, transformed from one of still, rural contemplation by the voice of the narrator as he recounts a bloody family saga – of feuds, fallen heroes and villains – taking place in the pictured landscape. Intermittent deep, sonorous sounds occur in breaks in the voiceover and as with Breakwell's *Repertory* – albeit differently regarding subject matter – the viewer of *Water Wrackets* is compelled to imagine the scenes of violence and bloodshed taking place in this idyllic landscape. Therefore, what clearly distinguishes *Water Wrackets* from *Stream Line* is the narrative structure produced by the soundtrack, appearing to forge the random compilation of calm scenes of nature into chronological order. Interestingly, however, Welsby's *Stream Line* has more of a chronological visual narrative, but imposes itself less on the viewer as he/she is allowed to navigate slowly along with the burbling sound of water as the camera makes its path along the stream.

Hall's *Vertical* (1970) and Greenaway's *Vertical Features Remake* (1978) provide further examples where two similar films reveal the soundtrack distinctly ordering the narrative. As with the previous two films, similarities are evident in the visual imagery, yet the films operate on vastly different levels due to the soundtrack. In *Vertical*, Hall explored the viewers' perception of perspective in film. By filming figures in landscapes from diverse camera angles or alongside vertical markers, Hall forces the viewer to question his/her reading of perspective, as the figures and the vertical markers sit at odds with accepted notions of perspective. Although *Vertical* has a soundtrack consisting of ambient sound, this in no way shapes any narrative aspects in the film.

Greenaway's *Vertical Features Remake* appears to be a direct reference to Hall's *Vertical*, with the narrative of the former being about a fictional character remaking a film based on instructions and fragments from an original, but lost, film. The film-within-the-film is made four times, each time following rigorous mathematical and structuring devices accompanied by a narrative voiceover recording the sequence of events. While Greenaway noted that he wanted to make a contribution to 'structuralism', his comment on the motivation behind the making of some early films clearly demonstrates a critique, as well as an engagement:

> At this particular time of making there was a great concern amongst English filmmakers for notions of structuralism. So in a sense, although the manufacture of images of English rustic landscape are serious enough, the way they've been arranged and the comments made upon it, has the feelings of being a mocking documentary.[86]

The visual images in *Vertical Features Remake* bear some resemblance to Hall's earlier *Vertical,* particularly with the focus on the vertical object. Landscape shots with poles, trees or other vertical objects construct a dialogue between the natural forms and the vertical shape. If *Vertical Features Remake* is watched silently, it operates in a similar fashion to Hall's *Vertical* as the viewer is urged to question what is perceived and how the perception of objects in relation to one another operates within the landscapes. In parodying the seriousness of structural filmmaking *Vertical Features Remake* is, according to Greenaway, 'both a celebration and a critique of structuralist theory, unthinkingly and stupidly dominant in film circles in the Seventies'.[87] The voiceover in *Vertical Features Remake* is instrumental in structuring the narrative as the complex story unfolds of how the film-within-the-film is to be constructed. This raises some pertinent points about the importance of a verbal soundtrack, not only in creating a linear account but also, in articulating an explicit narrative or account.

Although the soundtrack as narrative formation forms a key part in the narrative construction of dominant cinema, the experimental films focused on here also reveal some interesting ways in which the soundtrack complements (as in *Berlin Horse, Film No 1* and in Halford's films), subverts (as in Breakwell and Smith's films) or simply shapes a narrative through 'storytelling' as Greenaway's do, thus adding to the diversity in structural and material experimentation, which was far less ascetic and restrained of fun and playfulness than some accounts may imply. For further accounts of these forms of experimentation, the texts mentioned above by Gidal, Le Grice and Sitney, as well as Mark Webber's *Shoot Shoot Shoot* broadsheet (2002), Danino/Mazière *The Undercut Reader* (2003) and Hamlyn's *Film Art Phenomena* (2003), also reveal the extent of diversity in (mostly) LFMC filmmaking.

Critiques of the formal ideological position

In the mid-1970s doubts were raised about the radical and political nature of structural filmmaking. Anthony McCall announced his reservations at the Edinburgh Festival's 'International Forum of Avant-Garde Film' (1976) and published '1973–75. Closure', signalling a shift in his artistic direction, in the journal *Wallpaper* a year later.[88] In his unpublished statement McCall said:

> [A]vant-garde film, has slipped sideways into a network every bit as limiting, every bit as ideologically bound to a status quo, as the movie industry itself. The Museums of Modern Art have become our Odeons [sic] Leicester Square. Increasingly, the work is identified and practiced more as a visual style, than as a continuing exploration of the problematic of doing film, doing art, in this culture. Whatever political significance this work was beginning to acquire is now being negated by widespread promotion within the official system of art validation – one that occurs as a pervasive abstract imprint on an international scale, without authentic connection to the special social geography of each city, region or country.[89]

McCall, speaking from a position of affiliation with 'conceptual artists' working with film, criticised the co-option of these avant-garde practices into the gallery system, leading to a commercialism that newer experimental practices in the 1960s had sought to undermine (as discussed in Chapter 1 in relation to anti-commodification). During the same period, LFMC filmmaker Mike Dunford also criticised the LFMC's dominant theoretical position, with his Marxist/Leninist attack being particularly damning as it came from a fellow structuralist filmmaker. He admonished filmmakers (and theorists) of closely participating in the reproduction of the ideological function they defined themselves as being against, namely the dominant, commercial cinema.[90]

Gidal's theory/practice dualism would also come to undermine his filmmaking as some of his most ardent arguments, such as his attack on representation, and the disjunction between his theory and practice opened up additional avenues for criticism. Hamlyn, for example, observed that:

> Taken as a whole, Gidal's 'negative project' could be seen as paradoxical. He is against representation/reproduction and yet the large body of films constitutes a vigorous, even enthusiastic way of exploring

and developing the range of possible ways of not-representing, or, more accurately, withholding full or firm representations. On the negative view, one can see the myriad ways in which narration and illusionism can return and corrupt the project. They are always present, just 'outside', pushing on the door against which Gidal is leaning.[91]

Stephen Heath also questioned Gidal's uncompromising position as filmmaker/theorist in 'Afterword' (1979), identifying that the dismissal of all forms of filmmaking posed a significant dilemma:

> There is for Gidal a radical impossibility: *the history of cinema*. The fundamental criticism made of everyone from the Berwick Street Collective to Akerman, Oshima to LeGrice (even LeGrice), is that their films are part of that history, return its representation, that they are in that cinema, repeat its implications.[92] (Heath's emphasis)

The difficulty with Gidal's negation – especially against representation – is that the use of the film medium invariably creates a contradiction-in-terms. Unless the work was minimised to an extreme degree, as in Nam June Paik's *Zen for Film* (1964) or Anthony McCall's *Line Describing a Cone* (1973), then the film medium, particularly with filmed 'image' (as all of Gidal's films were), would be problematic. Perhaps the better solution for such negations could be found in McCall's *Long Film for Ambient Light* (1975), where no film was evident and was only referred to in the title, or better still in John Stezaker's 'idea for a film – concept committed to the page'.[93]

My approach to identifying some of the problems related to structural/material film, and its place in the dominant readings of this history, in no way intends to undermine Le Grice and Gidal's important theoretical (and filmic) positions that brought much richness to this decade, which Hamlyn's critique also recognised:

> In retrospect, it can be seen that Gidal's and Le Grice's anti-cinema polemics could not by themselves constitute a self-sufficient artistic theory, and this partly explains the decline of Structural film. However, their theories can usefully serve as a set of background beliefs to sustain a filmmaking which reinstates to its programme the investing of perception, exploring the peculiarities of the human eye, the experience of time and movement and their complex relationship to film technology.[94]

Certainly, their theories established many invaluable insights, forging important positions on the politics of representation and perception – and qualities inherent in film structure, process and materiality – with which contemporary filmmakers such as Hamlyn, Sherwin (collaborating with Lynne Loo), Butler/Mirza and others continue to engage. It has, however, been necessary to question the dominance of these positions as they not only stand in the way of accommodating more personal, expressive forms of 1970s filmmaking, they also deny a more solid understanding of the bedrock formed in the decade that has shaped (and continues to shape) the wider field in contemporary moving image.

Concluding thoughts

The examples presented in this chapter have identified a range of approaches to structural and material filmmaking, and recognised how readings of films could differ depending on how films were framed within theoretical discourses. The framing of films within specific theoretical discourses could imbue the viewer's approach to interpreting the film, and at times put a slant on the filmmaker's intentionality, as discussions surrounding Gidal's *Room Film 1973* revealed, as these did not always correlate with the viewer's reading of a film. It was also established how integral relationships between sound and image significantly shaped narrative construction. Certainly, theoretical discourses related to structural and material experimentation were important in opening up debate, discussion and film experimentation, as the examples shown here and which the dominant histories reveal, but these positions also required re-examining to ascertain their continued dominance in accounts of the histories. The asceticism and Gidal's 'anti-representation' in formal filmmaking also posed problems for the women filmmakers discussed in the following chapter, whose films are also sufficiently diverse in themselves, clearly demonstrating that no 'return to image' ever occurred. This is the way it was theorised, framed and has problematically continued to be perpetuated without question. Indeed, all those involved in building up the LFMC (and ensuring its longevity) and related structural and material frameworks for film experimentation should absolutely be recognised, but the lens of retrospective distance can also offer new views into the past that merit reconsideration.

6
Women and Film

This chapter explores the diversity in 1970s women's experimental film-making, considering how women engaged either explicitly with feminist discourses or followed their own directives to make experimental films, unconfined by historical precedents or legacies that might restrain their male counterparts. Films were informed by feminism, developments in the arts, formal experimentation and by film theories related to Marxism, psychoanalysis, semiotics and structuralism. Wider political and theoretical frameworks related to feminism and women's filmmaking are discussed at the outset to contextualise the complex spheres of influence. This will be followed by discussions prevalent in the 1970s, deliberating whether a feminine aesthetic existed, as these provide some particularly interesting frameworks for consideration. Thereafter, a range of experimental films will be discussed, focusing on the domestic, the gendered film text, the aesthetics of ephemerality and how history, language and ideology were used to question women's historically inscribed roles.

Political and theoretical frameworks for filmmaking

While the first wave of feminism focused on women's judicial rights, the second wave of 1960s feminism argued for gender equality in education and work, as well as access to free health- and childcare. Although a collective spirit – in both the US and Britain – consolidated the early stages of the Women's Movement, fragmentation intensified in the 1970s as differing priorities led to more specific feminist campaigning. Imelda Whelehan, however, noted:

> There may not have been one dominant definition of feminism, but all strands were rooted in the belief that women suffer injustice

because of their sex; and the emergence of women's liberation as not only a movement but an intellectual tendency too proved attractive to many women.[1]

The intellectual tendency was important for stimulating artists and filmmakers, manifesting itself in diverse discourses informing creative production. 'The personal is political' personified the Women's Movement, for despite the differing concerns of campaign groups and individuals, essentially all feminist politics necessitated the scrutiny of private life. The publication of influential feminist texts by Betty Friedan, Germaine Greer, Kate Millett and Juliet Mitchell (amongst others) raised awareness and further mobilised action, with British feminist magazines such as *Spare Rib*, *Red Rag* and *Shrew* also providing important platforms for dissemination. US feminist film journals also included *Women and Film* (1972–75) and *Camera Obscura* (from 1976), providing a voice for specific concerns.

One of the most influential essays for women filmmakers was almost certainly Laura Mulvey's seminal 'Visual Pleasure and Narrative Cinema' (1975), taking a Freudian approach to critique women's roles as objects of desire in dominant, 'Hollywood' cinema and opening up significant discourses for visual and intellectual engagement with film. D. N. Rodowick posited Mulvey's essay as 'the watershed article' in relation to women and film, identifying it as 'a polemic for an avant-garde feminist practice' and 'a key text of political modernism'.[2] He maintained that Mulvey's concerns should also be understood within the broader framework of feminist theory:

> In this respect Mulvey should be read in the context of the work by Juliet Mitchell, Julia Kristeva, Michèle Montrelay, Luce Irigaray, and other important thinkers, all of whom had published pathbreaking texts by the mid-70s. All of these writers, including Mulvey, introduced another important element. The psychoanalytic study of sexual difference was aimed not only at a critique of patriarchal culture; the reigning ideas of film and cultural theory were equally open to critique for how they represented (or forgot to represent) the concerns of feminism.[3]

Mulvey collaborated with theorist/filmmaker Peter Wollen on a number of films, putting into practice their interests in counter-cinema and avant-garde filmmaking. In their seminal *Riddles of the Sphinx* (1977) formal and aesthetic devices were utilised for its theoretically informed feminist premise. The film was framed through the Oedipus myth and centred on a mother's close relationship with her young child as they find a sense of separation and independence. The film takes an anti-narrative stance informed by the film theories of, amongst others, Jean-Luc Godard and Andre Bazin. In Mulvey's subsequent essay, 'Film, Feminism and the Avant-garde' (1978), she proposed further polemics and new possibilities for narrative filmic experimentation, citing Wollen's 'The Two Avant-gardes' and the useful examples Sergei Eisenstein, Dziga Vertov and Jean-Luc Godard provided in demonstrating integral links between form and content:

> Semiotics foregrounds language and emphasises both the crucial importance of the signifier (for a long time overlooked and subordinated to the signified) and the dual nature of the sign, thus suggesting the aesthetic mileage that can be gained by play on separation between its two aspects. For feminists this split has a triple action: aesthetic fascination with discontinuities; pleasure from disrupting the traditional unity of the sign; and theoretical advance from investigating language and the production of meaning.[4]

This semiotic expansion – rather than the reductionist position taken by conceptualists and structural/materialist filmmakers – would be essential for engaging with feminist discourses and was also outlined in feminist film theorist, E. Ann Kaplan's analysis:

> This confrontation entails making completely new use of cinematic form – organization of individual images (the entire mise en scène), the choice of camera angle, distance, lighting, etc., and ultimately even the technical equipment itself. All the audience's expectations are to be challenged and normal kinds of identification refused.[5]

Both Mulvey and Kaplan's assertions that political films needed to be made politically (as Godard had posited in his 1970 manifesto) informed possibilities without establishing specific modes of operation or prescriptive filmmaking aesthetics, and rather opened up diverse approaches for women's filmmaking.[6]

Not all women filmmakers, however, engaged with these discourses explicitly during the decade. At the LFMC, for example, where numerous films were made by women – certainly with an awareness of feminist discourses – filmmaking was (especially in the first half of the decade) mostly informed by hands-on engagements with film materiality, processing and printing, influenced by the predominant structural and materialist position. This is evident in films such as Annabel Nicolson's

Slides (1971), Lis Rhodes' *Light Music* (1975) and Gill Eatherley's *Hand Grenade* (1971). Increased politicisation, however, brought some changes, as Nicolson identified: 'our consciousness was changing very rapidly and there was a gap that was opening up'; and by the end of the decade – evident in Rhodes' *Light Reading* (1979) – more political feminist engagements with film came to the fore as women consolidated their position more firmly.[7]

The women's withdrawal from the 'Film as Film' exhibition (discussed in Chapter 1) and from the LFMC (in 1979) resulted in the formation of the women's film collective, Circles (1979). While women at the LFMC became more politicised Nicolson made it clear that the decision to withdraw from the LFMC was not taken lightly as it had generally been a supportive environment for women filmmakers:

> I think it was probably very painful for all concerned because we had all worked together and been allies. Certainly for myself I'd had plenty of support from the men in that group: critical support and practical support.[8]

This need for women to consolidate resources was, however, according to Whelehan, not uncommon practice in the 1970s:

> Most second wave feminism focused on social constructionist, rather than essentialist, arguments and therefore casting men as the 'enemy' was tacitly accepted as a temporary socio-historical subject positioning which would be open to transformation. Although perhaps the majority of feminists did not foresee total separatism as a workable long-term solution, they craved the autonomy to construct a movement for women.[9]

This would be important for mobilising Circles' activities in the 1980s, but it is also important to note that younger women filmmakers such as Anna Thew, Cordelia Swann and Jean Matthee continued working at the LFMC, producing diverse and provocative films in the 1980s on their own terms.

Specialised film events were important platforms for the development of feminist discourses in the 1970s, with the 'First International Women's Film Festival' taking place in New York in June 1972 and similar events following suit in London and Edinburgh. A season of 'Women's Cinema' (1973) at the NFT and Edinburgh Film Festivals (1976 and 1979) included women's programmes and discussions, with an LFMC seminar, 'Feminism, Fiction and the Avant-garde' (1978), presented by three editors from the US feminist film journal *Camera Obscura*. In their first issue, the editors had 'explicitly acknowledged their debt to the work of British feminist theorists of cinema and stated that they see themselves as following up on this initial research'.[10] Significantly, women filmmakers and activists also recognised the need to progress beyond the first stage of recovering women's lost histories and critically assessing sexism to find new ways of making films. Mulvey noted that she was struck 'by the historic conjuncture between feminist film theory, the *Camera Obscura* presentation, and the Co-op, home of avant-gardist film practice'.[11] Amidst the extensive activism and discussion in the 1970s some particularly interesting debates would emerge about politics, theory and aesthetics, which would be instrumental for women artists and filmmakers working in the 1970s and in subsequent decades.

Questions of a feminine aesthetic

The question 'Is there a feminine aesthetic?' provoked particularly interesting debates about patriarchy and language in the 1970s. This will be considered here in some depth as it opens up especially lively frameworks for discussion. The question was, for example, deliberated in a special women's issue of *Art and Artists* (1973), with Lucy Lippard stating:

> I, for one, am convinced this differentiation exists, but for every time I can be specific about it there are endless times in which it remains just out of reach. Perhaps it is impossible to pin it down or draw any but the most personal conclusions until women's place in society is indeed equalized and women's work can be studied outside of the confines of oppressive conditioning.[12]

Similar reservations to Lippard's about pinning down a specific aesthetic were deliberated throughout the decade, with debates preoccupying artists, filmmakers, critics and theorists. It was the central focus of an AIR Gallery seminar in 1977, including artists and critics such as Mary Kelly, Susan Hiller, Tina Keane and Caroline Tisdall, with Linda Mallett posing some pertinent questions:

> Is there, in fact, an especially female art practice and if so, how does it relate to the masculine mainstream? Is there an equivalent female aesthetic, either feminist or non-feminist?[13]

No clear answers were forthcoming at the event, but reviewer Sarah Kent, critical of the essentialist nature of these preoccupations, advocated for a need 'to adopt an optimistic and assertive stance in the world', rather than giving personal problems 'a status more important than they merited'.[14]

Mulvey's involvement with The History Group, (which also included Kelly, Juliet Mitchell and Sally Alexander), saw a group of women investigating feminism, psychoanalysis and film. While Mulvey had encouraged new approaches to women's filmmaking, she also questioned whether 'the very act of opposing traditional aesthetics and questioning male-dominated language generate[s] a new language and carr[ies] an aesthetic with it?'[15] In reference to research for women's events at film festivals, Mulvey had also hoped that a historical thread could be drawn to 'reveal a coherent aesthetic', as women's common experience of repression and exploitation in visual media had acted 'as a unifying element for women directors, however different their origins'.[16] It will be useful to deliberate these questions further as they reveal the complexity of the debates, providing some invigorating thoughts for 1970s women's experimental films.

In her article, 'Is there a Feminine Aesthetic?' (1976), Silvia Bovenschen used early literary examples to question the complexity of reconstructing a women's language firmly embedded within patriarchal language. She asked whether possibilities existed for women to redefine themselves within this:

> The analysis of linguistic structures, imagery, the forms and symbols of behaviour and communication, is tough work which has hardly begun. If women are to succeed in freeing themselves from old patterns, in conquering new terrain and – to finally return to the subject at hand – in developing different aesthetic forms, they can do this only on the basis of autonomy.[17]

Autonomy, however, could not mean the invention of a new language, as this was clearly impossible. Bovenschen, however, suggested that a feminine aesthetic was not determined by feminist *content* but rather that the *mode* of production could suggest a feminine perspective. She argued that women should not have to explicitly depict political feminist actions in their work as this would merely reduce it to the level of photo-journalism and outlined her conviction that unrestricted approaches to practice were essential to allow women to explore feminist discourses:

> I believe that feminine artistic production takes place by means of a complicated process involving conquering and reclaiming, appropriating and formulating, as well as forgetting and subverting.[18]

Bovenschen also noted that 'no formal criteria for "feminist art" can be definitively laid down', therefore enabling the categorical rejection of artistic norms, advocating for open-ended experimentation and preventing the 'renewal of the calcified aesthetics debate, this time under the guise of the feminist "approach"'.[19]

Clearly a tabula rasa – the creation of a new cinematic language, for example – was impossible. Yet perhaps the advantage women, somewhat ironically had, could be seen to exist in their exclusion from some established theoretical or critical discourses dominated by historically patriarchal frameworks. This, arguably, provided the liberty to experiment without building on established fields of reference. Some idea of what may be indicative of a feminine aesthetic can thus be found in the individual and personal approaches taken by women filmmakers.

For this discussion on the complex issues surrounding the existence of a feminine aesthetic Teresa de Lauretis' response to Bovenschen's article a numbers of years later provides some interesting developments. De Lauretis cited the twofold conclusion drawn in Bovenschen's opening paragraphs:

> Is there a feminine aesthetic? [...] Certainly there is, if one is talking about *aesthetic awareness* and *modes of sensory perception*. Certainly not, if one is talking about an unusual variant of artistic production or about a painstakingly constructed theory of art.[20] (Bovenschen's italics)

De Lauretis noted that the answer reflected some of the contradictions inherent in the previous 15 years of the Women's Movement, acknowledging that, on the one hand, an intrinsic condemnation of historical, patriarchal, bourgeois dominance had been necessary to forge a radical analysis, yet, on the other, a positive, political approach to women's social issues had also been essential to forward debates. She further identified that this was also indicative of the evident dichotomy in 1970s women's filmmaking, whereby either documentary-style approaches or more formal approaches engaging with form and content were taken to address women's issues.

De Lauretis was critical of the continued need 'to ask whether there is a feminine or female aesthetic, or a specific language of women's cinema', suggesting that this represented continuing to be 'caught in the master's house'.[21] In other words, if women's cinema continued to be positioned in opposition to men's cinema, this could lead to unproductive, essentialist positions, further serving to alienate women from the central debates. De Lauretis did not call for an indiscriminate rejection of the 'rigorous analysis and experimentation on the formal processes of meaning production', but instead advocated for the 'redefinition of aesthetic and formal knowledge' through feminist theory.[22] She argued that this should include attention to specific *details*, providing a feminine sense of identification for the spectator, and enabling an engagement with film from a specifically feminine perspective. This was to be understood as 'saying that a film whose visual and symbolic space is organised in this manner *addresses the spectator as a woman*, regardless of the gender of the viewers' (de Lauretis' emphasis).[23]

De Lauretis provided the example of Belgian filmmaker Chantal Akerman's *Jeanne Dielman, 23 Quai du Commerce – 1080 Bruxelles* (1975), suggesting that 'the pre-aesthetic is already fully aesthetic' in the film.[24] She argued that this was not due to the use of specific camera angles or particular narrative directives, but that the 'pre-aesthetic' paid specific attention to ordinary, mundane actions such as peeling potatoes or making coffee. While these did not hold the viewer in a state of suspense through narrative expectation, she argued that they formed a dialogue between temporality and insignificant actions:

> What the film constructs – formally and artfully, to be sure – is a picture of female experience, of duration, perception, events, relationships and silences, which feels immediately and unquestioningly true. And in this sense the 'pre-aesthetic' is *aesthetic* rather than *aestheticised*.[25] (de Lauretis' emphasis)

Akerman also supported de Lauretis' idea on the pre-aesthetic as she believed that few women had the confidence to follow through with their feelings in film, for instance by showing gestures for no other reason than wanting to do so. Akerman suggested that the difficulty lay in the *means* of expression, rather than in the content which was 'the most simple and obvious thing'.[26] She also asserted that women dealt with content forgetting 'to look for formal ways to express what they are and what they want, their own rhythms, their own way of looking at things'.[27] Akerman believed that not having contempt for her own feelings was 'the reason why I think it's a feminist film – not just what it says but *what* is shown and *how* it's shown' (de Lauretis' emphasis).[28]

Certainly, deliberating whether a feminine aesthetic existed in women's filmmaking was a complex task, resisting unproblematic conclusions. Further 1970s deliberations included discussions at the Edinburgh Film Festival's (1979) 'Feminism and Cinema' event, with Lesley Stern questioning whether 'formal experimentation can *inherently* be more *political*' or whether this only served to further alienate a broader audience, conflicting with the consciousness-raising feminists sought (Stern's italics).[29] This was one of the criticisms of the Berwick Street Collective's formally innovative campaign film *Nightcleaners* (1975), which sought to raise awareness about female office workers but was criticised for potentially alienating viewers due to its editing style. While Mulvey conceded that it appeared 'increasingly doubtful whether a unified tradition could be traced, except on the superficial level of women as content', the feminist film critic Patricia Erens outlined that 'for most viewers, films with strong [female] central characters and didactic messages have come to represent the feminist aesthetic, primarily because of their relationship with the women's movement'.[30] While Mulvey and Erens' analyses were perhaps useful in identifying the broader landscape of women's filmmaking, women's experimental films did not always explicitly centre on female characters. Nicolson revealed how women's approaches to filmmaking at the LFMC also differed significantly to other formal or documentary-informed approaches:

> We were thinking about what the films were saying, because we were in quite an odd position to, say, the feminist network. We weren't making films with a social, documentary content about women's experience. We were very sympathetic to it, but we weren't actually doing that. We were working in a more abstract way and exploring forms, but there wasn't a recognisable female content. So we were in this odd relationship to the rest of the feminist network, who couldn't see what we were doing, and our natural allies were the men at the Co-op, who we had grown up with, so to speak, artistically.[31]

By the end of the decade, however, experimental films such as the LFMC filmmaker Lis Rhodes' *Light Reading* (1979) and Sally Potter's *Thriller* (1979) would engage formally and aesthetically with feminist discourses successfully in less didactic form.

In a lecture given at the 'Oxford Women's Studies Committee' (1978) Mulvey reflected on women's involvement with feminism, theory and experimental filmmaking, concluding that a single approach or aesthetic language was not evident in women's filmmaking, making it easier to 'exemplify tendencies and movements', rather than claiming that an overriding aesthetic existed.[32] It will be useful to keep these deliberations in mind when considering the diversity of films discussed below, in order to identify tendencies or specific feminine traits. It is also evident from the films discussed that a 'return to image' did not occur at the end of the decade and that expressive, personal and image-rich filmmaking was ever-present in women's filmmaking throughout the 1970s.

Diversity in women's filmmaking

The domestic

The domestic, with the focus on women's historically-inscribed roles, provided a source of inspiration for a number of 1970s experimental films. And the 'feminine aesthetic', relating to attention to detail discussed by de Lauretis and Akerman, offered especially interesting points for deliberation. Joanna Davis's *Often During the Day* (1979) is a black-and-white film consisting of photographs and filmed footage which forms a record of minor events taking place in a kitchen. Hand-tinted photographs of seemingly mundane objects such as a tea-strainer, bread on the morning breakfast table or a cat's bowl are given focused attention, thereby rendering significant the objects (and residue of domestic activities) easily overlooked in the usual passage through the day. Davis explains the inspiration behind her film:

> I made the film because I had to stop ignoring the small daily tasks which seemed to occupy a large proportion of time, like washing up, cooking, caring for a space, jobs done in order that I could get on with my real work. For most women 'jobs done' in order that someone else can get on with the 'real work', in order that someone else can enter 'real life' and cope with 'real issues'.[33]

The film reveals a kind of meditation on the pleasures and frustrations of domestic life, with Akerman's comments about *Jeanne Dielman* being equally valid for Davis's film: 'I give space to things which were never, almost never, shown in that way [...] If you choose to show a woman's gestures so precisely, it's because you love them'.[34]

The soundtrack is important for contextualising 1970s socio-political events, with radio broadcasts announcing a bombing in Northern Ireland and playing the song 'Dancing in the City'. Significantly, a male voice also reads extracts from Annie Oakley's *Sociology of Housework* and Davis's voice describes the activities taking place in her kitchen, with painstaking attendance to detail relating to the topography of the kitchen and the minor events taking place within it.[35] Some comparisons can be drawn here with one of the circular pans in Mulvey/Wollen's *Riddles of the Sphinx* (1977), which takes a 360° view of a kitchen with a mother preparing scrambled eggs for her young child.

Rhodes' comment about Davis's film made during my interview with Rhodes sheds some interesting light on the conflicted feelings of domesticity Davis reveals in her film:

I mean it's about the male domination of space [...] I think that runs through it, doesn't it? I can't see how it doesn't, and indeed I think that is the case. And I suspect that one could say very much the same thing with *Jeanne Dielman* which I think is a very interesting film equally. In a sense to do with space, but also to do with economy.[36]

This notion of colonisation was also expressed by feminist historian Sheila Rowbotham in her influential feminist text *Woman's Consciousness, Man's World* (1973). In this way, the close examination of domestic space, which Akerman and Davis's films reveal, exposes the inherent anxieties about the male 'colonisation' of space, thereby setting up an emotionally ambivalent relationship to the domestic space, which is apprehended by the 'loving' and close attention to detailed care given, yet is also permeated by feelings of entrapment.

In the contemplation of the ordinary and domestic, the films satisfy Bovenschen's criteria for a feminine 'aesthetic awareness' in the utilisation of 'modes of sensory perception', particularly through the attention to detail given to formal aspects of filming and editing and in Davis's use of close-up, hand-tinted photographs, the pace and rhythm of the visual and audio 'narratives' and relationships between sound and image.[37] The 'modes of sensory perception' are located in the *details* of what is perceived in the space (kitchen), and how Davis acts on these using the camera to claim the intimate and homely space as her own. This is Davis's 'camera-eye', framing, fixing and paying attention to mundane objects such as the cat's food bowl, or to activities such as cutting bread. As Davis says, such things are often ignored yet 'occupy a big proportion of time'.[38]

The idea of personal filmic perception focused on ordinary activities centred on the home and 'ordinary' life is also particularly evident in Margaret Tait's unique approach to filmmaking. Her films *Tailpiece* (1976) and *Place of Work* (1976), discussed in Chapter 4, observed the detailed emptying of her family home, and close attention to detail is evident throughout Tait's films, exemplified particularly in earlier films such as *Portrait of Ga* (1952). Akerman's suggestion that women need to find their own way of looking at things is therefore particularly apt in relation to these women's approaches to filmmaking. In her discussion on *Jeanne Dielman*, Akerman further elaborated on these ideas, which are equally relevant to Davis' and Tait's films:

I give space to things which were never, almost never, shown in that way, like the daily gestures of a woman. They are the lowest in the hierarchy of film images [...] But more than the content, it's because of the style. If you chose to show a woman's gestures so precisely, it's because you love them. In some way you recognize those gestures that have always been denied and ignored.[39]

The loving attention to detail is epitomised in Tait's *Portrait of Ga* by the focus on her mother unwrapping a sticky sweet or stirring sugar into a cup of tea. Sensitive attention to detail is also evident in Tait's *Ariel* (1974), where small details in nature, such as a bird alighting on a branch, an earthworm in the soil or leaves blowing in the wind shed poetic light on the ordinary in nature. Tait's approaches to filmmaking also relate specifically to Bovenschen's concept of personal 'modes of sensory perception', as Sarah Neely elucidates:

Tait, who described her technique of 'breathing' with the camera and liked to use Lorca's phrase 'stalking the image' in reference to her own practices, allows the camera time to explore [...] she is preoccupied with catching the 'momentary', and 'subtle' gestures. Like the barely perceptible opening of the clover, Tait's breathing with the camera, or stalking the image, aims to give pause to the image, allowing for – as is the case with both of these portrait films [*Portrait of Ga* and *Hugh MacDiarmid* (1964)] – a glimpse of the real person.[40]

Perhaps it is this giving 'pause to the image', cherishing the understated, small gestures, as Davis does in *Often During the Day* and which Akerman and Tait see as being central to their filmmaking practices, that exemplifies Bovenschen's 'mode of sensory perception' – the *way* that filmmaking is approached, rather than only focusing on what is recorded or the mechanics of production.

The domestic act of sweeping in Gill Eatherley's expanded cinema work *Aperture Sweep* (1973) skilfully references both filmmaking (camera aperture and light) and domestic action and forms part of the 'Light Occupations' series (1973–4), as Eatherley explains: 'Light occupations in both senses of the word, light meaning lightweight or menial occupations, like sweeping, or light meaning the light from the sky, or light from a projector, artificial light'.[41] Eatherley interacted with the screened image of a shadowy figure in the act of sweeping, by sweeping the screen with a microphone attached to the broom. *Sweeping in Aperture Sweep* also resonates with Nicolson's *Sweeping the Sea* (1975), with both taking enigmatic and humorous approaches to this mundane and ordinary domestic action.

Further light-hearted, but more satirical approaches to domestic activities were taken in Helen Chadwick's little-known Super-8 trilogy (documentation of a live performance) *Domestic Sanitation, Bargain Bedroom Bonanza* and *Latex Glamour Rodeo* (1976), which focused on Chadwick and three friends performing, dressed in latex suits and enacting domestic activities such as vacuuming and dusting. The surreal scenario and bizarre charades included 'undergoing gynaecological probing in a dungeon-like living-room as Donny Osmond and an American voice promoting beauty products crackled from a nearby radio', creating a feminist polemic on the fixation of the media and society with female beauty.[42]

In Jayne Parker's *Free Show* (1979) and *RX Recipe* (1980), equally facetious domestic actions are performed in three acts by the actress Clare Winter: *Free Show*: 'Act I – Cutting liver; Act II – Ironing; Act III – Plucking Eyebrows'.[43] The play on danger and violence in these mundane domestic acts is further exaggerated by preceding 8mm clips of circus performances before each filmed action. *RX Recipe* is wonderful for its tongue-in-cheek humour, showing a woman lovingly cleaning and stuffing an eel. She then performs the same cleaning action on her legs before the film suggestively ends, insinuating that she might just perform the same 'stuffing' action on herself. The acerbic humour in Chadwick and Parker's films seems to embolden the points about women's oppression or 'enslavement' to the domestic. These sit in contrast to the quieter observed actions in Davis's film or the theoretically engaged earnestness of *Riddles of the Sphinx*. Thus, no singular way determined how women dealt with the domestic. Instead there was openness to finding voice in diverse modes of articulation.

An interesting contrast to the above films can be drawn with domestic actions performed by Le Grice in his *Time and Motion Study* (1976). The film of Le Grice washing the dishes was recorded by two cameras – one in medium-shot and the other with a wider view of the domestic space – and includes positive and negative colour film stock. In my interview with Le Grice he discussed his own film crisis in the late 1970s as being influenced by feminism, with some focus on the domestic in his trilogy of more narrative films, saying, 'my trilogy related to the issue of where women are placed in film, women's roles, etc. *Time and Motion Study*, of me washing the dishes, was influenced by men's and women's roles'.[44] Interestingly, through Le Grice's preoccupation with film materiality and film structuring processes, the content (domestic task) is given a rather more determined edge, appearing as if he has to provide evidence that he too takes part in mundane domestic duties historically ascribed to women. There is less of the 'loving' attention to detail that Davis,

Tait and Akerman reveal, but rather a double-insistence (two cameras) to record evidence of his actions, which interestingly relate to his comment on feelings of guilt as a male who needs to somehow demonstrate (physically) an engagement with feminist discourses/actions.

The gendered film text

The notion of a gendered film is clearly a debatable issue but in the context of discussions about a feminine aesthetic it provides some provocative thoughts for discussion. In de Lauretis' article she asked 'what formal, stylistic or thematic markers point to a female presence behind the camera?'[45] This question will be considered first in relation to Mary Kelly's *Antepartum* (1973) and Guy Sherwin's *Breathing* (1978), and second through comparative readings of Carolee Scheemann's *Fuses* (1964–67) and Stephen Dwoskin's *Moment* (1970).

The inherent simplicity in *Antepartum* and *Breathing* provides apposite room for investigation as both are short, silent and single-shot, black-and-white films of the same subject matter: a tightly-framed, heavily pregnant torso, not dissimilar to the abstracted subject matter of Susan Hiller's photographic work *10 Months* (1977–79). The camera in both films captures very subtle movements, with the common 'action' being the slight rise and fall of breath as the abdomen moves. In Kelly's film, further action in the form of hands occasionally stroking the abdomen takes place. While both are filmed from fixed camera positions, tightly framed on the pregnant torsos, the body in *Antepartum* is Kelly's own, while *Breathing* is of Sherwin's partner's pregnant form. In Kelly's film the camera is positioned below the pubic area, looking up at her pregnant belly, with the extremely tight framing creating an abstract image, strongly lit from above right, as Siona Wilson elucidates:

> In *Antepartum* the camera is positioned in close proximity to the woman's body. The body remains immobile except for the regular, rhythmic, rising and falling of her breath, and some possible (though hardly detectable) intrauterine movements. Like the camera, the body's position is more or less fixed; there is only slight movement, barely noticeable on the first viewing. Thus, there is a reciprocal mimetic relationship between the body and the camera; each remains more or less fixed and immobile except for some slight movement.[46]

Sherwin's film differs by being a side view of a prone body with a window in the background and a focus on Sherwin's continued preoccupation with light and time. Deke Dusinberre describes *Breathing* as follows:

The camera aperture is opened up and closed down in time with the natural breathing cycle. Subsequent changes in the light exposure and depth of field emphasise different aspects of the image, from skin surface (with subtle disruptions as the infant kicks) to the inversely symmetrical curve of a clothes line seen through the far window.[47]

While the content of both *Antepartum* and *Breathing* relate to the feminine (as intimate portraits of female experience), there are few observations revealing de Lauretis' gendered 'presence behind the camera' in the films, and clearly the strikingly similar films offer up no revelations about the gender of the filmmaker, nor do they provide fixed views relating to discourses on femininity, masculinity or the body. They are small, observed vignettes of experience revealing abstract views of a pregnant body. How the film is framed in exhibition, however, is significant. As Sherwin's *Breathing* forms part of his 'Short Film Series', the focus is more on cinematographic observation, using time/ duration and light with changes in aperture to synchronise with the breathing belly. The 'Short Film Series' can be screened in part and in any order, therefore whichever films precede or follow on from *Breathing* would also potentially offer different readings. *Antepartum*'s original screening was significantly framed within Marxist, feminist discourses as it was shown as part of a Super-8 dual-projection, with Kelly's other film consisting of a close-up of a female factory worker's arm operating machinery. The film therefore literally focused on women's labour – both biological and within the work force – providing provocative spaces for engagement.

While *Antepartum* and *Breathing* provide no direct indication of the gendered filmmaker, Schneemann's *Fuses* (1964–67) and Dwoskin's *Moment* (1970) may offer more distinctive considerations relating to de Lauretis' 'presence behind the camera'. Both centre on sexual acts, with *Fuses* including explicit imagery of heterosexual intercourse and *Moment* focusing on a woman masturbating.

Fuses (first screened in the UK at the Drury Lane Arts Lab, 1968) is a highly personal contemplation of Schneemann and her partner engaged in sexual intercourse, revealed through the nature of the imagery and the way Schneemann worked directly on the film material. *Fuses* was a response to Stan Brakhage's *Window Water Baby Moving* (1959) (a film of Brakhage's wife giving birth), as Schneemann felt that, 'the male persona or the male eye was [...] absorbing and repossessing an essential, unique female process' to the extent that the film 'became the birth giver'.[48] Schneemann felt compelled to take ownership of the female process for *Fuses*, identifying the importance of her role as both filmmaker and camerawoman:

> I did the filming even while I was participant in the action [...] Perhaps because it was made of her own life by a woman, *Fuses* is both a sensuous and equitable interchange; neither lover is 'subject' or 'object'.[49]

While the sexual action appears to be continuous in the 22-minute film, Schneemann amusingly observed that she was, in fact, having to wind out the Bolex camera every 30 seconds, saying, 'Honey I'm back! Where were we?'[50] She also, more seriously, offered further insights into her reasons for being both performer and camerawoman in *Fuses*:

> Partly I would never want to ask anyone else to do what I think I should do. I don't want to be in the hierarchical position of the director who had that separation between instruction, expectation and demand [...] So it was just an experiment: what happens if I use myself – because this is coming out of my lived experience and those sensations of it.[51]

A very important aspect of *Fuses,* revealing the materiality of the film medium, was Schneemann's reworking of the film print. She painted, scratched, baked and burnt it, dipped it in acid and left it outside in the elements, thereby rendering the explicit images to be partially obscured and transforming what would have been a 'conventional' pornographic film into a painterly and sensuous montage. Schneemann's awareness of the more austere aspects of structuralist filmmaking as being a predominantly male domain was also made evident in the text taken from her Super-8 film *Kitch's Last Meal* (1973–76) and used in her seminal *Interior Scroll* (1975) performance (pulled out of her vagina, unfurled like a film-strip and read to the audience), in which she said:

> I met a happy man / a structuralist filmmaker / – but don't call me that / it's / something else I do – / he said we are fond of you / you are charming / but don't / ask us / to look at your films / we cannot / there are certain films / we cannot look at / the personal clutter / the persistence of feelings / the hand-touch sensibility / the diaristic indulgence / the painterly mess.'[52]

Undoubtedly referring to her own films, Schneemann contended that personal, emotional and 'messy' content jarred with more formal,

unemotional (and mostly male) structuralist filmmaking. She amusingly ended the piece by saying that 'he told me he had lived / with
a "sculptress" I asked does / that make me a "film-makeress"? / "On
no," he said. / "We think of / you as a dancer."'[53] As an artist (and as
she also asserted about *Fuses*) Schneemann presented herself *exactly* as
she wanted to be seen – without compromise – differing significantly
to Dwoskin's subject in *Moment*.

Moment presents an interesting counterpoint to Schneemann's *Fuses*,
when considering the gendered 'presence behind the camera', and the
recording of intimate encounters on film. A number of Dwoskin's films
centre on the 'voyeuristic look' in film (as discussed in Chapter 4),
with Dwoskin's voyeuristic eye discussed, notably, as Paul Willeman's
'fourth look' in his 'Voyeurism, the Look and Dwoskin' essay.[54] Many
of the women in Dwoskin's short films are mute, with his scrutinising
'camera-eye' ever observant, although in his earlier film *Alone* (1963)
the woman's inner thoughts are revealed through her voice-over
monologue.

Moment consists of a continuous, fixed, close-up of a woman's head
lying on a red pillow. She is allegedly masturbating and comes to
orgasm, with only the subtleties of facial expressions revealing emo-
tions, and her hand periodically coming into frame as she smokes
a cigarette. Comparisons can be made with Andy Warhol's *Blow Job*
(1964), where all the suggested action is centred on the close-up of a
male face. Thus, as the viewer becomes implicated in the act of voyeurism, an uncomfortable self-reflective engagement occurs, differing to
the viewing of the dominant cinema whereby 'the viewer of Hollywood
cinema is allowed to imagine himself/herself as "invisible"'.[55] Here, the
viewer, through pleasure or discomfort, recognises his/her own voyeuristic viewing, but Curtis also suggested that 'like all [Dwoskin's] work
[it] says as much about the maker and the current viewer, as about its
ostensible subject'.[56]

The aesthetic 'look' of both *Fuses* and *Moment* differs significantly. *Fuses*
is painted over and worked on to slightly obscure or veil the explicit film
imagery, and *Moment*, despite a grainy quality to the image, is explicit in
what is not revealed of the woman's body but what the viewer 'sees' in
her expressions. The different viewing experiences are also attributable to
the editing and structuring of the film. While the continuous fixed shot
of *Moment* allows the viewer to stare and enter into the voyeuristic act
alongside the filmmaker, the fragmented and disrupted way of viewing
Fuses means that the viewer is constantly denied a detailed view of the
action, although as Kate Haug said, these glimpses and 'interference[s] of
the body' actually 'made it sexually charged'.[57]

These observations on *Antepartum, Breathing, Fuses* and *Moment* in no way propose that they reveal an *absolute* gendered film text, but I believe some 'formal, stylistic or thematic markers' can disclose something about the 'presence behind the camera'.[58] The knowledge of the gendered presence of the filmmaker also certainly changes the reading of the film, with the female nude historically presented in art usually for the titivation and voyeuristic scrutiny of the male viewer, whereas women's self-portraiture is more readily seen as a form of reclamation. Would we, for example, read *Moment* or *Fuses* differently if the filmmakers were, respectively, female and male? *Fuses* is understood in the terms under which it was made, which for Schneemann was very important, as she points out. This does not conclusively confirm any evidence in the film text about the gendered role of the filmmaker, but it opens up some thought-provoking readings, as does the screening context which raises issues around modes of interpretation, as the example with *Antepartum* revealed.

A feminine aesthetic of ephemerality

Tina Keane's *Shadow Woman* (1977) and Annabel Nicolson's *Sky for the Bird on the Roof of my Mind* (1973) and *Jaded Vision* (1973) include performance, pre-cinematic shadow-play and film screenings, thereby providing some interesting assertions for probing the existence of a feminine aesthetic. *Shadow Woman* (performed in a purposefully constructed gallery garden) focused on the mother–daughter relationship through game-playing. Performance was particularly important for Keane as it lent itself to an open-ended, experimental exploration of ideas within a prescribed structure:

> I've tried to combine the two – to mix the intellect with the intuitive part so that one has a structure within which one can be fairly spontaneous. The importance of not having a total script is actually trying to respond to the audience – see who is there.[59]

The first half of *Shadow Woman* had Keane placing mirrors on hopscotch numbers, with her shadow repeatedly falling across her young daughter playing hopscotch, whereas the second half focused on 'the passivity of waiting from the time of one's birth as a baby girl till the day of one's death as an old woman' through a reading of Faith Wilding's poem *Waiting*.[60] Keane later added a third part after reflecting on the rather sombre note it ended on, appearing to suggest the weight of women's inherited oppression. In the added section Keane read extracts from Virginia Woolf's *The Waves* while a film of the sun's reflections on water was screened, exuding the sought for 'optimism, it had the universe and it had energy, constant energy'.[61] The Super-8 footage was later used in Keane's film, *Shadow of a Journey* (1980), with the soundtrack including traditional forms of story-telling as women retold traumatic historical accounts of Highland clearances.

Some significant parallels, around questions of control, the predetermined and the incidental, were evident with Nicolson's 1970s performances, with Nicolson reflecting on these at a recent expanded cinema event:

> The importance of consideration, that there was an awareness of what would happen but it wasn't all predetermined. Within the performance space, the projection space, there was an openness. So whoever was doing the performance brings something else to it [...] I think the answer lies somewhere in my understanding of what performance is. It is the moment when things happen. It is the same with film in the sense that projecting is the moment when it all becomes real.[62]

Like Keane, Nicolson recognised that separation between audience and the performative event needed to be minimised in such experiential works, as they were more reliant on subtle gestures in the audience's responses. This was evident in Nicolson's *Sky for the Bird on the Roof of my Mind* (1973) where film loops were projected onto the roof and walls of Nicolson's studio, including an apparent bird projected onto a dusty mirror with 'bird' written on it. Another loop passed through a slide projector, casting vertical images of film frames from roof to ceiling. These images were then, in turn, projected onto the original precarious bird on the roof, illuminating it with light, with additional random flashes of reflected light catching the film loops caught in the light beams. Nicolson commented on the recurring image of the apparent bird, revealing how intuitive approaches to the space formed an integral part of her working process:

> Someone said the other day that everything was contained in that image, the projected image of the tiny bird. In fact it wasn't a bird, it was a crack in a glass roof. It's from years ago and recurs and recurs. It's mainly to do with listening to signs and seeing them manifest.[63]

In a similar way, *Jaded Vision* (1973) also utilised the space as a key part of the work, relying on the spontaneous interactions of audience, film and projection apparatus. *Jaded Vision* included the shadow of a paper bird, and floor-to-ceiling film loops presented either as a two- or three-screen film performance, with a microphone swung around creating strange bird-like sounds through feedback.

Although there were also male filmmakers who performed as part of their expanded cinema works, as Le Grice did in *Horror Film 1* (1971), Keane was insistent that the transient nature of such works was an especially female sensibility:

> You see, the whole idea of male art is very much tied to the idea of making art that will last for ever. So, in a sense they become monuments. I think that the art that comes from women is organic and not particularly lasting. I don't think women are thinking of trying to make themselves great artists with works that will last after their death, that will put them on a pedestal. It's to do with the whole NOW and LIVING.[64] (Keane's emphasis)

Whether the ephemeral nature of these works singled them out as ostensibly feminine was debatable, but the lack of documentation was certainly an issue concerning records for posterity, although Nicolson's sentiments about this echoed Keane's concerns:

> We were passionately interested in the projection situation, the live situation [...] So it wouldn't have occurred to us to document it. That was everything that we were shying away from. I also think it depends why you're performing and I think if you're trying to create a space for people to come into. In my case I was working in near darkness or very dim and working with quiet sounds. My dialogue was with the audience and not with the camera and I wouldn't have been able to work with someone recording.[65]

Certainly, performing with accommodations required for lighting and the self-consciousness of the camera would have rendered these as different works, so keeping the intentions without concerns for posterity and instead making artworks as momentary testaments make these particularly singular pieces. Nicolson does, however, regret that very few records exist of these works as their ephemerality means that 'there's very little trace and transient work doesn't leave much in its wake'.[66] Thus, they exist as specific moments in time, recorded more in the diffuseness of memory for the performers and viewers who were present.

History, language and ideology

Many of the films discussed above are either silent or have abstract/minimal soundtracks, but the films considered here include soundtracks which significantly (alongside the visual texts) open up discourses on feminist polemics. History, language and ideology are central to these films as they are used to polemically open up discussions on women's traditionally submissive roles as they interrogate patriarchal inscriptions of language. Sally Potter's *Thriller* (1979), Lis Rhodes' *Light Reading* (1978) and Susan Clayton/Jonathan Curling's *The Song of the Shirt* (1979) will be focused on, with Jeanette Iljon's *Focii* (1974) providing additional context. In *Thriller* Potter challenges the death of the heroine in Puccini's opera *La Bohème* as her death served primarily to satisfy the role of the grieving lover. In *Light Reading* Rhodes takes a dialectical approach, engaging with formal aspects of film structure and materiality, to question female subjectivity and women's historically oppressed position. *The Song of the Shirt* (1979) focuses on women's social/class status, work and low-pay, taking nineteenth-century needlewomen as a starting point to engage with these issues. The films draw attention to formal – and at times material – aspects of the medium itself and throughout these analyses the concept of the 'feminine aesthetic' will be kept in mind to continue probing discussions.

Thriller was informed by feminist texts such as Mulvey's 'Visual Pleasure' essay and Alfred Hitchcock's *Psycho* (1960), 'simultaneously critiqu[ing] and exploit[ing] the suspense thriller genre'.[67] According to Patricia Mellencamp, it 'begins where [Maya Deren's] *Meshes [of the Afternoon* (1943)] and *La Bohème* end'.[68] Potter challenges history and ideology by offering an alternative narrative for the original defenceless Mimi in the form of her confident, alter-ego Musetta. She defies her historically inscribed position, contesting her submissive position and murder, asking repeatedly 'why did I have to die?' Film historian, Sue Harper identified how Potter used binary oppositions to further polemicise the heroine's role as '[t]he film splits the heroine into good (Mimi) and bad (Musetta), into young (Mimi) and old (seamstress in the photograph), and most radically into white (Mimi) and black (Colette Laffont as Musetta)'.[69]

Thriller is filmed in grainy black-and-white and takes place in a bare attic (echoing Mimi's garret in *La Bohème*), with two female and two male actors performing choreographed actions which Potter said 'can be read in terms of sexual politics, specifically the role of the heroine in art'.[70] The mirror is central to *Thriller* as Mimi/Musetta frequently faces her reflected self as if in interrogation of her roles – historic and contemporary – also referencing psychoanalysis (self/reflected self) and historic *vanitas* paintings. Some parallels, in the way that dance/ movement, the mirror and the dual-self are used to question identity, can be drawn with Iljon's little-known *Focii* (1974) as her silent, 'sparse composition of one, then two dancers, convey[s] isolation, fear and curiosity'.[71] In *Thriller* Mimi/Musetta returns to her reflection to question and recognise, but in *Focii* she struggles to recognise her 'self' as she 'mimics the other figure, attempting to catch her out with rapid, erratic movements', thereby creating a sense of unease.[72]

In the opening scene of *Thriller* Mimi/Musetta sits on a chair, holding a book and laughing hysterically. This mocking, frenzied laughter is repeated in a later scene as Mimi/Musetta closes a journal (*Tel Quel*) containing the writings of Marx, Freud and Mallarmé and faces the camera. Potter elucidated on this critical commentary on the dominance of male theory over women's lives:

> Near the end of *Thriller*, an anonymous hand passes a book into the frame and Mimi reads from the introduction to the book, which is a structuralist text. That image is asking, 'What function does theoretical and analytical work have in understanding my life? Mimi's life? Cinema? What is the correct relationship between the complexities of theory and complexities of the image? And the answer in my film is laughter.[73]

It is the black Musetta, Harper says, that 'is the one to escape patriarchy, by laughter', and in her disavowal of Freud and Marx's theories Harper also identified the 'icons of male theoretical culture' as being as 'complicit as its works of art'.[74] Harper's analysis also alludes to the progressive fragmentation occurring within feminism in the late 1970s, with women beginning to focus more explicitly on issues related to race, class and sexual orientation which would dominate 1980s feminist discourses.

In *Light Reading* a significant focus on the sound/image relationship draws the viewer's attention to consider cinematic structuring devices, as the three-part film opens with a black screen (lasting almost three minutes) and Rhodes' voiceover. The sound/image dislocation imposes a greater sense of viewer reflexivity – unlike commercial cinema's audio-visual narrative linearity – compelling the viewer to observe the hierarchy of the auditory/visual stimuli, as Nancy Woods elucidates:

One consequence of this formal manoeuvre is the radical undermining of sight as the essential condition of the film's immediate intelligibility. This tactic precipitates a temporary shift of emphasis in the sensory registers by which film spectatorship is usually experienced, forcing the spectator to reconsider her/his habitual subjugation of sound to image.[75]

This undermining of sight points to cinema's very essence (the visual image) with Rhodes' negation of image prioritising the woman's voice and, arguably, also commenting on women's historical objectivity. Rhodes also appears to echo John Berger's discussion on female objectivity in his seminal 'Ways of Seeing' (1972), as Rhodes narrates in the film:

She watched herself being looked at. She looked at herself being watched but she could not perceive herself as the subject of the sentence as it was written. As it was read. The context defined her as the object of the explanation.[76]

In Berger's text he similarly deliberated:

Men look at women. Women watch themselves being looked at [...] The surveyor of women in herself is male: the surveyed female. Thus she turns herself into an object – and most particularly an object of vision: a sight.[77]

In my interview with Rhodes, she did not, however, directly accredit Berger, suggesting that 'one has things in one's ears. My feeling is: not necessarily [...] And if one is talking about how one [works] as an artist, you use everything that is sort of around'.[78] Rhodes, however, confirmed Gertrude Stein as a key literary source for *Light Reading*: 'I think that what I was reading at that time was some Gertrude Stein, so [...] the reference was very much her writing'.[79] Stein's poem 'Sonatina Followed by Another' is quoted in *Light Reading* and Rhodes' interest in Stein's writing was 'that in a way grammar is the problem, as much as anything else, in the sense of constructing meaning'.[80] Rhodes' use of language in *Light Reading* is not fixed, as she speaks in both first and third person, referring to 'she' in both singular and plural. Her monologue forms a score, complementing the rhythms and repetitions of the visual images, with tonal changes from indecision – asking advice on what to do – to decisiveness in providing concise directions for the printing of the film, thus offering no fixed sense of narrative. In the programme notes for 'Her Image Fades as Her Voice Rises' Felicity Sparrow's essay confirms the reasons for her seeming indecision as being to do with problems of women's oppression: '[t]he clues suggest it is language that has trapped her, meanings that have excluded her and a past that has been constructed to control her'.[81]

Rhodes exposed the structural procedures of the film's production, drawing attention to film materiality, with parts of an earlier film, *Amanuensis* (1973), forming the final part of *Light Reading*. Here film stock and a used typewriter ribbon were hand-wound and contact-printed with a light bulb, with parts of the film including traces of type-written letters and words scrolling through the screen. Segments were also re-filmed to create repetitions for the cyclic score, with the images and voice-over offering a lack of clarity or disclosure about events, as the tentative 'narrative' unfolds. Thus the film reads as a fragmented puzzle, offering little narrative certainty, yet raising questions about cinematic and verbal language, as Annette Kuhn elucidates:

> The repeated denial of meaning [...] is effectively an assertion of meaninglessness, a project of radical asceticized deconstruction [...] The repetitions, the radical refusal of semioticity, the unfixed nature of the space articulated by the film, all serve to operate against the kind of closure associated with a defined and homogenous filmic space.[82]

Providing a comprehensible narrative was never Rhodes' intention, as she explicitly exposed the mechanisms of the camera operations, revealing film materiality and processes of production. The camera, like a scanning 'eye', films the photographs in either fast-paced sequences or with slower, roving camera movements in close-up, moving either from left to right, right to left or from top to bottom. Images of rulers, scissors and hand-written numbers also reference the editorial, decision-making processes in filmmaking, as the voice-over provides instructions for printing and deliberates aspects of violence towards women.

The Song of the Shirt (the title of Thomas Hood's 1843 poem) similarly questioned language and ideology as Potter and Rhodes did in their films. It took the plight of nineteenth-century needlewomen as a starting point to engage with historical and contemporary concerns regarding women's social/class status, work and low-pay. Language and ideology are questioned with references to a range of historical male sources, including Richard Cobden and the Earl of Shaftsbury. Judith

Mayne identified how the authority of historical, male texts was undermined in *The Song of the Shirt,* and in her interview with Clayton also referred to Bovenschen's 'Is There a Feminine Aesthetic?' essay:

> Bovenschen describes the element of female resistance, however passive, that contributes to the work of art. In a sense much feminist work has been an attempt to exploit that resistance, to tease out its implications. The voice of *Thriller* is precisely that: it looks back at the text, takes whatever cracks there may be in the representation, and then attempts to take them to some kind of 'logical' feminist extreme. That voice is also present in *The Song of the Shirt* – not the authoritative voice you [Clayton] just described, but the voices of the two women who read the text and laugh about it.[83]

Thus, as in *Thriller,* laughter is used defiantly to challenge, rather than victimise, the injustices affiliated to women's historically inscribed status; operating, as Potter stated, to ask what the value of these texts are in defining women's lives.

The use of still photographs in all three films opens up some interesting spaces for discussion, with *The Song of the Shirt* and *Thriller* providing evidence of women's historical, oppressed position in society as working-class seamstresses. Archival photographs from an earlier theatre production of *La Bohème* and of needlewomen feature in *Thriller*; and in *The Song of the Shirt* still photographs illustrate a voice-over reading of a novel about a distressed needlewoman. E. Ann Kaplan made some pertinent observations about Potter's use of archival photographs as contributing to Mimi's inscribed mute role in the classical opera. These comments may be equally valid for the other two films discussed here:

> The space is deliberately 'frozen' in two senses; first, in that the shots are photographs of photographs of a stage performance ('signifiers of signifiers' as Jane Weinstock puts it), which sets them one stage further from the signified than a cinematic shot would normally be; secondly, in the literal sense that the figures do not move – occasionally the camera moves in for a close-up of some detail, e.g. Mimi 2's face, or a seamstress's hand, but this only accentuates the silent, passive aspect of the figures.[84]

Kaplan's observations are noteworthy in that they also relate to the interests of Sparrow and Rhodes in raising women's mute voices from history.

In *Light Reading* a rostrum camera was used to film photographs of an unmade, blood-stained bed, the bottom half of a male figure walking on a pavement and torn fragments of photographs. While these all provide indexical evidence, they offer no certainty but only clues to the possible crime or narrative events. Rhodes is glimpsed in photographic self-portraits, reflected in a small hand mirror and in a Polaroid photograph, problematising – as self-portraiture does – the duality of being both subject and object.

While an important objective in *The Song of the Shirt* was the re-inscription of women into history, Clayton believed that this was only proportionately possible. History, she said, could not materially be rewritten: 'you can try to explain why women are absent, but I don't think you can actually construct a female voice in a specific historical instance that has the power to explain its absence'.[85] Arguably, however, this is what women were attempting to do with these films, or at least they were challenging historical facts in order to reintegrate women into histories and give voice to their opinions on their own terms.

By contesting patriarchally inscribed grammatic form, Rhodes was also able to 'find' her own voice, and while *Light Reading* did not offer a 'single solution [...] there is a beginning. Of that she is positive'.[86] While the reinsertion of the women's voices into historical accounts offered some form of redress, Sparrow and Rhodes, like Clayton, questioned how much could in effect be changed:

> Where do we begin? There is the past, always, which we can re-read, re-frame, just as we can try and re-place Alice Guy and Germaine Dulac. But it's not just a question of balancing out the injustices: 'There is nothing connected with the staging of a motion picture that a woman cannot do as easily as a man', it goes deeper than these crimes of exclusion and unequal opportunities.[87]

While no clear solution was offered on how to make amends for women's exclusion, the important issue of challenging histories was clearly important. Sylvia Harvey similarly questioned how *The Song of the Shirt* provided a 'multiplicity of accounts' offering no explicit answer to the question, 'yes, but why did these things happen?'[88] She, however, identified that '[v]ery positively, though, what the film tries to do is ask who gets to write history and how do they do it?'[89] Harvey continued by suggesting that 'foregrounding the means of representation can help us to ask the question – who is representing, and for whom?'[90] This importantly also relates to questions asked in Rhodes' important 'Whose History?' essay (discussed in Chapter 1), where she similarly asked, '*who* makes history for *whom?*' (Rhodes' emphasis).[91] This is a question that *Thriller, The Song of the Shirt* and *Light Reading* all pose, as they address women's absence and prescribed roles, asking how it may be possible to make amendments or redress the balance.

Concluding thoughts

Although extensive research was undertaken to retrieve women's forgotten histories in the 1970s, and films addressed issues informed by feminist discourses in diverse ways, the likelihood of a common aesthetic was rather small. Researchers had initially been optimistic that 'a coherent aesthetic' could be revealed, but admitted that this was increasingly doubtful.[92] In Stern's review of the special women's event at the 1979 Edinburgh Film Festival (1979), she identified the importance of the diversity in women's experimentation:

> For what emerged with startling clarity is that films do not speak for themselves: there is no such thing as an essentially feminist film, there is no singular feminist position or critique. There is only difference. And differences are articulated in differing languages. This is integral to the dilemma of 'attempting to build a new language of film'.[93]

As the decade progressed, with further histories emerging through research by different groups of women, women also became more insistent about articulating their concerns outside of patriarchal structures. There is no doubt that this increased awareness resulted in the irresolvable difficulties emerging at the end of the decade in the Hayward Gallery's 1979 'Film as Film' exhibition (discussed in Chapter 1), leading to the women's split from the LFMC and the formation of the women's distribution centre and collective, Circles, in 1979. The Channel Four documentary, *Seeing for Ourselves: Women Working with Film* (1983), focused on the Circles group and the women involved explained how it provided a welcome, supportive network for women filmmakers, historians and theorists.[94]

A substantial amount of groundwork was done in the 1970s, coming to more concerted fruition in the 1980s, but increased fragmentation meant that more essentialist, political issues, such as race, class and sexuality, would become key concerns that further divided a cohesive position in the women's movement. What is revealed, through the complex discourses engaging women in resurrecting film histories and establishing their own positions in the 1970s, is the diversity of approach taken to explore experimental filmmaking. Furthermore, this importantly also reveals that there was no 'return to image' at the end of the 1970s, as this was central to many women's diverse and image-rich film practices.

Conclusion: (Re)cognitions and (Re)considerations for This History

In the opening passages to Nadine Gordimer's recent collection of short stories, she notes that '[t]he past is valid only in relation to whether the present recognises it'.[1] This recognition is, of course, central, to the any new historical unfolding or distillation. For without recognition, the history lies only as quiet and still as the mute sources the historian Keith Jenkins refers to and which the researcher attempts to make speak. This book has its origins in research undertaken for my doctoral thesis as part of a 1970s British cinema project. My love of 1970s experimental films, their earlier antecedents and later successors, which I had come across in my research as an artist/filmmaker (working with both film and video amongst other media) inspired me to take on the guise of historian and map this complex, but rich and beguiling field. At the outset it was the many diverse films which equally enthralled, intrigued or perplexed that spurred me on. The discovery that this history was in parts biased, misaligning certain filmmakers and failing to account for the actual diversity in the already established history of structural and material experimentation, was made plain by the recognition that the 'return to image' phrase – perpetuated throughout these histories – was simply not true. The accepted understanding that 'image' made a return at the end of the decade has allowed for a neat packaging of 1970s history – notably the theoretically informed dominant structural and material position – to set it apart from other types of filmmaking allegedly emerging at the end of the 1970s/ beginning of the 1980s. I imagine that one reason for this was the need to maintain a sense of authority and orthodoxy about the hard-core and earnest theoretical work – namely structural/materialist filmmaking – which could set it apart from (so as not to be tarnished by) a filmmaking full of image, intuition, chance and personal expression which Marxist-informed 1970s positions militated against.

This type of filmmaking, evident throughout the 1970s, reveals the joy and pleasure of filmmaking born out of a moment 'stalking' an image, capturing a world and fixing it for ever on the thousands of small frames that film *is*, as Dwoskin so celebrates in his 1975 book. This is the joy of filmmaking where the mapless filmmaker nevertheless points the film-charged camera into what catches the eye or ear or nose or tongue; filmmaking where the touch of the light on fresh film-stock forever fixes a moment. Filmmaking where the cinematographic structuring devices of the camera become willing partners in committing to celluloid anything that may catch the attention of the filmmaker by focusing or unfocusing, zooming in or out, by allowing an automatic light-meter to blacken the sky or bring into frame a celestial spilling of light. This is filmmaking where filmmakers could work like children in a room full of toys (the workshops) with noisy machines, chemicals and dust. A place where the precision of numbers and finely measured moments was required to ensure the possibility of an outcome, but one where the failures and mistakes equally made magical the marks etched into celluloid. This is the kind of filmmaking Tilda Swinton misses about Derek Jarman's films:

the mess
the vulgarity
the cant
the poetry
the edge
the pictures
Simon Fischer Turner's music
the real faces
the intellectualism
the science
the bad temperedness
the good temperedness
the cheek
the standards
the anarchy
the gaucheness
the romanticism
the classicism
the optimism
the activism
the challenge

the longueurs
the glee
the playfulness
the bumptiousness
the resistance
the wit
the fight
the colours
the grace
the passion
the goodness
the beauty[2]

All these things and more are what the filmmaker needed to take the sometimes crazed moment of inspiration and have the courage to bring this moment of conception to projection; a love and a true integrity of purpose, which I believe compelled *all* the 1970s filmmakers making up this history.

Certainly, the contexts of the times – the politics, the money (or lack thereof), the theory-building helping to define and articulate thoughts and points of view, education, where teaching became part of learning more – are essential for understanding what motivated this all to happen in the first place. It has therefore been important to recognise, as Mazière puts it, this 'web of support' and the 'nexus of education' outlined in Chapter 2, alongside some of the screenings, giving a flavour of the rich diversity in filmmaking. But it has also been essential to challenge what I believe to be a long-held mistaken view of this history, to make amends and to propose some new points of departure. What I found when I initially came to this history was a history devoid of the true recognition of films and filmmakers who were certainly present – the evidence is there in the multitude of films and in the paper trail of records housed so carefully within the archives – but whose works had been edged out from centre-stage illumination to fulfil some already well-conceived firm positions, populated at times by unswerving and dogmatic individuals or egos wanting to dig their heels firmly into the field of this history. It was therefore necessary to take such a nit-picking approach to what I found were the 'thorns in the side' of this history, as I have done in Chapter 1. I make my apologies. This is nothing personal. I am grateful that one of the 'culprits' encouraged me to do just that: to take to task some of his accounts of the decade. It is therefore hoped that my positioned approach – while certainly not *the* definitive history of the decade as it should be read alongside the other histories – can shed new light and bring illumination to this most marvellous decade in British experimental filmmaking. This is, however, not the end point. While this history fixes a new position on understandings of part of the recent past, it is also my intention that it lays the ground-work for further readings and understandings. I would, therefore, like to offer a point of departure to help untangle the highly complex field of contemporary moving image histories.

A proposition – Untangling histories: a point of departure

In the Introduction I mentioned that calling for medium-specific histories may not in fact be a bad thing. I was clear that this was not a call for medium-specific histories encapsulating themselves within fetishistic hierarchical conditions. Instead, my belief is that each of these histories could be laid out and investigated for clarity of purpose to untangle the wider field of moving image history. My hope is that the 'point of departure' offered here provides a certain road-map to be taken forward , rather than the mapless sea often required by the artist or filmmaker who needs just a hunch, an insight or intuition to leap forth into deep waters. Here is, instead, a proposition to begin to map the diverse strands making up the multiple histories of contemporary moving image. Before outlining this map, however, it will be necessary to once again draw on certain examples to get a sense of the terrain.

In his recent historical essay, Rees provided an in-depth survey of 'a still little-known aspect of British film and video art of the 1970s and beyond' in his search to find 'the shadows of the forgotten ancestors of new media practice'.[3] As I have indicated in this book, and as Rees writes in some detail in his essay, the history of contemporary moving image is to a large extent absent (although the gap, says Rees 'may now be closing'), with numerous artists, filmmakers and critics being una-ware of the history from which the new phenomenon of moving image allegedly 'exploded' onto the scene, first in the mid-1990s with gallery-based video installations, and again in the 2000s with the profusion of digital moving image technologies.[4] Rees outlined this by citing the art theorist, Michael Newman, who observed the following:

> In the first decade of the twenty-first century, it is practically impos-sible to walk round the gallery district of a major city, or visit a bien-nial, triennial or art fair, without seeing a large number of artworks containing images that move.[5]

The situation therefore remains: we have a profusion of moving image works with no attendant histories. And the question that needs asking is what is required to understand the historical trajectories for these works? My proposition for untangling these histories leads me to suggest a number of things.

Firstly, I think that we might take heed of what Rosalind Krauss says in her recently published collection of essays, *Perpetual Inventory* (2013). Krauss, on finding herself caught in Jean-François Lyotard's 'postmodern condition' in which the grand master narratives of history have been all but dispelled, argues that this has problematically taken along with it any sense of regard for medium specificity:

> The master narrative of modern art turns on the importance of specific aesthetic mediums understood as simultaneously empowering artistic practice and leveraging the works' possibility of meaning [...] This master narrative hit the wall of Lyotard's *Postmodern Condition* when certain aspects of artistic practice, such as conceptual art, jettisoned the use of a specific medium in order to juxtapose image and written text within the same work. The now-fashionable possibility of installation art followed in the wake of this dispatch of the medium. Installation is relentless in its refusal of specificity, filling galleries with mixtures of video images and taped narratives.[6]

Krauss calls for a return to medium-specificity as a condition for the critical examination of art, arguing that '[f]or the most part, *Perpetual Inventory* charts [her] conviction as a critic that the abandonment of the specific medium spells the death of serious art'.[7]

Secondly, we might note the important call for the recognition of film at the moment of its possible demise. Significantly, the threat of the demise of film (with the closure of film labs and now digital cinemas) has brought to attention the question of film and its history. Amongst the filmmakers, historians and critics calling for a recognition of the history of artists/experimental film, no doubt the Turner Prize nominated British artist, Tacita Dean, has figured in raising awareness about these issues. She started an on-line international petition in 2011, attempting to stop the closure of 16mm printing facilities at London's Soho Film Lab (without effect) and in 2014 met with UNESCO's Department of Intangible Cultural Heritage to make a plea for the recognition of film as a culturally specific historic medium. Dean's monumental 35mm film installation *FILM* (2011), in the Tate Gallery's Turbine Hall, also drew attention to many of the issues around the medium of film and its attendant 120-year history. In his introductory essay to Dean's exhibition catalogue, curator Nicolas Cullinan refers to Krauss' recent collection of essays, noting that she considers 'the "post-medium condition" to be a monstrous myth founded on the influence of 1960s structural filmmaking on broader forms of art practice, 'disclos[ing] the defining features of the medium itself', and as defined by the art critic Clement Greenberg for painting ('an embrace of its inherent flatness').[8] For film these included attributes specific to film, such as framing and focus. Taking his cue from Krauss, Cullinan pointed out that film should be recognised as distinct from digital moving image:

> The unique qualities of temporality, tone, contrast, colour depth, light and grain have not only defined the medium of analogue film historically, but now also delineate it against its digital heir and demand its preservation alongside new technologies. The latter simply cannot (nor should not try to) substitute or approximate the special temporal, aesthetic and philosophical qualities of contingent, flickering film.[9]

Cullinan also mentioned the disastrous consequences of assuming an analogue medium such as film could simply be updated through digital transfer 'without obliterating many of the key qualities of the original film' when he cited the critic Amy Taubin's 'superlative and excoriating' review of The Museum of Modern Art's exhibition of Andy Warhol's *Screen Tests*.[10] Warhol's films, Taubin observed, were astonishingly converted from 16mm to digital transfers with the 'gaps and interstices between the frames which structure and orchestrate Warhol's films, and upon which their languid choreography, pacing and tempo rest', obliterated.[11] Taubin asked whether this might be the first step towards allowing for digital substitution of not only films but also drawings, paintings and photographs. These issues about film, medium-specificity and the digital are important as they open up some detailed spaces for consideration. Again, this is not to hierarchise film over other moving image technologies, but to distinguish the differences.

Thirdly, we might take note of the complex diversity in contemporary moving image, with many artists or critics often having no awareness of its long and complex history. Besides the 1990s 'explosion' of video installation art in the gallery, the turn of the millennium also, as Rees noted, saw 'a flowering of experimental and expanded film and projection art', with diverse festivals taking place across Britain showing new and sometimes historical programmes.[12] Rees identified different types of contemporary experimentation, with some (but not all) being medium-specific, interrogating their own means of representation and exploring the properties inherent to the medium, whether made by mobile phone, film, video or other digital media.[13] Other works revealed a 'promiscuous merging of technologies' reaching back, he said, to the early days of cinema with predictions of a 'poly-expressive' cinema in Futurist manifestos (1916) and 'non-material materialism' in virtual imaging by El Lizzitzy (1925).[14] Other cross-disciplinary exploits included attempts at a graphic cinema putting painting in motion and the surrealist cinema of Dali/Buñuel in the 1920s. Diverse avant-garde cinemas came out of documentary movements in the 1930s, and by the 1960s/1970s artists such as Carolee Schneemann and Stan VanDerBeek worked in dynamic forms of mixed-media, performative, expanded cinema events using film, video, multiple screens, slides, etc. Rees continued that film's medium-specificity was, however, determined in the 1950s by the likes of Maya Deren and Stan Brakhage, who distinguished film as an independent art form separate from other disciplines such as painting or sculpture. This set the tone for 1960s/1970s medium-specific practices, also heightened by the 'new' video medium setting itself apart from film. Nevertheless, for conceptual artists working with film or video from the 1960s onwards an interrogation of the medium was *not* always integral to the work. And so the precedent for the 1980s/1990s 'meshing' and 'dissolving' of boundaries was set, which the eclecticism and diversity in contemporary moving image also reveals. While Rees did not call for medium-specificity as a mode of operation in his essay, it certainly appears to offer useful frameworks for historical analysis. My belief is that it could be a useful tool for uncovering and untangling the multiple histories making up contemporary moving image.

In George Clark's recent essay on the Tate's 'Assembly: A Survey of Artists' Film and Video 2008–2013' programmes, he asked what might be at stake in encouraging reflection on and taking stock of the past?[15] This is indeed an important question, particularly as Clarke observed that this crucial point in film and video development was marked by the 'increasing ambition and scale of artists' projects', the complexity in recent practices and the extraordinary diversity in moving image work.[16] 'Assembly', he said, came at the back of 'seismic shifts in the nature of producing and circulating images'.[17] Clark mentioned two highly ambitious London exhibitions, Dean's *FILM* (2011) and Christian Marclay's *The Clock* (2010), illustrating recent divergent practices: one medium-specific and 'about' film, the other drawing on the history of cinema in contemporary 24-hour digital format, which proposed 'equally momentous and complex possibilities for the future of moving image'.[18] Clark noted that instead of setting up oppositional aspects of moving image practice, *FILM* and *The Clock* propounded distinct future trajectories finding 'numerous analogies, companions and counter-proposals' across the diverse contemporary 'Assembly' programmes. These future trajectories also proposed, he said, 'equally momentous and complex possibilities for the future of moving image'.[19]

While these future trajectories are indeed certainly important as they lend a complete openness of possibility to experimentation, I also believe that these insist on equivalent historical trajectories by looking back. These future trajectories need Rees's 'shadows of the forgotten ancestors' to provide depth of understanding for the new innovations.[20] And for these historical trajectories I propose that medium-specific histories be drawn to untangle the histories. Krauss's conviction regarding medium-specificity is indeed an important point for consideration here. Not as a return to fetishistic medium-specific film*making* – unless this is integral to the artist's/filmmaker's process of working – but for teasing out the complex and multiple moving image histories. These include film, video, cinema, television, computer-generated art, animation, amateur filmmaking, mobile phones, etc. This should be done with an awareness of this current 'moment' of film and its potential demise, allowing for clarification in understanding distinctive aspects of contemporary moving image practice. Currently these histories exist as a homogenous mass of tangled threads. I believe that pulling out the individual threads and drawing each of these historical trajectories to the fore will aid a clarity of purpose, allowing for identifying points of intersection and overlap. By recognising these multiple but distinctive histories – and respecting the actual specificities defining them – more fluid critiques and analyses can be made to understand the richness, ambition and complexity of contemporary moving image. Certainly, the future trajectories must be able to move forward without the orthodoxies of encumbrance weighing down any need to produce works in a specific format, medium or overarching specification. But a knowledge of where these magical encounters with tricks of the light first emerged, whether sunlight and shadows, the etch of light into celluloid, the early humming buzz of computer-generated art or the curiosity of trying to find ghosts in the machine ... all these should be made apparent.

Notes

Introduction

1. Sam Rohdie, 'Metz and Film Semiotics: Opening the Field', *Jump Cut: A Review of Contemporary Media*, 2004, pp. 1–12; p. 1. www.ejumpcut.org/archive/onlinessays/JCO7folder/Metz.html.
2. Vanda Carter, 'Not Only Animation' in Michael Mazière and Nina Danino (eds), *The Undercut Reader: Critical Writings on Artists' Film and Video* (London: Wallflower Press, 2003), pp. 168–170; p. 168.
3. Rod Stoneman, 'Film-Related Practice and the Avant-garde' in *Screen*, Vol. 20, No. 3–4, 1979, pp. 40–57; p. 47.
4. Interview with Benjamin Cook, December 2008.
5. David Curtis, *A History of Artists' Film and Video in Britain* (London: BFI, 2007), p. 37.
6. Maxa Zoller, 'Interview: Maxa Zoller with Malcolm Le Grice' in *X-Screen: Film Installation and Actions of the '60s and '70s, Catalogue* (Wien: Walther König, 2003), pp. 136–147; p. 145.
7. Ibid.
8. Ibid.
9. Vicenti Todolí, 'Foreword' in *Open Systems: Rethinking Art c. 1970* (London: Tate, 2005), p. 6.
10. David Curtis, *A History of Artists' Film & Video in Britain*, op. cit., p. 3.
11. Margaret Dickinson, 'Introduction' in Margaret Dickinson (ed.), *Rogue Reels: Oppositional Film in Britain, 1945–90* (London: BFI, 1999), p. 4.
12. Duncan Reekie, *Subversion: The Definitive History of Underground Cinema* (London: Wallflower Press, 2007), p. 1.
13. D. N. Rodowick, *The Crisis of Political Modernism: Criticism and Ideology in Contemporary Film Criticism* (Berkeley: University of California Press, 1995), p. 1.
14. Stephen Dwoskin, *Film Is... The International Free Cinema* (London: Peter Owen, 1975), p. 23.
15. Jeff Nuttall, *Bomb Culture* (London: Paladin, 1968), p. 19.
16. Paul Cronin, 'The Ceremony of Innocence', *Sight and Sound*, Vol. 17, No. 3, March 2007, pp. 22–24; p. 22.
17. Ibid., p. 23.
18. Duncan Reekie, *Subversion: The Definitive History of Underground Cinema*, op. cit., p. 137.
19. D. N. Rodowick, 'Politics, Theory and the Avant-garde' in Nina Danino and Michael Mazière (eds), *The Undercut Reader, Critical Writings on Artists' Film and Video* (London: Wallflower Press, 2003), pp. 34–37; p. 35.

1 Questions of History

1. Marius Kwint, 'Introduction: The Physical Past' in Jeremy Aynsley, Christopher Breward and Marius Kwint (eds), *Material Memories: Design and Evocation* (Oxford: Berg, 1999), pp. 1–16; p. 1.

2. Paul Feyerabend, *Against Method* (London: Verso, 2010), p. 1. First published 1975.
3. Robert Musil, *The Man Without Qualities* (London: Picador, 1997), p. 392. First published 1943.
4. Malcolm Le Grice, 'The History We Need' and Lis Rhodes, 'Whose History?' in Deke Dusinberre and A.L. Rees (eds), *Film as Film: Formal Experiment in Film 1910–1975* (London: Arts Council/Hayward Gallery, 1979), pp. 113–120; David Curtis, *Which History?* Tate International Council Conference, London, 1 June, 2001. http://www.studycollection.co.uk/whichhistory.html
5. Keith Jenkins, *Rethinking History* (London: Routledge, 2003). p. 7.
6. Ibid., p. 46.
7. Michael O'Pray, 'The Elusive Sign: From Asceticism to Aestheticism' in *The Elusive Sign* (London: Arts/British Council, 1987), p. 10.
8. Walter Grasskamp, 'For Example, *Documenta*, or, How is Art History Produced?' in Reesa Greenberg, Bruce W Ferguson and Sandy Nairne (eds), *Thinking about Exhibitions* (London: Routledge, 1996), pp. 67–78; p. 68.
9. Ibid.
10. Ibid.
11. Derek Jarman, *Dancing Ledge* (Minnesota: University of Minnesota Press, 2010), p. 118.
12. David Curtis, 'Artists' Films' in *Studio International,* Vol. 193, 1977, pp. 24–25; p. 24.
13. Ibid.
14. D. N. Rodowick, *The Virtual Life of Film* (Massachusetts: Harvard University Press, 2007), P. 26.
15. David Curtis, 'English Avant-garde Film: An Early Chronology' in *A Perspective on English Avant-garde Film* (London: Arts Council, 1978), pp. 9–18; p. 9.
16. Interview with Benjamin Cook at LUX, London, December 2008.
17. Ibid.
18. Lucy Reynolds, 'Minor Cinema: Artists Film and Video: Books by David James and David Curtis' in *Millennium Film Journal*, No. 52, Winter 2009/2010, http://mfj-online.org/journalPages/MFJ52/Reynolds.htm. No page numbers.
19. Phillip Drummond, 'Introduction' in *Film as Film, Formal Experiment in Film: 1910–1975* (London: Arts Council/Hayward Gallery, 1979), pp. 5–6; p. 5.
20. Ibid.
21. Malcolm Le Grice, 'The History We Need' in *Film as Film: Formal Experiment in Film: 1910–1975*, op. cit., pp. 113–117; p. 113.
22. Ibid., p. 114.
23. Nicolson and Rhodes were the only women on the 'Film as Film' committee, although Felicity Sparrow, Jane Clarke, Jeanette Iljon, Mary Pat Leece, Pat Murphy and Susan Stein contributed research.
24. Lis Rhodes, 'Whose History?' in *Film as Film: Formal Experiment in Film: 1910–1975*, op. cit., pp. 193–197; p. 119.
25. Ibid., p. 120.
26. David Curtis, *Which History?*, op. cit., p. 1.
27. Ibid., p. 1.
28. Ibid., p. 1.
29. Ibid., p. 2.

30. Ibid., p. 3.
31. A.L. Rees, 'Video and the Argument from Design', www.rewind.ac.uk/ rewind/index.php, pp. 10 of 12.
32. Ibid.
33. Malcolm Le Grice, 'Vision: First Festival of Independent British Cinema', *Studio International*, Vol. 186, October 1973, pp. 148–149; p. 148. Cited in David Curtis, *A History of Artists' Film and Video in Britain*, op. cit., p. 60.
34. Michael Mazière interview with Malcolm Le Grice in Mazière, *Institutional Support for Artists' Film and Video in England 1966–2003*, p. 6 of 14. http:// www.studycollection.co.uk/maziere/interviews/LeGrice.html.
35. Ibid.
36. David Curtis, *A History of Artists' Film & Video in Britain*, op. cit., p. 294.
37. Ibid., p. 60.
38. Conrad Atkinson, 'Artist's Information' in *Live in Your Head: Concept and Experiment in Britain 1965–75* (London: Whitechapel, 2000), pp. 44–45; p. 45.
39. A.L. Rees, *A History of Experimental Film and Video* (London: BFI, 1999), p. 78.
40. P. Adams Sitney, *Visionary Film: The American Avant-Garde, 1943–2000* (New York: Oxford University Press, 2003), p. xii.
41. A.L. Rees, 'No Psychodrama Please, We're British', audio recordings of symposium, Tate Gallery. Sourced Hyman Kreitman Reading Rooms, Tate Britain.
42. Ibid.
43. Ibid.
44. A.L. Rees, 'Underground 3: Reviewing the Avant-garde', *Monthly Film Bulletin*, Vol. 50, No. 597, October 1983, pp. 288; p. 288.
45. Ibid.
46. Ibid., p. 286.
47. Ibid., p. 288.
48. Michael O'Pray, 'The Elusive Sign: From Asceticism to Aestheticism', op. cit., pp. 7–10; p. 8.
49. Ibid., p. 10.
50. Ibid., p. 8.
51. Ibid., p. 10.
52. Michael O'Pray, 'Expanded Cinema and the New Romantic Movement of the 1980s' in Steven Ball, David Curtis, A.L. Rees and Duncan White (eds), *Expanded Cinema: Art, Performance and Film* (London: Tate, 2011), pp. 62–71; p. 66.
53. Ibid., p. 8.
54. Michael O'Pray, *Avant-garde Film: Forms, Themes and Passions* (London: Wallflower, 2003), p. 107. New Romantic Movement: approx.1979–1986.
55. David Curtis, *A History of Artists' Film and Video in Britain*, op. cit., p. 289.
56. *Glitterbug* on BBC 2 *Arena*. (London: A Basilisk Communications Ltd./BBC Co-production, 1994).
57. Ibid.
58. Michael O'Pray, 'Introduction' in Michael O'Pray (ed.), *The British Avant-garde Film: 1926–1995* (Luton: Luton University Press, 1996), pp. 1–28; p. 18.
59. Michael O'Pray, *Avant-garde Film: Forms, Themes and Passions*, op. cit., p. 110.
60. Simon Filed and Michael O'Pray, 'Imagining October, Dr. Dee and Other Matters', *Afterimage*, 12, Autumn 1985, pp. 40–58; p. 50.

61. Margaret Tait, 'Film-poem or Poem-film: A Few Notes about Film and Poetry' in Benjamin Cook and Peter Todd (eds), *Subjects and Sequences: A Margaret Tait Reader* (London: LUX, 2004), pp. 132–133; p. 133.
62. David Curtis, *A History of Artists' Film and Video in Britain*, op. cit., p. 236; Nicky Hamlyn, 'From Structuralism to Imagism: Peter Gidal and His Influence in the 1980s' in Nina Danino and Michael Mazière, *The Undercut Reader: Critical Writings on Artists' Film and Video*, op. cit., pp. 233–238. Hamlyn's article was first published in *Undercut*, 19, Spring 1999.
63. Interview/discussion with Malcolm Le Grice, London, February 2008.
64. Peter Wollen, 'Alternative Sounds and Images' in *Between Imagination and Reality* (London: ICA, 1990), pp. 5–7; p. 5.
65. Lucy Reynolds, *A Certain Sensibility: Cerith Wyn Evans and John Maybury, ICA* Accessed 23 February 2001, www.luxonline.org.uk/histories/1980–1989/a_certain_sensibility.html.
66. Ibid.
67. Ibid.
68. A.L. Rees, *A History of Experimental Film and Video*, op. cit., p. 78.
69. Ibid.
70. Ibid., p. 90.
71. Peter Wollen, 'Alternative Sounds and Images' in *Between Imagination and Reality*, op. cit., pp. 5–7; p. 5.
72. Michael O'Pray, 'The Elusive Sign: From Asceticism to Aestheticism', op. cit., p. 10.
73. Michael O'Pray, 'Expanded Cinema and the New Romantic Film Movement of the 1980s', op. cit., pp. 62–71; p. 64.
74. Ibid.
75. Ibid., p. 65.
76. Ibid., p. 66.
77. Ibid.
78. Julia Knight, 'Material, Materials, Materials: Questions of Technology and History' in Nina Danino and Michael Mazière (eds), *The Undercut Reader: Critical Writing on Artists' Film and Video*, op. cit., pp. 17–21, p. 17.
79. Ibid., p. 18. Knight cites Deke Dusinberre, 'Deke Dusinberre on British Avant-garde Landscape Films', *Undercut*, No. 7/8, Spring 1983, p. 49.
80. Julia Knight, 'Material, Materials, Materials: Questions of Technology and History', op. cit., p. 18.
81. Ibid., p. 19. Knight cites Barbara Meter, 'From Across the Channel and 15 Years' in *The Undercut Reader: Critical Writings on Artists' Film and Video* (London: Wallflower Press, 2003), pp. 241–243.
82. Derek Jarman, letter to Ron Haseldon for 'A Festival of Expanded Cinema' application, 1975. BAFVSC, 1976 file.
83. Peter Greenaway DVD, introduction to films, *The Early Films of Peter Greenaway 2*. (London: BFI Video Publishing, 2003).
84. Ibid., p. 19.
85. Ibid.
86. Keith Jenkins, *Rethinking History*, op. cit., p. 46.
87. Lis Rhodes, 'Thoughts in Various Histories, 1978–2008: On the Possessive' in *Oberhausen Short Film Festival Catalogue 2008* (Oberhausen: Karl Maria Laufen, 2008), pp. 151–155; p. 152.

2 Institutional Frameworks and Organisational Strategies

1. Michael Maziere, *Institutional Support for Artists' Film and Video in England 1966–2003*, op. cit., pp. 1–41; p. 17.
2. Ibid.
3. David Curtis, 'The Economics of the Independent Film', *Cinema*, 2, 1969, pp. 2–4; p. 2.
4. Duncan Reekie, *Subversion: The Definitive History of Underground Cinema*, op. cit., p. 113.
5. Margaret Dickinson (ed.), *Rogue Reels: Oppositional Film in Britain, 1945–90*, op. cit., p. 41.
6. Ibid., and 'The Cinema Workshops: New Models of Cinema' in Rod Stoneman and Hilary Thompson (eds), *The New Social Function of Cinema Catalogue: British Film Institute Productions '79/80* (London: BFI, 1981), pp. 140–155.
7. Fernando Solanas and Octavio Getino, 'Towards a Third Cinema: Notes and Experiences for the Development of a Cinema of Liberation' in Michael T. Martin (ed.), *New Latin American Cinema: Theory, Practices and Transcontinental Practices, Volume One* (Detroit: Wayne State University Press, 1997), pp. 33–58.
8. Ibid., p. 53.
9. Ibid., p. 49.
10. Archie Tait, 'ICA: London – Decolonising the Unconscious' in *The New Social Function of Cinema Catalogue: British Film Institute Productions '79/80*, op. cit., pp. 72–75.
11. Organising Committee for IFA Conference, 'Independent Film-Making in the 70s' in Margaret Dickinson (ed.), *Rogue Reels: Oppositional Film in Britain, 1945–90*, op. cit., p. 133.
12. Ibid., p. 132.
13. Independent Video Association (IVA) formed 1975. Incorporated into IFA (1983), thus becoming the IFVA.
14. Sylvia Harvey, *Independent Cinema?* (Stafford: West Midlands Arts, 1978), p. 19.
15. Organising Committee for IFA Conference, 'Independent Film-Making in the 70s', op. cit., p. 129.
16. A.L. Rees, *A History of Experimental Film and Video*, op. cit., pp. 92.
17. Ibid.
18. A.L. Rees, 'Experimenting on Air: UK Artists' Film on Television' in Laura Mulvey and Jamie Sexton (eds), *Experimental British Television* (Manchester: Manchester University Press, 2007), pp. 146–165; p. 151.
19. John Wyver, *Vision On: Film, Television and the Arts in Britain* (London: Wallflower Press, 2007), p. 108.
20. Ibid.
21. Ibid., p. 103.
22. David Curtis, 'English Avant-garde Film: An Early Chronology' in *A Perspective in English Avant-Garde Film*, op. cit., pp. 9–19; p. 18.
23. Ibid., p. 16.
24. Ibid., p. 105.
25. Changed to Artists' Film and Video Subcommittee in 1976.

26. A.L. Rees, *A History of Experimental Film and Video*, op. cit., p. 92.
27. Michael Mazière, List 'L2: Total Artists Funded' in *Institutional Support for Artists' Film and Video in England 1966–2003*, op. cit., list 2.
28. David Curtis and Rodney Wilson, *Perspectives on British Avant-garde Film* (London: Hayward, 1977), loose leaf catalogue.
29. David Curtis, *A History of Artists' Film & Video in Britain*, op. cit., p. 68.
30. Henry K. Miller, 'The Slade School and Cinema: Part Two', *Vertigo*, Vol. 3, No. 5, Spring 2007, pp. 65–67, p. 66.
31. 'Experimental Film Fund 1952–59' in John Ellis (ed.), *Catalogue of BFI Productions 1951–76* (London: BFI, 1977), The quotation is sourced from David Curtis, *A History of Artists' Film & Video in Britain*, op. cit., p. 62.
32. John Ellis, 'Production Board Policies', *Screen*, Vol. 17, No. 4, Winter 1976/1977, pp. 9–23; p. 9.
33. David Curtis, *A History of Artists' Film & Video in Britain*, op. cit., p. 62.
34. David Curtis, 'The Economics of the Independent Film', *Cinema*, 2, 1969. Sourced BAFVSC.
35. Christophe Dupin, *The British Film Institute as a sponsor and producer of non-commercial film: a contextualised analysis of the origins, administration, policy and achievements of the BFI Experimental Film Fund (1952–1965) and Production Board (1966–1979)*, doctoral thesis (London: Birkbeck College, University of London, 2005), p. 263.
36. Ibid.
37. Ibid., p. 264.
38. Ian Christie interview, Michael Mazière, *Institutional Support for Artists' Film and Video in England 1966–2003*, op. cit., p. 3.
39. Malcolm Le Grice interview, Michael Mazière, *Institutional Support for Artists' Film and Video in England 1966–2003*, op. cit., p. 4.
40. Michael Mazière, *Institutional Support for Artists' Film and Video in England 1966–2003*, Lists L2, op. cit.
41. Ibid., and Christophe Dupin, *The British Film Institute*, op. cit.
42. Ian Christie interview, Michael Mazière, *Institutional Support for Artists' Film and Video in England 1966–2003*, op. cit., p. 3.
43. Michael Mazière, *Institutional Support for Artists' Film and Video in England 1966–2003*, op. cit., p. 18.
44. David Curtis, *A History of Artists' Film & Video in Britain*, op. cit., p. 68.
45. Michael Mazière interview with Malcolm Le Grice, *Institutional Support for Artists' Film and Video in England 1966–2003*, op. cit., p. 6 of 14.
46. John Wyver, *Vision On: Film, Television and the Arts in Britain*, op. cit., p. 103.
47. David Curtis, *A History of Artists' Film & Video in Britain*, op. cit., p. 74.
48. Ibid., p. 68.
49. John Wyver, *Vision On: Film, Television and the Arts in Britain*, op. cit., p. 106.
50. Christophe Dupin, *The British Film Institute*, op. cit., p. 213.
51. Ibid., footnote 80.
52. David Curtis, *A History of Artists' Film & Video in Britain*, op. cit., p. 74.
53. Christophe Dupin, *The British Film Institute*, op. cit., p. 212, footnote 75.
54. Malcolm Le Grice interview, Michael Mazière, *Institutional Support for Artists' Film and Video in England 1966–2003*, op. cit., p. 4.
55. David Curtis, *A History of Artists' Film & Video in Britain*, op. cit., p. 68.
56. Ibid., p. 291.

57. David Curtis, *A History of Artists' Film and Video in Britain*, op. cit., p. 28.
58. Derek Jarman, *Dancing Ledge*, op. cit., p. 120.
59. Gray Watson, programme notes: 'London Super-8 Film Group', ICA October 1975. Sourced BAFVSC.
60. Michael O'Pray, 'Derek Jarman Filmography', *Afterimage*, 12, Autumn 1985, pp. 16–21; p. 16.
61. Stephen Dwoskin, *Film Is: The International Free Cinema*, op. cit., p. 52.
62. Ibid.
63. 'Perspectives on British Avant-Garde Film' (1977) and 'Film as Film: Formal Experiment in Film 1910–1975' (1979), at the Arts Council's Hayward Gallery.
64. Rod Stoneman and Hilary Thompson, 'Editorial Introduction' in Rod Stoneman and Hilary Thompson (eds), *The New Social Function of Cinema Catalogue: British Film Institute Productions '79/80*, op. cit., pp. 6–7, p. 7.
65. Dickinson was aware of Jonas Mekas' *Film Culture* magazine, contributing the essay 'This Documentary Business', *Film Culture*, October 1957.
66. David Curtis, *A History of Artists' Film and Video in Britain*, op. cit., p. 25 and *Vertigo* magazines four-part history by Henry K. Miller, 'The Slade School and Cinema', *Vertigo*, 2007.
67. David Curtis, *A History of Artists' Film and Video in Britain*, op. cit., p. 25
68. David Curtis, 'English Avant-garde Film: an Early Chronology' in Michael O'Pray, *The British Avant-garde Film: 1926–1995*, op. cit., pp. 101–119; p. 109.
69. Malcolm Le Grice, 'Interview with Malcolm Le Grice' in Michael Mazière, *Institutional Support for Artists' Film and Video in England 1966–2003*, op. cit., p. 14.
70. Ibid.
71. Ibid.
72. Ibid., p. 16.
73. David Curtis, 'English Avant-garde Film: An Early Chronology' in *Studio International*, November/December, pp. 176–82; p. 182.
74. Interview with Benjamin Cook, LUX, London, December 2008.
75. Ibid.
76. David Curtis (ed.), *Film-makers on Tour* (London: Arts Council, 1980), November 1980, loose-leaf prospectus.
77. David Curtis, *A History of Artists' Film and Video in Britain*, op. cit., p. 68.
78. A.L. Rees, 'Experimenting on air: UK Artists' Film on Television' in Laura Mulvey and Jamie Sexton (eds), *Experimental British Television*, op. cit., pp. 146–165; p. 152.
79. David Curtis, *A History of Artists' Film and Video in Britain*, op. cit., p. 241.
80. Ibid.
81. Phil Hardy, Claire Johnston, Paul Willeman, 'Edinburgh 76 Magazine: Introduction' in Margaret Dickinson (ed.), *Rogue Reels: Oppositional Film In Britain, 1945–90*, op. cit., pp. 138–140, p. 138.
82. Tony Rayns, 'Reflected Light', *Sight and Sound*, Vol. 74, Winter 1973, pp. 16–19.
83. Jonas Mekas, 'Movie Journal', *The Village Voice*, 4 October 1973. Sourced BAFVSC.
84. Tony Rayns, 'Reflected Light', op. cit. p. 18.

85. 'Polemic: Extract from the Festival Programme of the First Festival of Independent British Cinema' in Margaret Dickinson (ed.), *Rogue Reels Oppositional Film in Britain, 1945–90*, op. cit., p. 137.
86. Malcolm Le Grice, 'Vision: First Festival of Independent British Cinema', *Studio International*, May/June 1975, pp. 224–225; p. 224.
87. Ibid.
88. Ibid.
89. David Curtis, Rodney Wilson and committee, 'Introduction' to 'Perspectives on British Avant-garde Film' op. cit., loose-leaf exhibition catalogue.
90. Deke Dusinberre, 'A Perspective on English Avant-Garde Film' in *A Perspective on English Avant-Garde Film*, op. cit., pp. 7–8; p. 7.
91. A.L. Rees, *A History of Experimental Film and Video*, op. cit., p. 83.
92. David Curtis, *A History of Artists' Film and Video in Britain*, op. cit., p. 96.
93. Ibid., p. 95.
94. Deke Dusinberre, 'Festival of Expanded Cinema: An Introduction' in *The Festival of Expanded cinema* (London: Arts Council/ICA, 1976), exhibition catalogue. Sourced BAFVSC.
95. Jeff Keen in *The Festival of Expanded Cinema*, op. cit.
96. Ibid.
97. Derek Jarman, letter to Ron Haseldon, ICA 1976. Sourced BAFVSC.
98. Ian Breakwell, application form, ICA 1976. Sourced BAFVSC.
99. William Raban, 'Expanded Cinema 1st–10th April', http://www.luxonline. org.uk/articles/expanded _cinema(1).html.
100. Lucy Reynolds, 'Defining Filmaktion', http://www.studycollection.co.uk/ filmaktion/Frameset31.html.
101. Deke Dusinberre, 'Making the Avant-Grade [sic]', *Time Out*, 1–7 June 1979, pp. 14–15; p. 14.
102. 'Film London – Third International Avant-Garde Festival' in National Film Theatre (NFT) booklet, June 1979, pp. 2–10. Sourced BAFVSC.
103. Deke Dusinberre, 'Making the Avant-Grade [sic]', op. cit., p. 14.

3   Experimental Film and Other Visual Arts

1. Daniel Marzona, *Conceptual Art* (Cologne: Taschen, 2006), p. 7.
2. A.L. Rees, *A History of Experimental Film and Video*, op. cit., p. 66.
3. Clive Phillpot and Andrea Tarsia, 'Introduction' in *Live in Your Head: Concept and Experiment in Britain 1965–75*, op. cit., pp. 6–7; p. 7.
4. Stuart Sillars, 'Is It Possible for Me to Do Nothing as My Contribution?' in Bart Moore-Gilbert (ed.), *The Arts in the 1970s: Cultural Closure?* (London: Routledge, 1993), pp. 259–280; p. 259.
5. John A. Walker, *Left Shift: Radical Art in 1970s Britain* (London: I.B. Tauris, 2002), p. 3.
6. Stephen Dwoskin, *Film Is: The International Free Cinema*, op. cit., p. 50.
7. Clive Phillpot and Andrea Tarsia, 'Introduction' in Clive Phillpot and Andrea Tarsia (ed.), *Live in Your Head: Concept and Experiment in Britain 1965–75*, op. cit., pp. 17–23; p. 17.
8. Sol LeWitt, 'Paragraphs on Conceptual Art' in Charles Harrison and Paul Wood (eds.), *Art in Theory 1900–1990: An Anthology of Changing Ideas*

(Oxford: Blackwell, 2000), pp. 834–837; p. 836. First published in *Artforum* in, Vol. 5, No. 10, Summer 1967, pp. 79–83.

9. Joseph Kosuth, 'Art after Philosophy' in Charles Harrison and Paul Wood (eds), *Art in Theory 1900–1990: An Anthology of Changing Ideas*, op. cit., pp. 840–850; p. 844.
10. Ibid.
11. Deke Dusinberre, *English Avant-garde Cinema: 1966–1974*, MPhil thesis (London: London University College, 1974), p. 14.
12. A.L. Rees 'Conditions of Illusionism', *Screen*, 3/18, Autumn 1977; pp. 41–54; p. 49.
13. Deke Dusinberre, 'St George in the Forest' in *A Perspective in English Avant-garde Film*, op. cit., pp. 43–48; p. 46.
14. Jonathan Walley, 'Modes of Film Practice in the Avant-garde' in Tanya Leighton, *Art and the Moving Image: A Critical Reader* (London: Tate 2008), pp. 182–199; p. 192.
15. Annabel Nicolson, 'Artist as Filmmaker', *Art and Artists*, Vol. 7, No. 9, Issue 81, December 1972, pp. 20–26; p. 20.
16. Ibid.
17. Ibid.
18. Interview: Annabel Nicolson and David Curtis, 'Shoot Shoot Shoot' rushes I/V1 2001. Viewed at BAFVSC.
19. Annabel Nicolson, 'The Early Years of the Film Co-op' in Jackie Hatfield and Stephen Littman (eds), *Experiments in Moving Image* (Luton: EpiGraph, 2004), pp. 12–19. Exhibition catalogue. First published in *Light Years, Film-makers Co-op Anniversary Programme*, 1986.
20. Brian O'Doherty, *Inside the White Cube: the Ideology of the Gallery Space* (Santa Monica: The Lapis Press, 1986), p. 14.
21. Gareth Buckell, 'Shoot Shoot Shoot: The LFMC and the Film Culture of Sixties Britain', *Filmwaves*, Issue 31, 2006, pp. 36–40; p. 38.
22. John A. Walker, *Left Shift: Radical Art in 1970s Britain*, op. cit., p. 97.
23. David Curtis, *A History of Artists' Film and Video in Britain*, op. cit., p. 39.
24. Ibid., p. 39 and p. 50 (reference 60).
25. Maxa Zoller, 'Interview: Maxa Zoller with Malcolm Le Grice' in *X-Screen: Film Installation and Actions of the '60s and '70s*, op. cit., pp. 136–147, p. 144.
26. Ibid.
27. A.L. Rees, 'Expanded Cinema and Narrative: A Troubled History' in Steven Ball, David Curtis, A.L. Rees and Duncan White, *Expanded Cinema: Art, Performance and Film*, op. cit., pp. 12–21; p. 21.
28. Malcolm Le Grice, *Experimental Cinema in the Digital Age* (London: BFI, 2001), p. 319.
29. Malcolm Le Grice, 'Real time/space', *Art and Artists*, December, 1972, pp. 39–43; p. 39.
30. Malcolm Le Grice, *Experimental Cinema in the Digital Age*, op.cit., p. 160.
31. Annabel Nicolson, 'Artist as Filmmaker', op cit., p. 23.
32. A.L. Rees, 'Video and the Argument from Design' in Jackie Hatfield and Stephen Littman (eds), *Experiments in Moving Image*, op. cit., pp. 4–6; p. 4.
33. Theo von Doesburg and Standish Lawder, 'Film as Pure Form' in *Form*, Summer 1966. http://isites.harvard.edu/fs/docs/icb.topic235120.files/vanDoesbergFilmForm.pdf p. 9. Essay first published in 1929.

34. Stan VanDerBeek, '"Culture: Intercom" and Expanded Cinema: A Proposal and Manifesto' in Tanya Leighton (ed.), *Art and the Moving Image: A Critical Reader,* op. cit., pp. 72–74; p. 74. First published in *Film Culture,* Spring 1966.
35. Ibid., p. 73.
36. Maxa Zoller, 'Interview: Maxa Zoller with Malcolm Le Grice' in *X-Screen: Film Installation and Actions of the '60s and '70s,* op. cit., pp. 136–147, p. 146.
37. 'Filmaktion at Walker Art Gallery', Lucy Reynolds, http://www.studycollection.co.uk/filmaktion/Frameset13.html.
38. Michael O'Pray, 'Derek Jarman: The Art of Films/Films of Art' in *Derek Jarman: A Portrait: Artist, Film-maker, Designer* (London: Thames and Hudson, 1996), pp. 65–75; p. 65. Exhibition catalogue.
39. Entry from Jarman's notebook, 30 March 1983, Phoenix House, Box 23, BFI Special Collections.
40. Chrissie Iles, 'Derek Jarman' in Isaac Julien (curator), *Derek Jarman: Brutal Beauty* (London: Serpentine Gallery, 2008); pp. 64–73; p. 69.
41. Michael O'Pray, 'Derek Jarman's Cinema: Eros and Thanatos', *Afterimage,* No. 12, Autumn 1985, pp. 6–15; p. 9.
42. Peter Wollen, 'Blue', *New Left Review,* November/December 2000, pp. 120–133; p. 124.
43. Gray Watson, 'An Archaeology of Soul' in Roger Wollen (ed.), *Derek Jarman: A Portrait, Artist, Film-maker, Designer* (London: Thames and Hudson, 1996), pp. 33–48; p. 43. Exhibition catalogue.
44. Peter Wollen, 'Blue', *New Left Review,* op. cit., p. 133.
45. Deke Dusinbere, 'On Expanding Cinema', *Studio International,* Vol. 190, July to November, 1975, pp. 220–224; p. 222.
46. Jeremy Spenser, 'Jenny Okun' in Annabel Nicolson (ed.), *Readings,* No. 2, 1977, pp. 4–5, p. 4.
47. Peter Wollen, 'The Two Avant-Gardes', *Studio International,* Vol. 190, 978, November/December 1975, pp. 171–175.
48. Standish D. Lawder, *The Cubist Cinema* (New York, New York University Press, 1975), p. 21.
49. Ibid., p. 21 and p. 22.
50. Malcolm Le Grice, *Abstract Film and Beyond* (London: Studio Vista, 1977), p. 128.
51. Email correspondence with William Raban, 23 June 2009.
52. William Raban, *Angles of Incidence,* http://www.luxonline.org.uk/artists/william_raban/angles_of_incidence.html.
53. Malcolm Le Grice, *Abstract Film and Beyond,* op. cit., p. 129.
54. Ron Haseldon, *Tracking Cycles* (1975), cited from cover of video held in BAFVSC.
55. Malcolm Le Grice, *Experimental Cinema in the Digital Age,* op. cit., p. 165.
56. Guy Sherwin, *Optical Sound Films* (London: Lux, 2007), p. 15.
57. Nicky Hadley, 'Anne Rees-Mogg: Conjuring Tricks', http://www.luxonline.org.uk/artists/anne_rees-mogg/essay(3).html.
58. Guy Sherwin interview, January 2009.
59. David Curtis, *A History of Artists Film and Video in Britain,* op. cit., p. 217.
60. Ibid., p. 235.
61. Deke Dusinberre, 'See Real Images!', *Afterimage,* No. 8/9, Winter 1980/1981, pp. 87–107; p. 99.

62. A.L. Rees, *A History of Experimental Film and Video*, op. cit., p. 85.
63. Deke Dusinberre, 'See Real Images!', op. cit., p. 99.
64. A.L. Rees, 'Locating the LFMC: The First Decade in Context' in *Shoot Shoot Shoot: The First Decade of the London Film-makers' Co-operative and British Avant-garde Film 1966–76* (London: Lux, 2002), p. 8.
65. Roger Wollen, 'Introduction: Facets of Derek Jarman' in *Derek Jarman: A Portrait, Artist, Film-maker, Designer*, op. cit., pp. 15–31, p. 18.
66. Ibid.
67. Sebastian Coe, *Like a Fiery Elephany: The Story of B. S. Johnson* (London: Picador, 2004), p. 373.
68. David Curtis, *A History of Artists Film and Video in Britain*, op. cit., p. 220.
69. A.L. Rees, 'Locating the LFMC: The First Decade in Context' op. cit., p. 8.
70. David Curtis, *A History of Artists Film and Video in Britain*, op. cit., p. 216.
71. Ibid., p. 99.
72. Ibid., p. 148. Notes 10.
73. Peter Wollen, 'Chris Welsby' in DVD booklet (London: Illuminations, 2005).
74. Ibid., p. 96. Curtis is citing Deke Dusinberre from programme notes for 'Avant-garde British Landscape Films', Tate Gallery, March 1975.
75. David Curtis, *A History of Artists Film and Video in Britain*, op. cit., 95.
76. David Curtis, 'English Avant-garde Film: An Early Chronology' in *A Perspective on English Avant-garde Film*, op. cit., pp. 9–18; p. 18.
77. Ibid.
78. Annabel Nicolson, *Escaping Notice* (Yorkshire: Arc Press, 1977). Edition of 500 artists' books.
79. Ibid.
80. Letter from Annabel Nicolson, dated 22 April 2009.
81. Branden W. Joseph, 'Sparring with the Spectacle' in *Anthony McCall: The Solid Light Films and Related Works* (Göttingen: Steidl Publishers, 2004), pp. 36–142; p. 118.
82. Ibid., p. 120.
83. Jonathan Walley, 'An Interview with Anthony McCall' in *Anthony McCall: The Solid Light Films and Related Works*, op. cit., pp. 146–163; p. 149.
84. Annabel Nicolson, 'Artist as Filmmaker', op.cit., p. 22.
85. Ibid., p. 23.
86. David Dye and Simon Field, 'David Dye: An Interview with Simon Field', *Art and Artists*, Vol. 7, No. 9, December 1972, pp. 16–19; p. 16.
87. Ibid., p. 18.
88. Ibid., p. 17.
89. Jonathan Walley, 'The Material of Film and the Idea of Cinema: Contrasting Practices in Sixties and Seventies Avant-garde Film', *October*, Issue 103, 2003, pp. 15–30; p. 18.
90. Ibid., p. 22.
91. Ibid., p. 23.
92. Anthony Mccall, 'Long Film for Ambient Light: Notes in Duration' in *Anthony McCall: The Solid Light Films and Related Works*, op. cit., p. 99.
93. Ibid.
94. Deke Dusinbere, 'On Expanding Cinema', *Studio International*, Vol. 190, 1975, pp. 220–224; p. 224.

95. Annabel Nicolson and Sylvia Paskin, *Films for Women* (London: BFI Publishing, 1986). Copy of the text provided by Nicolson.
96. Tony Hill, 'Statement' in *Live in Your Head: Concept and Experiment in Britain 1965–75*, op. cit., pp. 100–101; p. 100.
97. Jonathan Walley, 'The Material of Film and the Idea of Cinema: Contrasting Practices in Sixties and Seventies Avant-garde Film', op. cit. p. 19.

4 Visionary, Mythopoeia and Diary Films

1. P. Adams Sitney, *Visionary Film: The American Avant-garde 1943–1978* (New York, Oxford University Press, 1978). First published in 1974.
2. American academics like psychologist Richard Bucke and psychologist/philosopher William James investigated Eastern 'sciences' related to mysticism. Richard Bucke, *Cosmic Consciousness* (1901) and William James, *The Varieties of Religious Experience: A Study in Human Nature* (1902).
3. Jay Stevens, *Storming Heaven: LSD and the American Dream* (London: Harper Collins, 1993), p. 79.
4. Jeff Nuttall, *Bomb Culture*, op. cit., p. 183.
5. Ibid.
6. Duncan Reekie, *Subversion: The Definitive History of Underground Cinema*, op. cit., p. 137.
7. Henrik Hendrikson, 'Monkey's Birthday' in *Perspectives on British Avant-garde Film* (London: Arts Council/Hayward, 1977). Loose leaf exhibition catalogue.
8. Janey Walkin, 'Interview with Anne Rees-Mogg' in *The Undercut Reader: Critical Writings on Artists' Film and Video*, op. cit., pp. 71–75' p. 72.
9. P. Adams Sitney, *Visionary Film: The American Avant-garde 1943–1978*, op. cit., p. 21.
10. Ibid., p. 150.
11. Ibid., p. 164.
12. Ibid., p. 173.
13. Ibid., p. 360.
14. Jonas Mekas, 'Diaries, Notes and Sketches' programme for 'A Season of Diary Films: Hill, Mekas, Breakwell, McBride', ICA, March–April 1977.
15. Pam Cook, 'The Point of Expression in Avant-Garde Film' in Elizabeth Cowie (ed.), *Catalogue British Film Institute productions: 1977–1978*, op. cit., pp. 53–56; p. 53.
16. Ibid.
17. David Curtis, *A History of Artists' Film and Video in Britain*, op. cit., p. 181.
18. Jane Arden, 'Notes on Vibration' (London: BFI, 2009). DVD booklet.
19. P. Adams Sitney, *Visionary Film: The American Avant-garde 1943–1978*, op. cit., p. 21.
20. Jane Arden, 'Notes on Vibration', op. cit.
21. Chris Darke, 'Mind Games' in *Anti-Clock* (London: BFI, 2009), pp. 1–3, p. 2. DVD booklet.
22. Ibid., p. 3.
23. William Fowler, 'Encounters with Central Bazaar', in *Central Bazaar* (London: BFI, 2009), pp. 2–6; p. 3. DVD booklet.
24. Claire Monk, 'Always Too Early' in *Separation* (London: BFI, 2009), pp. 1–4; p. 2. DVD booklet.

25. William Fowler, 'Encounters with Central Bazaar', in *Central Bazaar*, op. cit., p. 3. DVD booklet.
26. Ibid., p. 5.
27. Ibid.
28. Penny Slinger, 'The Other Side of the Underneath', in *The Other Side of the Underneath* (London, BFI, 2009), pp. 4–10; p. 5 and 8. DVD booklet.
29. Paul Willeman, 'Voyeurism, the Look and Dwoskin', *Afterimage*, No. 6, Summer 1976, pp. 40–51; p. 47.
30. A.L. Rees, 'Stephen Dwoskin', luxonline, http://www.luxonline.org.uk/artists/stephen_dwoskin/essay(2).html.
31. Stephen Dwoskin, 'Statement' in *Central Bazaar*, op. cit., p. 1. DVD booklet.
32. Jonas Mekas, 'Central Bazaar' in *Central Bazaar* op. cit., pp. 12–13; p. 12. DVD booklet. Originally published in *Soho News*, 7 April 1977.
33. Alice L. Hutchison, *Kenneth Anger: A Demonic Visionary* (London: Black Dog Publishing, 2004), p. 164.
34. A.L. Rees, *A History of Experimental Film and Video*, op. cit., p. 79.
35. Alice L. Hutchison, *Kenneth Anger: A Demonic Visionary*, op. cit., p. 165.
36. Gary Lachman, 'Kenneth Anger: The Crowned and Conquering Child' in *Magick Lantern Cycle: Kenneth Anger* (London: BFI, 2009), pp. 10–22; p. 20. DVD booklet.
37. Alice L. Hutchison, *Kenneth Anger: A Demonic Visionary*, op. cit., p. 164.
38. Ibid.
39. Rowland Wymer, *Derek Jarman* (Manchester: University of Manchester Press, 2005), p. 28.
40. Derek Jarman, *The Last of England* (London, Constable, 1987), p. 22 and 36.
41. Barry Miles, 'The Naked Lunch in my Life' in Oliver Harris and Ian Macfadyen (eds), *Naked Lunch @ 50: Anniversary Essays* (Illinois, Southern Illinois University Press, 2009); pp. 114–122; p. 119.
42. John Wyver, *Derek Jarman*, op. cit., p. 8.
43. Gary Lachman, 'Kenneth Anger: The Crowned and Conquering Child' in *Magick Lantern Cycle: Kenneth Anger*, op. cit.; p. 15.
44. Alice L. Hutchison, *Kenneth Anger: A Demonic Visionary*, op. cit., p. 176.
45. Derek Jarman's personal notebook, entry dated '30th March 1983 Phoenix House', BFI Special Collections Library.
46. Derek Jarman, *Dancing Ledge*, op. cit., p. 121.
47. Ibid.
48. John Wyver, *Derek Jarman*, op. cit., p. 30.
49. Derek Jarman, *Dancing Ledge*, op. cit., p. 122.
50. Ibid., p. 118.
51. Ibid.
52. Ibid., p. 116.
53. Ibid.
54. Margaret Tait, 'On "stalking the image"' in Peter Todd and Benjamin Cook (eds), *Subjects and Sequences: A Margaret Tait Reader*, op. cit., p. 89.
55. P. Adams Sitney, *Visionary Film: The American Avant-garde 1943–1978*, op. cit., p. 360.
56. Nick Kimberley, 'Introduction' in Ian Breakwell, *Diary 1964–1985* (London: Pluto Press, 1986), p. 8.
57. Ibid., p. 9.

58. Ibid., p. 8.
59. Ibid., p. 67.
60. Nick Kimberley, 'Obituary: Ian Breakwell', *The Guardian*, Friday 21 October 2005.
61. Jonathan Coe, *Like a Fiery Elephant: The Story of B. S. Johnson* (London: Picador, 2004).
62. Johnson monologue in *Fat Man on the Beach*.
63. Jonathan Coe, *Like a Fiery Elephant: The Story of B. S. Johnson*, op. cit., p. 62.
64. Johnson monologue in *Fat Man on the Beach*.
65. Email correspondence with Jonathan Coe, dated 16 October 2007.
66. David Curtis, 'Britain's Oldest Experimentalist ... Margaret Tait' in *Vertigo*, Vol. 1, No. 9, 1999, http://www.closeupfilmcentre.com/vertigo_magazine/volume-1-issue-9-summer-1999/britain-s-oldest-experimentalist-margaret-tait/. No page numbers.
67. Ali Smith, 'The Margaret Tait Years' in Peter Todd and Benjamin Cook (eds), *Subjects and Sequences: A Margaret Tait Reader*, op. cit., pp. 7–27; p. 9.
68. Sarah Neely, 'Stalking the Image: Margaret Tait and Intimate Filmmaking Practices', *Screen*, Vol. 49, No. 2, pp. 216–221; p. 219.
69. Margaret Tait, 'On "stalking the image"' in Peter Todd and Benjamin Cook (eds), *Subjects and Sequences: A Margaret Tait Reader*, op. cit., p. 89.
70. Catherine Russell, *Experimental Ethnography: The Work of Film in the Age of Video* (London: Duke University Press, 1999), p. 285.
71. Margaret Tait, 'Tailpiece' in Peter Todd and Benjamin Cook (eds), *Subjects and Sequences: A Margaret Tait Reader*, op. cit., p. 165.
72. Jo Comino, 'Short Films: Place of Work', *Art and Artists*, October 1983, Vol. 50, No. 597, pp. 284–287; p. 285.
73. Ibid.
74. Margaret Tait is quoted in Mike Leggett's programme notes for her LFMC screening on 30 November 1977. Sourced BAFVSC.
75. Nick Wadley, 'Anne Rees Mogg', http://www.luxonline.org.uk/artists/anne_rees-mogg/essay(1).html.
76. Nick Wadley, 'Anne Rees Mogg', op. cit.
77. Janey Walkin, 'Interview with Anne Rees-Mogg' in *The Undercut Reader: Critical Writings on Artists' Film and Video*, op. cit., pp. 71–75, p. 72.
78. Henrik Hendrikson, 'Monkey's Birthday' in *Perspectives on British Avant-garde Film*, op. cit. Loose leaf exhibition catalogue.
79. David Curtis, *A History of Artists' Film and Video in Britain*, op. cit., p. 179.
80. Henrik Hendrikson, 'Monkey's Birthday' in *Perspectives on British Avant-garde Film*, op. cit.
81. David Larcher on REWIND, op. cit.
82. Henrik Hendrikson, 'Monkey's Birthday' in *Perspectives on British Avant-garde Film*, op. cit.
83. Steve Dwoskin, 'Mare's Tail', *Afterimage*, No. 2, Autumn 1970, pp. 40–43; p. 43.
84. Phone interview with John Akomfrah, 16 April 2014.
85. Gray Watson, 'An Archaeology of Soul' in Roger Wollen (ed.), *Derek Jarman: A Portrait Artist, Film-maker, Designer*, op. cit., pp. 33–48; p. 47.
86. Chrissie Iles, 'Derek Jarman' in *Derek Jarman: Brutal Beauty*, Serpentine Gallery exhibition catalogue, op. cit., pp. 4–73; p. 64.
87. Janey Walkin, 'Interview with Anne Rees-Mogg' in *The Undercut Reader: Critical Writings on Artists' Film and Video*, op. cit., pp. 71–75; p. 73.

88. Hamid Naficy, *An Accented Cinema: Exilic and Diasporic Filmmaking* (New Jersey, Princeton University Press, 2001), p. 143.
89. Gray Watson, 'An Archaeology of Soul' in Roger Wollen (ed.), *Derek Jarman: A Portrait Artist, Film-maker, Designer*, op. cit., p. 47.
90. Steve Dwoskin, 'Mare's Tail', op. cit., pp. 40–43; p. 43.

5 Experiments with Structure and Material

1. A.L. Rees, *A History of Experimental Film and Video*, op. cit., p. 80.
2. Ibid., p. 77.
3. Malcolm Le Grice, *Experimental Cinema in the Digital Age*, op. cit., p. 165.
4. Deke Dusinberre, 'Structural Asceticism' in 'Perspectives on British Avant-Garde Film', op. cit., loose-leaf programme notes.
5. Deke Dusinberre, *English Avant-garde Cinema 1966–1974*, op. cit., p. 58.
6. Michael Mazière, *Institutional Support for Artists' Film and Video in England 1966–2003*, op. cit., p. 14.
7. A.L. Rees, *A History of Experimental Film and Video*, op. cit., p. 81.
8. David Curtis, *A History of Artists' Film and Video in Britain*, op. cit., p. 219.
9. Ibid.
10. Peter Gidal, *Structural Film Anthology* (London: BFI, 1978), p. 14. First published in 1976.
11. Malcolm Le Grice, *Experimental Cinema in the Digital Age*, op. cit., p. 70.
12. Duncan Reekie, *Subversion: The Definitive History of Underground Cinema*, op. cit., p. 177.
13. Mark Webber, 'Chronology of Events and Developments 1966–76' in Mark Webber (ed.), *Shoot Shoot Shoot* broadsheet, op. cit., p. 6.
14. Annabel Nicolson, 'Canada Fragments', *Art and Artists*, Vol. 8, No. 1, April 1973, pp. 29–33. Le Grice's debates with Brakhage and Sitney in Malcolm Le Grice, *Experimental Cinema in the Digital Age*, op. cit., pp. 85–127 and pp. 134–152 respectively.
15. Mark Webber, 'Chronology of Events and Developments 1966–76' in Mark Webber (ed.), *Shoot Shoot Shoot* broadsheet, op. cit., p. 6.
16. Ibid.
17. Malcolm Le Grice, *Experimental Cinema in the Digital Age*, op. cit., p. 54.
18. Ibid., p. 64.
19. Mark Webber, 'Chronology of Events and Developments 1966–76' in *Shoot Shoot Shoot*, op. cit., p. 7.
20. David Curtis, 'English Avant-Garde Film: An Early Chronology' in *A Perspective on English Avant-Garde Film*, op. cit., pp. 9–18; p. 9.
21. Ibid.
22. P. Adams Sitney, *Visionary Film: The American Avant-Garde 1943–1978*, op. cit.
23. Ibid., p. 370.
24. Ibid., p. 369.
25. Callie Angell, *The Films of Andy Warhol: Part II* (New York: Whitney, 1994), p. 10.
26. P. Adams Sitney, *Visionary Film: The American Avant-Garde 1943–1978*, op. cit., p. 371.
27. A.L. Rees, *A History of Experimental Film and Video*, op. cit., p. 77.

28. P. Adams Sitney, *Structural Film* in *Visionary Film: American Avant-Garde 1943–1978*, op. cit., p. 374.
29. David Curtis, *Experimental Cinema: A Fifty-Year Evolution* (New York: Universe Books, 1971), p. 152.
30. George Maciunas, 'Some Comments on *Structural Film* by P. Adams Sitney (*Film Culture No. 47, 1969)*' reproduced in Tanya Leighton, *Art and the Moving Image: A Critical Reader*, op. cit., pp. 54; p. 54.
31. Malcolm Le Grice, *Experimental Cinema in the Digital Age*, op. cit., p. 14. The essay 'Thoughts on Recent Underground Film' was first published in *Afterimage*, 1972.
32. Ibid.
33. Malcolm Le Grice, 'Thoughts on Recent Underground Film' in *Experimental Cinema in the Digital Age*, op. cit., pp. 14–26.
34. Ibid., p. 140.
35. Peter Gidal, 'Theory and Definition of Structural/Materialist Film' in Peter Gidal (ed.), *Structural Film Anthology*, op. cit., p. 1.
36. Interview with Peter Gidal, June 2007.
37. Peter Gidal, 'Theory and Definition of Structural/Materialist Film' in Peter Gidal (ed.), *Structural Film Anthology*, op. cit., p. 1.
38. A.L. Rees, *A History of Experimental Film and Video*, op. cit., p. 82.
39. A.L. Rees, 'Projecting Back – UK film and video installation in the 1970s' *Millennium Film Journal*, No. 52 (winter 2009/10), http://mfj-online.org/journalPages/MFJ52/Rees.htm. No page numbers.
40. Nina Danino and Michael Mazière, *The Undercut Reader*, op. cit., *Light Years: A Twenty Year Celebration* (Arts Council: 1986).
41. Malcolm Le Grice, 'A Reflection on the History of the London Film-makers Co-op' in Michael Mazière (ed.), *Light Years: A Twenty Year Celebration*, catalogue for screenings 1986, London. pp. 26–27, p. 26.
42. A.L. Rees, 'Locating the LFMC' in Mark Webber, *Shoot Shoot Shoot*, op. cit., p. 8. Exhibition catalogue.
43. Paul S. Arthur, 'Structural Film: Revisions, New Versions and the Artifact: Part Two', *Millenium Film Journal*, No. 4/5, Summer/Fall 1979, pp. 122–134; p. 128.
44. A.L. Rees, *A History of Experimental Film and Video*, op. cit., p. 82.
45. Constance Penley, *Future of an Illusion: Film, Feminism and Psychoanalysis* (Minneapolis: University of Minnesota Press, 1989), p. 5.
46. Malcolm Le Grice, *Experimental Cinema in the Digital Age*, op. cit., p. 4.
47. Ibid., p. 134.
48. Peter Gidal, *Structural Film Anthology*, op. cit., p. iv.
49. Peter Gidal, 'Structural Films', programme notes: 'Structural Film Retrospective'. Sourced BAFVSC.
50. A.L. Rees, *A History of Experimental Film and Video*, op. cit., p. 83.
51. Constance Penley, *Future of an Illusion: Film, Feminism and Psychoanalysis*, op. cit., p. 4.
52. Peter Gidal, 'Theory and Definition of Structural/Materialist Film' in Peter Gidal (ed.), *Structural Film Anthology*, op. cit., p. 4.
53. Constance Penley, *Future of an Illusion: Film, Feminism and Psychoanalysis*, op. cit., p. 13.

54. John Du Cane, 'Film and Video: The Third Part of Gallery House's Survey of the Avant-Garde in Britain', *Time Out*, 13–19 October 1972.
55. Stan Brakhage, 'On Silent Sound' in *Stan Brakhage: An American Independent Filmmaker: An Exhibition of Films Toured by the Arts Council of Great Britain* (London: Arts Council, 1980), pp. 29.
56. Peter Wollen, 'The Two Avant-gardes' in Michael O'Pray, *The British Avant-Garde Film: 1926–1995*, op. cit., p. 137.
57. Malcolm Le Grice, *Experimental Cinema in the Digital Age*, op. cit., p. 301.
58. David Miller, *Paragraphs On Some Films by Annabel Nicolson Seen in March, 1973*. Sourced BAFVSC.
59. Ibid.
60. Nicky Hamlyn, *Film Art Phenomena* (London: BFI, 2003), p. 35.
61. Ibid.
62. Deke Dusinberre, 'The Ascetic Task: Peter's Gidal's *Room Film 1973*' in Peter Gidal (ed.), *Structural Film Anthology*, op. cit., pp. 109–113; p. 109.
63. Peter Gidal, 'Artists' Statement' in Deke Dusinberre and David Curtis (eds), *A Perspective on English Avant-garde Film*, op. cit., pp. 73–74, p. 58.
64. A.L. Rees, *A History of Experimental Film and Video*, op. cit., p. 86.
65. Jonas Mekas, 'Movie Journal', *The Village Voice*, 25 October 1973, pp. 87.
66. Malcolm Le Grice, *Experimental Cinema in the Digital Age*, op. cit., p. 74.
67. Nicky Hamlyn, 'From Structuralism to Imagism: Peter Gidal and His Influence in the 1980s' in *The Undercut Reader: Critical Writings on Artists' Film and Video*, op. cit., pp. 233–238; p. 235.
68. Peter Gidal, 'Artists' Statement' in Deke Dusinberre and David Curtis (eds), *A Perspective on English Avant-garde Film*, op. cit. pp. 73–74, p. 58.
69. Stan Brakhage, *Essential Brakhage: Selected Writings on Filmmaking* (New York: McPherson, 2001), p. 12. 'Metaphors on Vision' essay first published in *Film Culture* in 1963.
70. Ibid.
71. A.L. Rees, *A History of Experimental Film and Video*, op. cit., p. 69.
72. Ibid.
73. Paul Arthur, Structural Film: Revisions, New Versions, and the Artifact', *Millenium Film Journal*, Vol. 1, No. 2, Spring/Summer 1978.
74. William C. Wees, *Light Moving in Time: Studies in the Visual Aesthetics of Avant-Garde Film* (California: University of California Press, 1992), p. 103.
75. Ibid., p. 101.
76. 'Structural/Materialist' – *Shoot Shoot Shoot: The First Decade of the London Film-makers' Co-operative and British Avant-garde Film 1966–76*. Video rushes of introductions to screenings at Tate Gallery. Sourced BAFVSC.
77. Mike Sperlinger, 'Ian Breakwell', luxonline, p. 1–4; p. 1. http://www.luxonline.org.uk/artists/ian_breakwell/essay(1).html.
78. A.L. Rees, *A History of Experimental Film and Video*, op. cit., p. 117.
79. David Curtis, *A History of British Artists Film and Video*, op. cit., p. 197.
80. Mike Sperlinger, 'Ian Breakwell', luxonline, op. cit., p. 1–4; p. 1.
81. Paul Arthur, 'Structural Film: Revisions, New Versions and the Artifact: Part Two', *Millennium Film Journal*, op. cit., pp. 122–134; p. 133 (note 13).
82. Catherine Russell, *Experimental Ethnography: The Work of Film in the Age of Video*, op. cit., p. 287.

83. Peter Greenaway, *Introduction to Early Films No. 1* (London: BFI Video Publishing, 2003). DVD booklet.
84. David Curtis, *A History of British Artists Film and Video*, op. cit., p. 235.
85. Welsby on Luxonline. http://www.luxonline.org.uk/artists/chris_welsby/ stream_line.html.
86. Peter Greenaway, *Introduction to Early Films No. 1*, op. cit., Greenaway's introduction to the film.
87. Peter Greenaway, *Introduction to Early Films No. 2* (London: BFI, 2003). DVD booklet.
88. '1973–75. Closure' was published in *Wallpaper* in June 1976. Branden W. Joseph, 'Sparring with the Spectacle: Parts 1–5' in Christopher Eamon (ed.), *Anthony McCall: The Solid Light Films and Related Works*, op. cit., pp. 36–77; p. 39.
89. Ibid.
90. Duncan Reekie, *Subversion: The Definitive History of Underground Cinema*, op. cit., p. 177.
91. Nicky Hamlyn, 'From Structuralism to Imagism: Peter Gidal and His Influence in the 1980s' in Michael Mazière and Nina Danino (eds), *The Undercut Reader: Critical Writings on Artists' Film and Video*, op. cit., pp. 233–238; p. 234.
92. Stephen Heath, 'Afterword', *Screen*, Vol. 20, No. 2, Summer 1979, pp. 93–99; p. 94.
93. David Curtis, *A History of Artists' Film and Video*, op. cit., p. 213.
94. Nicky Hamlyn, 'Structuralist Traces' in Michael O'Pray (ed.), *Avant-Garde Film 1926–1995: An Anthology of Writings* (London: Arts Council/Luton University Press, 1996), pp. p. 234.

6   Women and Film

1. Imelda Whelehan, *Modern Feminist Thought: From the Second Wave to 'Post-Feminism'* (Edinburgh: Edinburgh University Press, 1996), p. 11.
2. D. N. Rodowick, *The Crisis of Political Modernism: Criticism and Ideology in Contemporary Film Criticism*, op. cit., p. xxi.
3. Ibid.
4. Laura Mulvey, 'Film, Feminism and the Avant-Garde' in Michael O'Pray (ed.), *The British Avant-garde Film: 1926–1995: An Anthology of Writings*, op. cit., pp. 199–216; p. 211.
5. E. Ann Kaplan, 'Aspects of British Feminist Film Theory: A Critical Evaluation of Texts by Claire Johnson and Pam Cook', *Jump Cut*, 2, 1974, pp. 52–55. www.ejumpcut.org/archive/onlinessays/jc12–13folder/britfemtheory.html, p. 4 of 14.
6. Jean-Luc Godard, 'What is to be done?', *Afterimage*, No. 1, April 1970. No page numbers.
7. Nicolson interview with David Curtis for 'Shoot Shoot Shoot' documentary. Video rushes I/V 1, 2001. Sourced BAFVSC.
8. Ibid.
9. Imelda Whelehan, *Modern Feminist Thought: From the Second Wave to 'Post-Feminism'*, op.cit., p. 177.
10. 'Feminism, Fiction and the Avant-garde' conference, 6–7 May 1978. Arts Council funding application 13 March 1978.Sourced BAFVSC.

11. Laura Mulvey, 'Film, Feminism and the Avant-Garde' in Michael O'Pray (ed.), *The British Avant-garde Film: 1926–1995: An Anthology of Writings*, op. cit., pp. 199–216; p. 209.
12. Lucy Lippard, 'Why Separate Women's Art?', *Art and Artists*, Vol. 8, No. 7, October 1973, pp. 8–9; p. 9.
13. Sarah Kent, review of 'Towards a Feminist Perception of Women's Practise in Art at AIR Gallery 2th February' in Annabel Nicolson and Paul Burrell (eds), *Readings*, No. 2, 1977. p. 11.
14. Ibid.
15. Laura Mulvey, 'Film, Feminism and the Avant-Garde' in Michael O'Pray (ed.), *The British Avant-garde Film: 1926–1995: An Anthology of Writings*, op. cit., pp. 199–216; p. 200.
16. Ibid., p. 202.
17. Silvia Bovenschein, 'Is There a Feminine Aesthetic?' in *New German Critique*, No. 10, Winter 1977, pp. 111–137; p. 124.
18. Ibid., p. 134.
19. Ibid.
20. Teresa de Lauretis, 'Aesthetic and Feminist Theory: Rethinking Women's Cinema' in *New German Critique*, No. 34, Winter 1985, pp. 154–175, p. 154.
21. Ibid., p. 158.
22. Ibid.
23. Ibid., p. 161.
24. Ibid., p. 159.
25. Ibid.
26. Ibid. Akerman is cited by de Lauretis.
27. Ibid.
28. Ibid., p. 160.
29. Lesley Stern, 'Feminism and Cinema-Exchanges', *Screen*, Vol. 20, Winter 1979/1980, pp. 89–105; p. 95.
30. Laura Mulvey, 'Film, Feminism and the Avant-Garde' in Michael O'Pray (ed.), *The British Avant-garde Film: 1926–1995: An Anthology of Writings*, op. cit. p. 202 and Patricia Erens, 'Towards a Feminist Aesthetic: Reflection-Revolution-Ritual' in Patricia Erens (ed.) *Sexual Stratagems: The World of Women in Film* (New York: Horizon Press, 1979), pp. 156–167; p. 161.
31. Nicolson interview with David Curtis for 'Shoot Shoot Shoot' documentary. Video rushes I/V 1, 2001. Sourced BAFVSC.
32. Laura Mulvey, 'Film, Feminism and the Avant-Garde', op. cit., pp. 199–216; p. 213.
33. Joanna Davis discussing *Often During the Day* in *Seeing for Ourselves: Women Working in Film* (1983) Channel Four documentary. Sourced BAFVSC.
34. Teresa de Lauretis, 'Aesthetic and Feminist Theory: Rethinking Women's Cinema', op. cit., p. 174. Akerman is cited by de Lauretis.
35. Annie Oakley, *Sociology of Housework* (London: Wiley-Blackwell, 1974).
36. Interview with Lis Rhodes at British Library, London, December 2008.
37. Silvia Bovenschein, 'Is There a Feminine Aesthetic?', op. cit. p. 136.
38. Joanna Davis, statement on the video cover of *Often During the Day*. Sourced BAFVSC.
39. Teresa de Lauretis, 'Aesthetic and Feminist Theory: Rethinking Women's Cinema', op. cit, p. 159. Akerman is cited in de Lauretis.

40. Sarah Neely, 'Stalking the Image: Margaret Tait and Intimate Filmmaking Practices', *Screen*, 2008, Vol. 49, No. 2, pp. 216–221; p. 219.
41. Gill Eatherley in Annabel Nicolson, 'The Early Years of the Film Co-op' in Jackie Hatfield and Stephen Littman (eds), *Experiments in Moving Image*, op. cit., pp. 12–19, p. 15.
42. Andy Beckett, 'What a Swell Party it Was', *The Independent*, 2 June 1996.
43. Jayne Parker, 'Free Show', *theFrame*, Jayne Parker DVD (London: BFI, 2005).
44. Interview/discussion with Le Grice at BAFVSC. February 2008.
45. Teresa de Lauretis, 'Aesthetic and Feminist Theory: Rethinking Women's Cinema', op. cit., p. 158.
46. Siona Wilson, 'From Women's Work to the Umbilical Lens: Mary Kelly's Early Films', *Art History*, 31/1, 2008, pp. 79–102; p. 89.
47. Deke Dusinbere, 'Short Film Series', *Art and Artists*, No. 50, October 1983, pp. 286–287; p. 287.
48. Carolee Schneemann, *Imaging Her Erotics: Essays, Interviews, Projects* (Massachusetts: The MIT Press, 2003), p. 123.
49. Ibid., p. 45.
50. Interview Carolee Schneemann and Duncan White, New York, April 2008. p. 7, http://www.rewind.ac.uk/expanded/Narrative/Interviews_files/SchneemannTS.pdf.
51. Ibid.
52. Carolee Schneemann, *Imaging Her Erotics: Essays, Interviews, Projects*, op. cit., p. 159.
53. Ibid.
54. Paul Willeman, 'Voyeurism, the Look and Dwoskin' in *Afterimage*, 6, 1976, pp. 40–51; p. 47.
55. Ibid., p. 41.
56. David Curtis, *A History of Artists' Film and Video in Britain*, op. cit., p. 249.
57. 'Interview with Kate Haug' in *Carolee Schneemann: Imaging Her Erotics: Essays, Interviews, Projects*, op. cit., pp. 21–44; p. 43.
58. Teresa de Lauretis, 'Aesthetic and Feminist Theory: Rethinking Women's Cinema', op. cit., p. 158.
59. Natasha Morgan, 'Tina Keane: Shadow Woman' in Rozsika Parker and Griselda Pollock (eds), *Framing Feminism: Art and the Women's Movement 1970–1985*, op. cit., pp. 287–288; p. 288.
60. Natasha Morgan, 'Shadow Woman', *Spare Rib*, 1977, No. 675, pp. 26–27; p. 27.
61. Ibid.
62. 'Expanded Cartography and the New Live Cinema' seminar at Central St Martins College of Art and Design, London, 20 May 2009. Video transcript. BAFVSC.
63. 'Max Eastley Talking to Annabel Nicolson'. Text provided by Annabel Nicolson.
64. Natasha Morgan, 'Shadow Woman', *Spare Rib*, 1977, No. 675, pp. 26–27; p. 27.
65. Interview between Annabel Nicolson and David Curtis, rushes for 'Shoot Shoot Shoot', I/V (2001). Sourced BAFVSC.
66. Ibid.
67. Scott MacDonald, *A Critical Cinema 5: Interviews with Independent Filmmakers* (California: University of California Press, 1998), p. 398.
68. Patricia Mellencamp, *Indiscretions: Avant-garde Film, Video and Feminism* (Indianapolis: Indiana University Press, 1990), p. 152.

69. Sue Harper, *Women in British Cinema: Mad, Bad and Dangerous to Know* (London: Continuum, 2000), p. 201.
70. Sally Potter Arts Council grant application, 19 September 1977, BAFVSC.
71. Marina Vishmidt, 'Jeanette Iljon' on luxonline, accessed on 6 April 2011, pp. 1–5; p. 3. www.luxonline.org.uk/artists/jeanette_iljon/essay(3).html.
72. Ibid.
73. Scott MacDonald, *A Critical Cinema 5: Interviews with Independent Filmmakers*, op. cit., p. 407.
74. Sue Harper, *Women in British Cinema: Mad, Bad and Dangerous to Know*, op. cit., p. 201.
75. Nancy Woods, 'On Light Reading', *Circles Distribution*, unpublished programme notes, 1981–1984. Cited in Peter Gidal, *Materialist Film* (London: Routledge, 1990), p. 71.
76. Voiceover in *Light Reading*.
77. John Berger, *Ways of Seeing* (London: Penguin, 1972); p. 47.
78. Interview with Lis Rhodes, British Library, London, November 2008.
79. Ibid.
80. Ibid.
81. Lis Rhodes and Felicity Sparrow, 'Imprisoned in Dependency or the Violence of Meaning' in 'Her Image Fades as Her Voice Rises' (London, Arts Council Great Britain, 1983).
82. Annette Kuhn is cited in Peter Gidal, *Materialist Film,* op. cit., p. 45.
83. Peter Lehman and Judith Mayne, 'The Song of the Shirt: An Interview with Susan Clayton', *Wide Angle*, Vol. 6, No. 3, 1981, pp. 68–75; p. 73.
84. E. Ann Kaplan, 'Night at the Opera', *Millennium Film Journal*, Winter 1981/1982, p. 116.
85. Ibid.
86. Lis Rhodes and Felicity Sparrow, 'Imprisoned in Dependency or the Violence of Meaning', op. cit.
87. Ibid.
88. Sylvia Harvey, An Introduction to 'The Song of the Shirt', op. cit., p. 46.
89. Ibid.
90. Ibid., p. 48.
91. Lis Rhodes, 'Whose History?' in *Film as Film: Formal Experiment in Film: 1910–1975*, op. cit., pp. 119–120; p. 120.
92. Laura Mulvey, 'Film, Feminism and the Avant-Garde' in Michael O'Pray (ed.), *The British Avant-garde Film: 1926–1995: An Anthology of Writings*, op. cit., p. 202.
93. Lesley Stern, 'Feminism and Cinema-Exchanges', op. cit., pp. 89–105; p. 93.
94. *Seeing for Ourselves: Women Working with Film* (1983), Channel Four documentary. Sourced BAFVSC.

Conclusion: (Re)cognitions and (Re)considerations for This History

1. Nadine Gordimer, *Beethoven was One-Sixteenth Black* (London: Bloomsbury, 2008) p. 7.
2. Tilda Swinton, 'No known address ... or ... Don't look down ...' in *Derek Jarman: Brutal Beauty*, op. cit., pp. 10–17; p. 17.

3. A.L. Rees, 'Projecting Back: UK Film and Video Installation in the 1970s', *Millennium Film Journal*, No. 52, Winter 2009/2010. http://mfj-online.org/journalPages/MFJ52/Rees.htm. No page numbers.
4. Ibid.
5. Ibid.
6. Rosalind E. Krauss, *Perpetual Inventory* (Massachusetts: MIT Press, 2010), p. xiii.
7. Ibid.
8. Nicholas Cullinan, 'Film Still' in *FILM* (London: Tate, 2011), pp. 8–13; p. 9.
9. Ibid.
10. Ibid.
11. Ibid., p. 13.
12. A.L. Rees, *A History of Experimental Film and Video* (London: BFI, 2011). p. 140. 2nd Edition.
13. Ibid., p. 140.
14. Ibid.
15. George Clark, 'The Luminous View' in *Tate etc*, No. 30, Spring 2014, pp. 57–59.
16. Ibid., p. 57.
17. Ibid.
18. Ibid.
19. Ibid.
20. A.L. Rees, 'Projecting Back: UK Film and Video Installation in the 1970s', op. cit., http://mfj-online.org/journalPages/MFJ52/Rees.htm. No page numbers.

Bibliography

Books and exhibition catalogues

Angell, Callie, *The Films of Andy Warhol: Part II* (New York: Whitney, 1994).

Berger, John, *Ways of Seeing* (London: Penguin, 1972).

Brakhage, Stan, *Stan Brakhage: An American Independent Filmmaker: An Exhibition of Films Toured by the Arts Council of Great Britain* (London: Arts Council, 1980).

Brakhage, Stan, *Essential Brakhage: Selected Writings on Filmmaking* (New York: McPherson, 2001).

Breakwell, Ian, *The Artist's Dream: Stories and Pictures by Ian Breakwell* (London: Serpent's Tail, 1988).

Coe, Jonathan, *Like a Fiery Elephant: The Story of B.S. Johnson* (London: Picador, 2004).

Cullinan, Nicholas (ed.), *Tacita Dean: FILM* (London: Tate, 2011).

Curtis, David, *Experimental Cinema* (New York: Universe Books, 1971).

Curtis, David, *A History of Artists' Film and Video in Britain* (London: BFI Publishing, 2007).

Dwoskin, Stephen, *Film Is: The International Free Cinema* (London: Peter Owen, 1975).

Feyerabend, Paul, *Against Method* (London: Verso, 2010), p. 1. First published 1975.

Gidal, Peter, *Structural Film Anthology* (London: BFI, 1976).

Gidal, Peter, *Materialist Film* (London: Routledge, 1989).

Gordimer, Nadine, *Beethoven was One-Sixteenth Black* (London: Bloomsbury, 2008).

Hamlyn, Nicky, *Film Art Phenomena* (London: BFI, 2003).

Harper, Sue, *Women in British Cinema: Mad, Bad and Dangerous to Know* (London: Continuum, 2000).

Harvey, Sylvia, *Independent Cinema?* (Stafford: West Midlands Arts, 1978).

Harvey, Sylvia, *May '68 and Film Culture* (London: BFI, 1980).

Hewison, R., *Too Much: Art and Society in the Sixties 1960–75* (London: Methuen, 1988).

Hutchison, Alice L., *Kenneth Anger* (London: Black Dog Publishing, 2004).

Jarman, Derek, *Dancing Ledge* (Minneapolis: University of Minnesota Press, 2010). First published 1983.

Jenkins, Keith, *Re-thinking History* (London: Routledge, 2003).

Krauss, Rosalind, *Perpetual Inventory* (Massachusetts: MIT Press, 2010).

Larner, Melissa (ed.), *Derek Jarman: Brutal Beauty* (London: Koenig Books, 2008).

Lawder, Standish D., *The Cubist Cinema* (New York: New York University Press, 1975).

Le Grice, Malcolm, *Abstract Film and Beyond* (London: Studio Vista, 1977).

Le Grice, Malcolm, *Experimental Cinema in the Digital Age* (London: BFI Publishing, 2001).

Marzona, Daniel, *Conceptual Art* (Cologne: Taschen, 2006).

Mellencamp, Patricia, *Indiscretions: Avant-garde Film, Video and Feminism* (Indianapolis: Indiana University Press, 1990).

Musil, Robert, *The Man Without Qualities* (London: Picador, 1997). First published 1943.

Naficy, Hamid, *An Accented Cinema: Exilic and Diasporic Filmmaking* (New Jersey, Princeton University Press, 2001).

Nuttall, Jeff, *Bomb Culture* (London: Paladin, 1968).

Oakley, Annie, *Sociology of Housework* (London: Wiley-Blackwell, 1974).

O'Doherty, Brian, *Inside the White Cube: the Ideology of the Gallery Space* (Santa Monica: The Lapis Press, 1986).

O'Pray, Michael, *Avant-garde Film: Forms, Themes and Passions* (London: Wallflower, 2003).

Penley, Constance, *Future of an Illusion: Film, Feminism and Psychoanalysis* (Minneapolis: University of Minnesota Press, 1989).

Reekie, Duncan, *Subversion: The Definitive History of Underground Cinema* (London: Wallflower Press, 2007).

Rees, A.L., *A History of Experimental Film and Video* (London: BFI, 2011). First published 1999.

Rodowick, D. N., *The Crisis of Political Modernism: Criticism and Ideology in Contemporary Film Criticism* (Berkeley: University of California Press, 1995).

Russell, Catherine, *Experimental Ethnography: The Work of Film in the Age of Video* (London: Duke University Press, 1999).

Schneemann, Carolee, *Imaging Her Erotics: Essays, Interviews, Projects* (Cambridge: The MIT Press, 2003).

Sitney, P. Adams, *The Avant-Garde Film: Reader of Theory and Criticism* (New York: New York University Press, 1978).

Sitney, P. Adams, *Visionary Film: The American Avant-garde 1943–1978* (New York, Oxford University Press, 1978). First published in 1974.

Sitney, P. Adams, *Visionary Film: American Avant-Garde 1943–1978* (New York: Oxford University Press, 2002). First published 1974.

Stevens, Jay, *Storming Heaven: LSD and the American Dream* (London: Harper Collins, 1993).

Walker, John A., *Left Shift: Radical Art in 1970s Britain* (London: I. B. Tauris, 2002).

Wees, William C., *Light Moving in Time: Studies in the Visual Aesthetics of Avant-Garde Film* (California: University of California Press, 1992).

Whelehan, Imelda, *Modern Feminist Thought: From the Second Wave to 'Post-Feminism'* (Edinburgh: Edinburgh University Press, 1996).

Wollen Peter, *Signs and Meanings in the Cinema* (London, Secker & Warburg, 1972).

Wymer, Rowland, *Derek Jarman* (Manchester: University of Manchester Press, 2005).

Wyver, John, *Vision On: Film, Television and the Arts in Britain* (London: Wallflower Press, 2007).

Edited collections

Ball, Steven, Curtis, David, Rees, A.L. and White, Duncan (eds), *Expanded Cinema: Art Performance Film* (London: Tate 2011).

Brunsdon, Charlotte (ed.), *Films for Women* (London: BFI, 1986).

Comer, Stuart (ed.), *Film and Video Art* (London: Tate, 2009).

Cook, Benjamin and Todd, Peter (eds), *Subjects and Sequences: A Margaret Tait Reader* (London: LUX, 2004).

Cowie, Elizabeth (ed.), *British Film Institute Productions Catalogue: 1977–1978* (London: BFI, 1978).

Curtis, David (ed.), *A Directory of British Film & Video Artists* (London: Arts Council, 1995).

Curtis, David and Dusinberre, Deke (eds), *A Perspective on English Avant-Garde Film* (London: Arts/British Council, 1978).

Curtis, David and Wilson, Rodney (ed.), *Perspectives on British Avant-Garde Film* (London: Hayward, 1977).

Danino, Nina and Mazière, Michael (eds), *The Undercut Reader: Critical Writings on Artists' Film and Video* (London: Wallflower Press, 2003).

De Lauretis, Teresa and Heath, Stephen (eds), *Cinematic Apparatus* (London: Macmillan Press, 1980).

Dickinson, Margaret (ed.), *Rogue Reels: Oppositional Film in Britain, 1945–90* (London: BFI, 1999).

Dusinberre, Deke and Rees, A.L. (ed.), *Film as Film: Formal Experiment in Film 1910–1975* (London: Arts Council/Hayward Gallery, 1979).

Eamon, Christopher (ed.), *Anthony McCall: The Solid Light Films and Related Works* (Göttingen: Steidl, 2005).

Ellis, John (ed.), *Catalogue of BFI Productions 1951–76* (London: BFI, 1977).

Erens, Patricia (ed.) *Sexual Stratagems: The World of Women in Film* (New York: Horizon Press, 1979).

Greenberg, Reesa, Ferguson, Bruce W. and Nairne, Sandy (eds), *Thinking about Exhibitions* (London: Routledge, 1996).

Harris, Oliver and Macfadyen, Ian (eds), *Naked Lunch @ 50: Anniversary Essays* (Illinois, Southern Illinois University Press, 2009).

Harrison, Charles and Wood, Paul (eds), *Art in Theory 1900–1990: An Anthology of Changing Ideas* (Oxford: Blackwell, 2000).

Hatfield, Jackie (ed.), *Experimental Film and Video: An Anthology* (Eastleigh: John Libbey Publishing, 2006).

Hatfield, Jackie and Littman, Stephen (eds), *Experiments in Moving Image* (Luton: EpiGraph, 2004).

Knight, Julia and Thomas, Peter (eds), *Distribution and Promotion of Alternative Moving Image* (Bristol: Intellect, 2012).

Leighton, Tanya (ed.), *Art and the Moving Image: A Critical Reader* (London: Tate/Afterall, 2008).

Moore-Gilbert, Bart (ed.), *The Arts in the 1970s: Cultural Closure?* (London: Routledge, 1993).

Mulvey, Laura and Sexton, Jamie (eds), *Experimental British Television* (Manchester: Manchester University Press, 2007).

O'Pray, Michael (ed.), *Avant-Garde Film 1926–1995: An Anthology of Writings* (Luton, University of Luton, 1996).

Parker, Rozsika and Pollock, Griselda (eds), *Framing Feminism: Art and the Women's Movement 1970–1985* (London: Pandora Press, 1987).

Phillpot, Clive and Tarsia, Andrea (eds), *Live in Your Head: Concept and Experiment in Britain 1965–75* (London: Whitechapel, 2000).

Sitney P. Adams (ed.), *Film Culture: An Anthology* (London: Secker & Warburg, 1971).

Sitney, P. Adams (ed.), *The Avant-Garde Film: A Reader of Theory and Criticism* (New York: New York University Press, 1978).

Stangos, Nikos (ed.), *Concepts of Modern Art* (London: Thames and Hudson, 1994).

Stoneman, Rod and Thompson, Hilary (eds), *British Film Institute Productions Catalogue: The New Social Function of Cinema: '79/'80* (London: BFI, 1981).

Webber, Mark (ed.), *Shoot Shoot Shoot: The First Decade of the London Filmmaker's Co-operative and British Avant-garde Film 1966–76* (London: LUX, 2002).

Wollen, Roger (ed.), *Derek Jarman: A Portrait, Artist, Film-maker, Designer* (London: Thames and Hudson, 1996).

Essays and chapters in edited collections

Barrett, Cyril, 'Kinetic Art' in Nikos Stangos (ed.), *Concepts of Modern Art* (London: Thames and Hudson, 1994), pp. 213–223.

Carter, Vanda, 'Not Only Animation' in Michael Mazière and Nina Danino (eds), *The Undercut Reader: Critical Writings on Artists' Film and Video* (London: Wallflower press, 2003), pp. 168–170.

Cook, Pam, 'The Point of Expression in Avant-Garde Film' in Elizabeth Cowie (ed.), *Catalogue British Film Institute productions: 1977–1978* (London: BFI, 1978), pp. 53–56.

Curtis, David, 'English Avant-Garde Film: An Early Chronology' in *A Perspective on English Avant-Garde Film* (London: Arts Council, 1978), pp. 9–18. First published in *Studio International*, November/December 1975.

Danino, Nina, 'The Intense Subject' in Nino Danino and Michael Mazière (eds), *The Undercut Reader: Critical Writings on Artists' Film and Video* (London: Wallflower press, 2003), pp. 8–12.

Darke, Chris, 'Mind Games' in *Anti-Clock* DVD (London: BFI, 2009), pp. 1–3.

Dusinberre, Deke, 'The Ascetic Task: Peter's Gidal's *Room Film 1973*' in Peter Gidal (ed.), *Structural Film Anthology* (London: BFI, 1976), pp. 109–113.

Dusinberre, Deke, 'A Perspective on English Avant-Garde Film' in *A Perspective on English Avant-Garde Film* (London: Arts Council/British Council, 1978), pp. 7–8.

Dusinberre, Deke, 'St George in the Forest' in *A Perspective in English Avant-garde Film* (London: Arts Council, 1978), pp. 43–48.

Fowler, William, 'Encounters with Central Bazaar', in *Central Bazaar* DVD (London: BFI, 2009), pp. 2–6.

Gidal, Peter, 'Technology and Ideology in/through/and Avant-Garde Film: An Instance' in Teresa de Lauretis and Stephen Heath (eds), *Cinematic Apparatus* (London: Macmillan Press, 1980), pp. 151–165.

Grasskamp, Walter, 'For Example, *Documenta*, or, How Is Art History Produced?' in Reesa Greenberg, Bruce W Ferguson and Sandy Nairne (eds), *Thinking about Exhibitions* (London: Routledge, 1996), pp. 67–78.

Hamlyn, Nicky, 'From Structuralism to Imagism: Peter Gidal and his Influence in the 1980s' in Michael Mazière and Nina Danino (eds), *The Undercut Reader: Critical Writings on Artists' Film and Video* (London: Wallflower Press, 2003), pp. 233–238.

Harvey, Sylvia, An Introduction to 'The Song of the Shirt' in Charlotte Brunsdon, *Films for Women* (ed.) (London: BFI, 1986), pp. 44–48.

Haug, Kate, 'Interview with Kate Haug' in *Carolee Schneemann: Imaging Her Erotics: Essays, Interviews, Projects* (Massachusetts: The MIT Press, 2003), p. 21–44.

Hendrikson, Henrik, 'Monkey's Birthday' in *Perspectives on British Avant-garde Film* (London: Hayward, 1977), loose leaf.

Iles, Chrissie, 'Derek Jarman' in Larner, Melissa (ed.), *Derek Jarman: Brutal Beauty* (London: Koenig Books, 2008), pp. 64–73.

Jenkins, Bruce, 'Fluxfilms in Three False Starts' in Tanya Leighton (ed.), *Art and the Moving Image: A Critical Reader* (London: Tate Publishing, 2008), pp. 53–71.

Joseph, Branden W. 'Sparring with the Spectacle: Parts 1–5' in Christopher Eamon (ed.), *Anthony McCall: The Solid Light Films and Related Works* (Göttingen: Steidl, 2005), pp. 36–77.

Kimberley, Nick, 'Introduction' in Ian Breakwell, *Diary 1964–1985* (London: Pluto Press, 1986), p. 8.

Knight, Julia, 'Materials, Materials, Materials: Questions of Technology and History', in Nino Danino and Michael Mazière (eds), *The Undercut Reader* (London: Wallflower Press, 2003), pp. 17–21.

Kosuth, Joseph, 'Art after Philosophy' in Charles Harrison and Paul Wood (eds), *Art in Theory 1900–1990: An Anthology of Changing Ideas* (Oxford: Blackwell, 2000), pp. 840–850.

Kwint, Marius, 'Introduction: The Physical Past' in Jeremy Aynsley, Christopher Breward and Marius Kwint (eds), *Material Memories: Design and Evocation* (Oxford: Berg, 1999), pp. 1–16.

Lachman, Gary 'Kenneth Anger: The Crowned and Conquering Child' in *Magick Lantern Cycle: Kenneth Anger* DVD (London: BFI, 2009).

Le Grice, Malcolm, 'The History We Need' in Deke Dusinberre and A.L. Rees (eds), *Film as Film: Formal Experiment in Film: 1910–1975* (London: Arts Council/Hayward, 1979), pp. 113–117.

LeWitt, Sol, 'Paragraphs on Conceptual Art' in Charles Harrison and Paul Wood (eds), *Art in Theory 1900–1990: An Anthology of Changing Ideas* (Oxford: Blackwell, 2000), pp. 834–837.

Miles, Barry, 'The Naked Lunch in my Life' in Oliver Harris and Ian Macfadyen (eds), *Naked Lunch @ 50: Anniversary Essays* (Illinois: Southern Illinois University Press, 2009), pp. 114–122.

Monk, Claire, 'Always Too Early' in *Separation* DVD (London: BFI, 2009), pp. 1–4.

Morgan, Natasha, 'Tina Keane: Shadow Woman' in Rozsika Parker and Griselda Pollock (eds), *Framing Feminism: Art and the Women's Movement 1970–1985*, op. cit., pp. 287–288.

Mulvey, Laura, 'Film, Feminism and the Avant-Garde' in Michael O'Pray (ed.), *The British Avant-garde Film: 1926–1995: An Anthology of Writings* (Luton, University of Luton, 1996), pp. 199–216.

Newman, Michael, 'Moving Image in the Gallery Since the 1990s' in Stuart Comer (ed.), *Film and Video Art* (London: Tate, 2009), pp. 86–121.

Nicolson, Annabel, 'Artists' Statement' in Deke Dusinberre and David Curtis (eds), *A Perspective on English Avant-garde Film* (London: Arts/British Council, 1978), pp. 73–74.

Nicolson, Annabel, 'The Early Years of the Film Co-op' in Jackie Hatfield and Stephen Littman (eds), *Experiments in Moving Image* (Luton: EpiGraph, 2004), pp. 12–19.

O'Pray, Michael, 'The Elusive Sign: From Asceticism to Aestheticism', in *The Elusive Sign* (London: Tate, 1987), pp. 7–10.

O'Pray, Michael, 'The Art of Films/Films of Art' in Roger Wollen (ed.), *Derek Jarman: A Portrait: Artist, Film-maker, Designer* (London: Thames and Hudson, 1996), pp. 65–75.

Parker, Jayne, 'Free Show' in *theFrame*, Jayne Parker DVD (London: BFI, 2005).

Phillpot, Clive and Tarsia, Andrea, 'Introduction' in Clive Phillpot and Andrea Tarsia (eds), *Live in Your Head: Concept and Experiment in Britain 1965–75* (London: Whitechapel, 2000), pp. pp. 6–7.

Rees, A.L., 'Locating the LFMC: the First Decade in Context' in *Shoot Shoot Shoot: The First Decade of the London Film-makers' Co-operative and British Avant-garde Film 1966–76* (London: Lux, 2002), pp. 8.

Rees, A.L., 'Video and Argument from Design', in Jackie Hatfield (ed.), *Experiments in Moving Image* exhibition catalogue (Luton: Epigraph Publications, 2004), pp. 4–5.

Rees, A.L., 'Foreword' in Jackie Hatfield (ed.), *Experimental Film and Video: An Anthology* (Eastleigh: John Libbey Publishing, 2006), pp. x–xi.

Rees, A.L., 'Experimenting on Air: UK Artists' Film on Television' in Laura Mulvey and Jamie Sexton (eds), *Experimental British Television* (Manchester: Manchester University Press, 2007), pp. 146–165.

Rhodes, Lis, 'Whose History?' in Deke Dusinberre and A.L. Rees (ed.), *Film as Film: Formal Experiment in Film: 1910–1975* (London: Arts Council/Hayward, 1979), pp. 119–120.

Rhodes, Lis, 'Thoughts in Various Histories, 1978–2008: On the Possessive' in *Oberhausen Short Film Festival Catalogue 2008* (Oberhausen: Karl Maria Laufen, 2008), pp. 151–155.

Rodowick, D. N., 'Theory and the Avant-garde' in Nina Danino and Michael Mazière (eds), *The Undercut Reader, Critical Writings on Artists' Film and Video* (London: Wallflower Press, 2003), pp. 34–37.

Sillars, Stuart, 'Is it possible for me to do nothing as my contribution?' in Bart Moore-Gilbert (ed.), *The Arts in the 1970s: Cultural Closure?* (London: Routledge, 1993), pp. 259–280.

Smith, Ali, 'The Margaret Tait Years' in Peter Todd and Benjamin Cook (eds), *Subjects and Sequences: A Margaret Tait Reader* (London: LUX, 2004), pp. 7–27.

Swinton, Tilda, 'No known address ... or ... Don't look down ...' in *Derek Jarman: Brutal Beauty* (London: Koenig Books, 2008), pp. 10–17.

Tait, Archie, 'ICA: London – Decolonising the Unconscious' in Rod Stoneman and Hilary Thompson (eds), *The New Social Function of Cinema: British Film Institute Productions Catalogue '79/'80* (London: BFI publishing, 1981) pp. 72–75.

Todolí, Vicenti, 'Foreword' in *Open Systems: Rethinking Art c. 1970* (London: Tate, 2005), p. 6.

VanDerBeek, Stan, '"Culture: Intercom" and Expanded Cinema: A Proposal and Manifesto' in Tanya Leighton (ed.), *Art and the Moving Image* (London: Tate Publishing, 2008), pp. 72–74.

Walkin, Janey, 'Interview with Anne Rees-Mogg' in Nina Danino and Michael Mazière (eds), *The Undercut Reader: Critical Writings on Artists' Film and Video* (London: Wallflower Press, 2003), pp. 71–75.

Walley, Jonathan, 'An Interview with Anthony McCall' in Christopher Eamon (ed.), *Anthony McCall: The Solid Light Films and Related Works* (Göttingen: Steidl Publishers, 2004), pp. 146–163.

Walley, Jonathan, 'Modes of Film Practice in the Avant-Garde' in Tanya Leighton (ed.), *Art and the Moving Image* (London: Tate Publishing, 2008), pp. 182–199.

Watson, Gray, 'An Archaeology of Soul' in Roger Wollen (ed.), *Derek Jarman: A Portrait, Artist, Film-maker, Designer* (London: Thames and Hudson, 1996, pp. 33–48.

Webber, Mark, 'Chronology of Events and Developments 1966–76' in Mark Webber (ed.), *Shoot Shoot Shoot: The First Decade of the London Film-makers' Co-operative and British Avant-garde Film 1966–76* (London: Lux, 2002), p. 6–7.

Wollen, Peter, 'Alternative Sounds and Images' in *Between Imagination and Reality* (London: ICA, 1990), pp. 5–7.

Wollen, Roger, 'Introduction: Facets of Derek Jarman' in Roger Wollen (ed.), *Derek Jarman: A Portrait, Artist, Film-maker, Designer* (London: Thames and Hudson, 1996), pp. 15–31.

Zoller, Maxa, 'Interview: Maxa Zoller with Malcolm Le Grice' in *X-Screen Catalogue*, Museum Moderne Kunst Stiftung Ludwig (Wien: Walther König, 2003), pp. 136–147.

Articles

Arthur, Paul S., 'Structural Film: Revisions, New Versions, and the Artifact', *Millenium Film Journal*, Vol. 1, No. 2, Spring/Summer 1978, pp. 124–132.

Arthur, Paul S., 'Structural Film: Revisions, New Versions And The Artifact: Part Two' *Millenium Film Journal*, No. 4/5, Summer/Fall 1979, pp. 122–134.

Beckett, Andy, 'What a Swell Party it Was', *The Independent*, 2 June 1996.

Bovenschen, Silvia, 'Is There a Feminine Aesthetic?', *New German Critique*, No. 10, Winter 1977, pp. 111–137.

Bruce, Tim, 'Fred Drummond Come in from the Cold Film Co-op Feb 16th', *Readings*, No. 2, March 1977, p. 5.

Buckell, Gareth, 'Shoot Shoot Shoot: The LFMC and the Film Culture of Sixties Britain', *Filmwaves*, Issue 31, 2006, pp. 36–40.

Child, Sarah, 'Fred Drummond at the Co-op', Annabel Nicolson, *Readings*, No. 2, March 1977, p. 5.

Clark, George, 'The Luminous View', *Tate etc*, No. 30, Spring 2014, pp. 57–59.

Comino, Jo, 'Short Films: Place of Work', *Art and Artists*, Vol. 50, No. 597, October 1983, pp. 284–287.

Cottringer, Anne 'On Peter Gidal's Theory and Definition of Structural/Materilist Film', *Afterimage*, No. 6, Summer 1976, pp. 86–95.

Cronin, Paul, 'The Ceremony of Innocence', *Sight and Sound*, Vol. 17, No. 3, March 2007, pp. 22–24.

Curtis, David, 'Artists' Films', *Studio International*, Vol. 193, 1977, pp. 24–25.

Curtis, David, 'Curating a Century of Artists' Film in Britain' *Filmwaves*, No. 22, Summer/Autumn 2003, pp. 54–55.

Danino, Nina, 'A Century of Artists' Film in Britain: A Response to the Curatorial Rationale', *Filmwaves*, No. 22, Summer/Autumn 2003, pp. 56–57.

de Lauretis, Teresa, 'Aesthetic and Feminist Theory: Rethinking Women's Cinema', *New German Critique*, No. 34, Winter 1985, pp. 154–175.

Du Cane, John, 'Film and Video: The Third Part of Gallery House's Survey of the Avant-Garde in Britain', *Time Out*, 13–19 October 1972.

Durgnat, Ray, 'The London Film-maker's Co-op', *International Times*, Vol. 1, No. 2, 1968, pp. 7; p. 7.

Dusinbere, Deke, 'On Expanding Cinema', *Studio International*, Vol. 190, July–November 1975, pp. 220–224.

Dusinberre, Deke, 'Consistent Oxymoron', *Screen*, Vol. 18, No. 2, Summer 1977, pp. 79–89.

Dusinberre, Deke, 'Making the Avant-Grade' [sic], *Time Out*, 1–7 June 1979, pp. 14–15.

Dusinberre, Deke, 'See Real Images!', *Afterimage*, No. 8/9, Winter 1980/1981, pp. 87–107.

Dusinberre, Deke 'Short Film Series', *Art and Artists*, No. 50, October 1983, pp. 286–287.

Dwoskin, Stephen, 'Mare's Tail', *Afterimage,* No. 2, Autumn 1970, pp. 40–43.

Dwoskin, Stephen, 'A Little Bit of Then', *Filmwaves*, No. 24, Spring 2004, pp. 18–21.

Ellis, John, 'Production Board Policies', *Screen*, Vol. 17, No. 4, Winter 1976/1977, pp. 9–23.

Field, Simon and O'Pray, Michael, 'Imagining October, Dr. Dee and Other Matters', *Afterimage*, No. 12, Autumn 1985, pp. 40–58.

Gidal, Peter, 'Letter from Peter Gidal', *Afterimage*, No. 7, Summer 1978, pp. 120–123.

Gidal, Peter, 'Time Regained (Sort Of): A Century of Artists' Film in Britain', *Tate Magazine*, No. 6, 2003.

Godard, Jean-Luc, 'What is to be done?', *Afterimage*, No 1, April 1970. No page numbers.

Heath, Stephen, 'Afterword', *Screen*, Vol. 20, No. 2, Summer 1979, pp. 93–99.

Kaplan, E. Ann, 'Aspects of British Feminist Film Theory: A Critical Evaluation of Texts by Claire Johnson and Pam Cook', *Jump Cut*, No. 2, 1974, pp. 52–55.

Kent, Sarah, 'Towards a Feminist Perception of Women's Practice in Art at AIR Gallery 2th February' in Annabel Nicolson and Paul Burrell (eds), *Readings*, No. 2, 1977, p. 11.

Le Grice, Malcolm, 'REALTIME/SPACE', *Art and Artists*, December, 1972, pp. 39–43.

Le Grice, Malcolm, 'Vision: The London Festival of Avant-garde Film', *Studio International*, Vol. 186, No. 960, November 1973, pp. 188–189.

Le Grice, Malcolm, 'Film', *Studio International*, Vol. 193, 1977, pp. 4–6.

Lippard, Lucy, 'Why Separate Women's Art?', *Art and Artists*, Vol. 8, No. 7, October 1973, pp. 8–9.

Mekas, Jonas, 'Movie Journal', *The Village Voice*, 27 September–25 October 1973.

Miller, Henry K., 'The Slade School and Cinema: Part Two', *Vertigo*, Vol. 3, No. 5, Spring 2007, pp. 65–67.

Morgan, Natasha, 'Shadow Woman', *Spare Rib*, No. 675, 1977, pp. 26–27.

Nicolson, Annabel, 'Artist as Filmmaker', *Art and Artists*, December 1972, pp. 20–27.

Nicolson, Annabel, 'Canada Fragments', *Art and Artists*, Vol. 8, No. 1, April 1973, pp. 29–33.

O'Pray, Michael, 'Derek Jarman's Cinema: Eros and Thanatos', *Afterimage*, No. 12, Autumn 1985, pp. 6–15.

O'Pray, Michael, 'Derek Jarman Filmography', *Afterimage*, No. 12, Autumn 1985, pp. 16–21.

Rayns, Tony, 'Reflected Light', *Sight and Sound*, 43, No. 1, Winter 1973/74, pp. 16–19.

Rees, A.L., 'Conditions of Illusionism', *Screen*, Vol. 18, No. 3, Autumn 1977, pp. 41–54.

Rees, A.L., 'Projecting Back – UK Film and Video Installation in the 1970s', *Millennium Film Journal*, No. 52, Winter 2009/2010.

Sparrow, Felicity, 'Light Illusions: Artists and Cinema; Filmmakers and Galleries', *Vertigo*, Vol. 1, No. 2, Spring 2001. On-line source. No page numbers.

Sparrow, Felicity, 'A Century of Artists' Film in Britain or the Hybrid Black Box', *Filmwaves*, No. 22, Summer/Autumn 2003, pp. 61–62.

Spenser, Jeremy, 'Jenny Okun' in Annabel Nicolson (ed.), *Readings*, No. 2, 1977, pp. 4–5.

Stern, Lesley, 'Feminism and Cinema-Exchanges', *Screen*, Vol. 20, Winter 1979/1980, pp. 89–105.

Thomas, Peter, 'The Struggle for Funding: Sponsorship, Competition and Pacification', *Screen*, Vol. 47, No. 4, 2006, pp. 461–467.

Walley, Jonathan, 'The Material of Film and the Idea of Cinema: Contrasting Practices in Sixties and Seventies Avant-garde Film', *October*, Issue 103, 2003, pp. 15–30.

Willeman, Paul, 'Voyeurism, the Look and Dwoskin', *Afterimage*, No. 6, Summer 1976, pp. 40–50.

Wilson, Siona, 'From Women's Work to the Umbilical Lens: Mary Kelly's Early Films', in *Art History*, Vol. 31, No. 1, 2008, pp. 79–102.

Wood, Jason, 'Andi Engel', *Vertigo*, Vol. 3, No. 4, Winter 2007, pp. 69.

Index

Printed and bound by CPI Group (UK) Ltd, Croydon, CR0 4YY